D1237538

SHAKESPEARE AND GARRICK

Much has been written about the acting style of David Garrick, the eighteenth century's greatest actor-manager, but this book, unusually, claims a place for him within Shakespeare studies as a *literary* as well as a *theatrical* figure. It analyses several of Garrick's alterations of Shakespeare's plays in which he took the lead, and traces his close involvement with the major Shakespeare editors of the period, including his friend Samuel Johnson. Admirers claimed that Garrick's performances illuminated the playtexts better than the commentaries of scholarly editors. His reputation as Shakespeare's living representative and best interpreter was so high that he was involved in most Shakespeare-related projects of his day, not least the Jubilee at Stratford. While Garrick lived, the imminent divorce of 'stage' and 'page' could not take place. Cunningham shows how vital a resource Garrick's collection of early plays in English has been to generations of Shakespeare scholars.

Vanessa Cunningham was awarded an MBE for Services to Cardiff University in 2000, and became a Fellow of the University in 2001. She is the author, with John Goodwin, of *Cardiff University: A Celebration* (2001).

Roubiliac's statue of Shakespeare. Made in 1758 to adorn Garrick's temple at Hampton, it now stands in the British Library. Garrick was almost certainly the model.

SHAKESPEARE AND GARRICK

VANESSA CUNNINGHAM

CAMBRIDGE UNIVERSITY PRESS
Cambridge, New York, Melbourne, Madrid, Cape Town, Singapore, São Paulo, Delhi

Cambridge University Press
The Edinburgh Building, Cambridge CB2 8RU, UK

Published in the United States of America by Cambridge University Press, New York

www.cambridge.org
Information on this title: www.cambridge.org/9780521889773

First published 2008

Printed in the United Kingdom at the University Press, Cambridge

A catalogue record for this publication is available from the British Library

Library of Congress Cataloguing in Publication data

Cunningham, Vanessa.
Shakespeare and Garrick / Vanessa Cunningham.
p. cm.
Includes bibliographical references and index.
ISBN 978-0-521-88977-3 (hardback : alk. paper)
1. Garrick, David, 1717–1779. 2. Garrick, David, 1717–1779 – Influence.
3. Shakespeare, William, 1564–1616 – Criticism, Textual. 4. Shakespeare, William,
1564–1616 – Criticism and interpretation – History – 18th century. 5. Shakespeare, William,
1564–1616 – Stage history – 1625–1800. 6. Drama – Editing – History – 18th century.
I. Title.

PR3070.C86 2008
822.3′3 – dc22

2007050989

ISBN 978-0-521-88977-3 hardback

Contents

List of illustrations *page* vi
Acknowledgements vii

Prologue: Garrick's alterations of Shakespeare – a note on texts 1

1 Garrick and Shakespeare – before the divorce of stage and page 3

2 The contexts of Garrick's alterations of Shakespeare 13

3 'To give the actor more eclat' – Garrick's earliest alterations of Shakespeare 43

4 'Re-bottling' Shakespeare – Garrick in mid-career (1753–1768) 76

5 (Entr'acte): Celebrating Shakespeare on page and stage in 1769 106

6 'Parental and filial capacities' – *King Lear* and *Hamlet* 119

Epilogue: Garrick's legacy to Shakespeare studies 162

Notes 171
Bibliography 207
Index 226

Illustrations

Frontispiece: Roubiliac's statue of Shakespeare.
1. Garrick in the role of Kitely in *Every Man in His Humour.* 38
2. Garrick and Hannah Pritchard in Garrick's alteration of *Macbeth.* 56
3. Garrick and George Anne Bellamy in the tomb scene of Garrick's alteration of *Romeo and Juliet.* 67
4. Shakespeare, Tragedy and Comedy advance to welcome Garrick to Parnassus, while fellow actors mourn his passing. 92
5. Stratford-on-Avon, 7 September 1769; Garrick and the Drury Lane choir and orchestra perform the Ode. 108
6. Garrick in his alteration of *King Lear.* 126
7. Garrick as Hamlet sees his father's ghost. 141
8. Garrick's preparation copy for his alteration of *Hamlet.* 146

Acknowledgements

Many people have helped me in the preparation of this book. In particular, Professor Martin Coyle of Cardiff University has been an invaluable source of encouragement and advice over many years. The staff of the University Library, especially Tom Dawkes and Peter Keelan, have also been proactively and unfailingly helpful. I am grateful to Marcus Risdell at the Garrick Club for generously giving both time and advice to help me select illustrations for the book. Abroad, I have met with enthusiastic assistance, especially from Jim Kuhn at the Folger Shakespeare Library in Washington, and from Earle Havers at the Boston Public Library. I thank Sarah Stanton and Rebecca Jones at the Cambridge University Press for their friendly guidance.

The support and interest of family and friends has encouraged me to keep going with the project. Special thanks go to Mike and Barbara Green for help with French translation. Above all, I thank my husband, Norman Cunningham, who has been my travelling companion, progress chaser, critic and editor. Without his back-up, this book would never have been completed.

PROLOGUE

Garrick's alterations of Shakespeare – a note on texts

The great majority of the versions of Shakespeare's plays made by David Garrick and published during his management of Drury Lane (1747–1776) are described on their title pages as 'alterations', or as having been 'alter'd for performance'.[1] The two operas (*The Fairies*, 1755, and *The Tempest*, 1756) are said to be 'taken from Shakespear', while *Antony and Cleopatra*, published in 1758 and generally credited jointly to Edward Capell and Garrick (though not attributed to either on the title page), is distinguished from the others by its description as 'an historical Play, written by William Shakespeare: fitted for the Stage by abridging only'. Despite the fact that Harry William Pedicord and Fredrick Louis Bergmann, modern editors of Garrick's plays, entitle their two volumes of Shakespeare-derived texts 'adaptations',[2] 'alteration' is certainly the preferable term for discussion of Garrick's performance versions of Shakespeare's plays, since throughout the eighteenth century 'alter' was used far more commonly than 'adapt'.

Garrick, according to Pedicord and Bergmann, is believed to have been involved in the altering of some twenty-two plays by Shakespeare over the course of his professional career. In their collected edition they reproduce the dozen that they consider can be authenticated.[3] The present work discusses a selection of alterations that span Garrick's professional career. Two are from the early years (*Macbeth*, *Romeo and Juliet*) and two from the middle period (*Florizel and Perdita*, *Antony and Cleopatra*). Although Garrick seems to have tinkered with *King Lear* and *Hamlet* throughout his career, he worked most intensively on them towards its close; they therefore represent the late stage of his career. This chronological approach makes it possible to explore whether any trends – for example, towards greater faithfulness to Shakespeare's language or respect for his plots – are discernible in Garrick's alterations over time. Another strong reason for choosing these six plays is that in each, at least initially, Garrick himself played the leading role.

The base text used is the only complete edition of Garrick's *Plays*, that of Pedicord and Bergmann (1980–1982), with its modernised spelling and punctuation; quotations from their edition are preceded by 'G'. Inevitably, the gain in ease of access and reference is at the expense of the sense of immediacy generated by the excited punctuation and lavish capitalization of the eighteenth-century editions. Garrick often straightforwardly referred to the plays upon which his alterations were based as the 'originals'. Occasional use of the shorthand term 'original' in this book should not be seen as under-estimating the complexities facing editors who seek to establish authoritative texts. Quotations from Shakespeare are from a modern edition, the Oxford *Complete Works*,[4] selected not least because of its recognition that '[t]heatre is an endlessly fluid medium' and that performance was 'the end to which they [the plays] were created'.[5]

CHAPTER I

Garrick and Shakespeare – before the divorce of stage and page

When SHAKESPEARE dy'd, he left behind
No mortal of an equal mind.
When GARRICK play'd, he liv'd again,
Unrival'd'mongst the sons of men.
But GARRICK dies! and (mark the sequel)
THE WORLD WILL NEVER SEE THEIR EQUAL.

The above poem by William Oland appeared in *The Gentleman's Magazine* in 1779.[1] It is just one of numerous tributes published that year to mark the death of David Garrick, England's celebrated actor-manager-dramatist, and is typical in placing Garrick's name on an equal footing with Shakespeare's. Garrick's fame as an actor has persisted to this day: a well-known London club and numerous theatres, drama groups and pubs still bear his name. Since his death, few decades have passed without the publication of yet another Garrick biography; this book is not intended to add to the list. Nevertheless, the basic outline of his life, though well known, needs to be briefly retold.

Of Huguenot descent and the son of an army officer, Garrick was born in Hereford in 1717 and brought up in Lichfield in a family of four boys and three girls, in which money was always short. David and his younger brother George were two of the three pupils of the short-lived school set up at Edial by fellow Lichfield resident Samuel Johnson. The friendship of Johnson and Garrick, though often under strain, lasted until the actor's death in 1779. In 1737 they set out together for London to seek their fortunes; Johnson had written a tragedy and Garrick was supposed to study for a legal career. Johnson's struggles to survive in the capital as a writer were lengthy and painful but Garrick, after an attempt to establish himself as a wine merchant, rapidly achieved the fame that Johnson longed for. Since boyhood he had been stage-struck, and in 1741 he became a professional actor.

The young player's success in both tragedy and comedy was immediate and spectacular. Audiences were especially struck by the contrast between the mannered, rhetorical style of acting adopted by contemporaries such as James Quin and the young Garrick's much more naturalistic approach. As his first biographer, Thomas Davies, put it: 'he banished ranting, bombast and grimace; and restored ease, simplicity and genuine humour'.[2] In 1747, at the age of 30, he became joint patentee of the Theatre Royal in Drury Lane, a managerial role that continued, along with those of performer, dramatist and alterer of plays, until his retirement in 1776. Garrick is credited for his attempts to bring respectability and order to the theatre. His thirty-year marriage to Eva Maria Veigel, a Viennese dancer, was a very close and happy one, though the couple had no children. In his lifetime Garrick was hugely celebrated. Fêted in the highest circles of British and European society, he was frequently painted, both in character and in private life, by leading artists, and his image was reproduced in prints, on porcelain figurines and even on trays and tea caddies. The impact of his startlingly original acting style upon audiences is often recorded in novels of the period; of these, Partridge's response to his Hamlet, in Fielding's *Tom Jones*, is probably the best known.[3] His health was always poor. His death from uraemia in 1779, at the age of 61, was followed by a funeral of almost royal magnificence and a torrent of tributes and eulogies in the press.

The contribution made by Shakespeare to the growth of Garrick's reputation is hard to overstate. Indeed, some of his contemporary admirers would have reversed the names in the previous sentence. Garrick had abundant reason to be grateful to the author who had provided him with many of his most acclaimed roles, of which Richard III (in Cibber's alteration) in his London debut season of 1741–1742 was just the first. Over the thirty-five years of his acting career, he triumphed as Benedick in *Much Ado about Nothing* (113 performances),[4] Hamlet (90), King Lear (85) and, of course, Richard III (83). While manager of Drury Lane he appeared in his own alterations as Romeo (60 performances), Macbeth (37), Posthumus in *Cymbeline* (23) and Leontes in *The Winter's Tale* (23). The only leading Shakespearean roles he attempted in which he was not acclaimed were Antony (6 performances) and Othello (3). Shakespeare not only brought Garrick fame, riches and social position, but he also offered the actor magnificent opportunities to practise his art, and Garrick's letters demonstrate the immense care with which he studied the texts in order to tease out the finest nuances of meaning, and so determine where emphases, pauses and breaths should occur in performance. Because of similarities in their backgrounds, Garrick may well have felt a strong personal identification with Shakespeare. Both left Midlands homes at a young age to seek fame in the capital. Garrick became an actor who wrote plays, Shakespeare a playwright who also acted. Both progressed up the social ladder and gained the highest professional eminence and royal patronage. Both were involved in the management of the companies that formed the settings for their theatrical achievements, and both survived to a prosperous and comfortable retirement in private life.

How genuinely heartfelt Garrick's frequently professed devotion to Shakespeare actually was can never be known for sure; it certainly provided a very useful professional stance. Throughout the eighteenth century, the process of establishing Shakespeare as the supreme Bard of the nation accelerated. As manager, Garrick seized the opportunities offered by the rising tide of bardolatry,[5] and enthusiastically presented himself to the public as the high priest at Shakespeare's shrine. In the prologue with which he opened Drury Lane's 1750–1751 season, he declared: 'Sacred to Shakespeare was this spot design'd, / To pierce the heart, and humanize the mind.'[6] In 1755 he purchased a villa at Hampton and built there, beside the Thames, a temple to Shakespeare, designed by Robert Adam, to house memorabilia and a statue of his idol. Garrick's identification in the public mind as Shakespeare's chief representative could only intensify when, in 1769, he presided over and master-minded every detail of the famous (or infamous) Jubilee at Stratford-upon-Avon.

Nowadays, Garrick is only a marginal figure in the scholarly world of Shakespeare studies. Few modern works concerned with eighteenth-century editors of Shakespeare pay him much attention. Simon Jarvis's single mention of Garrick is as authority for a word in Johnson's *Dictionary*,[7] while Marcus Walsh makes three brief references in passing.[8] The actor-manager lies quite outside the field of reference of such specialists, and any interest that his peripheral figure holds for them lies only in the fact that he made his collection of old English plays available to contemporary editors of Shakespeare, including Samuel Johnson, George Steevens and Edward Capell. Yet, in his lifetime, his domination of the theatre, his literary pursuits and his close relationships with contemporary writers and editors were such that few important Shakespeare-related projects could happen without his involvement, and a generation of playgoers came to 'know' Shakespeare primarily through Garrick's alterations. Evidence of his wide-ranging dominance is found even in Walsh's three passing mentions. He speaks of the eighteenth century's 'divinization' of the figure of Shakespeare, which 'reached its zenith' in Garrick's Ode for the Stratford Jubilee, and gives examples of 'editorial discourse' throughout the century in which 'the texts of Shakespeare

are insistently figured as sacred, reverend, scriptural'. Second, he cites Garrick's alteration of *Hamlet* (misdated to 1773) as an example of one of the 'few survivals of printed texts annotated as promptbooks' (strictly speaking it was a preparation copy, not a promptbook). Third, when dealing with the development of glossaries of Shakespeare, Walsh gives as an example the specimen annexed to Richard Warner's *A Letter to David Garrick, Esq., Concerning a Glossary to the Plays of Shakespeare* of 1768, which sought Garrick's endorsement of his proposed work. These three brief references provide glimpses of one whose influence was such that, in his own person, he linked domains that succeeding generations would fence off from one another. Later actors – Henderson and Kemble, for example – made collections of rare old plays, but after Garrick none had the authority personally to hold together the soon-to-be-separate worlds of editing and performing Shakespeare.

Garrick's claim that Shakespeare was the god of his idolatry occasionally earned him ridicule from his intimates. Boswell gives an account of Garrick in 1769 rising with 'tragick eagerness' to the bait of Johnson's praising Congreve above Shakespeare.[9] But to his public there was nothing unreasonable in the idea that the brilliance of his performances signalled a unique insight into the mind of his idol. Garrick was early accorded the status of an expert on Shakespeare. In February 1744, for example, 'P. W.' wrote to him: 'As you seem to me to be a very good judge of Shakspeare, and have often given us his true sense and meaning where his learned editors could give us neither, I shall submit to your judgment a line in "Hamlet", which, in my opinion, is wrong placed in all the editions that I have seen.'[10] Garrick was credited by admirers with interpretative powers surpassing those of his editors:

> Dull Menders of a Syllable,
> a learned, motley Train,
> The Page with vague Conjectures fill;
> and puzzle, not Explain:
> In thy [Garrick's] Expression Shakespeare's Meaning shines,
> Thou finest Commentator on his Lines![11]

Significantly, the anonymous writer of this tribute sees acting and editing as a single tradition and has little doubt that Garrick's stage can gloss Shakespeare's page and reveal its meaning.

In the eighteenth century the term 'editor' was more broadly defined than it is today, and in the eyes of his contemporaries Garrick would have been regarded as an editor of Shakespeare. In his advertisement to the third edition (1753) of his version of *Romeo and Juliet*, Garrick called himself 'the present editor', and later he referred to his alteration of *Cymbeline* (published 1762) as 'this edition'. Pope, writing in 1725 when Garrick was eight, had used 'stage-editors' to mean player-alterers. In commenting on the notorious 'table of green fields' crux in *Henry V* (II.iii.16–17), he said: 'This nonsense got into all the following editions by a pleasant mistake of the Stage-editors, who printed from the common piece-meal Parts in the Play-house.'[12] Johnson used a shortened version of that very quotation ('This nonsense got into all the editions by a mistake of the stage editors') to illustrate his definition of 'editor' in his Dictionary of 1755. An editor, he said, was a 'Publisher: he that revises or prepares any work for publication'. But when defining 'publish', Johnson had placed the literary connotations second. The word's primary meaning, he said, was to 'discover to mankind; to make generally and openly known; to proclaim; to divulge' – exactly the service that Garrick's admirers saw him as performing for Shakespeare by revealing the plays to an ever-wider public. In this sense Garrick could be counted in his own day as honouring Shakespeare as publisher and editor, as well as actor.

Strict boundaries had not yet been set between those who served Shakespeare in the study and in the theatre. As editor, Pope had not actually re-written the plays, but he had not hesitated to update Shakespeare's vocabulary or to demote to footnotes passages he personally considered unworthy, often attributing them to interpolations by 'the players'. However, his squabbling successors over the next half-century, though they may not have realised it, were feeling their way towards the devising and adopting of generally accepted standards and methodologies for editing. This process of professionalisation was actually impeded by Garrick's pre-eminence in matters Shakespearean. Over the thirty-five years of his career, 'page' was striving to separate from 'stage', but their divorce was prevented by the authoritative figure of the great alterer-actor-manager who enjoyed public recognition as Shakespeare's supreme interpreter.

In the centuries since Garrick's death, two accounts, over-simple but persistent, of his relationship with Shakespeare have predominated. The first hails Garrick as the great restorer to the stage of plays not seen in their original forms since Shakespeare's day; the second, paradoxically, condemns him for choosing to stage travesties when he could have presented what Shakespeare actually wrote. The first of these myths – Garrick the great rescuer of Shakespeare – was widely circulated in Garrick's lifetime and fostered by his earliest biographers, Thomas Davies and Arthur Murphy,[13] both of whom had had the incomparable advantage of having worked professionally with their subject: Davies as a member of the Drury Lane company, Murphy as a successful and prolific playwright. Davies recalls: 'But when in the revival of Shakespeare's plays, he [Garrick] complied with the general taste as well as his own, he was determined to restore him to his genuine splendour and native simplicity, unincumbered with the unnatural additions, and gaudy trappings, thrown upon him by some writers who lived in the reign of Charles the Second.'[14] Murphy quotes Dr Browne's tribute, written in 1776 upon Garrick's retirement:

> A great genius hath arisen to dignify the stage, who, when it was sinking into the lowest insipidity, restored it to the fullness of its antient splendour, and, with a variety of powers beyond example, established nature, Shakespeare, and himself.[15]

Garrick's monument in Westminster Abbey, erected in 1797 eighteen years after his death, perpetuates the myth. It shows him in the act of 'throwing aside a curtain, which discovers a medallion of the great Poet [. . .] The curtain itself is designed to represent the Veil of Ignorance and Barbarism, which darkened the drama of the immortal bard till the appearance of Garrick.'[16] The inscription plays up the theme of Garrick as restorer of Shakespeare from oblivion:

> Tho' sunk in death the forms the Poet drew,
> The Actor's genius bade them breathe anew.
> Tho', like the Bard himself, in night they lay,
> Immortal Garrick call'd them back to day.

The second myth – Garrick the vandal – emerges in biographies of the nineteenth century, a period when devotion to Shakespeare could only be envisaged in terms of strict faithfulness to his writings. Percy Fitzgerald, for example, pays very little attention to Garrick's alterations of Shakespeare, and Shakespeare is not even listed in his index.[17] The exception is Garrick's 'hacked and hewed' alteration of *Hamlet.* Like James Boaden before him,[18] Fitzgerald is shocked that, at the close of his career Garrick, who had 'done so much for Shakspeare', could commit such sacrilege as 'that famous and Gothic mutilation of "Hamlet", the outrageous hewing to pieces of the noble play'.

Even more indignant was Joseph Knight, who saw Garrick's 'perversions of Shakespeare's texts' as his 'crowning disgrace'.[19] Knight condemned Garrick for hypocritically posing 'as the great defender of Shakespeare, oblivious of the fact that he had continually, with no feeling of shamefacedness, promoted his own kitchen drudge of a muse to occupy the same eminence with the muse of Shakespeare'. Garrick's first biographer of the twentieth century, Mrs Clement Parsons (1906), followed the line of her predecessors in deploring his 'inexcusable stupidity' in retaining Tate's happy ending to *King Lear*.[20] As for his *Hamlet*: 'Could obtuseness go further?' Frank Hedgcock, too, agreed that Garrick's 'travesty of *Hamlet*' was just 'the most celebrated' of 'all Garrick's nefarious attempts on Shakespeare's pieces'.[21] The counter-view – Garrick the restorer – is heard again from the 1920s. Shakespeare scholar George Odell had no doubts that alteration was always to be deplored but, refreshingly, was prepared to give Garrick credit for turning the tide against it.[22] W. J. Macqueen Pope, in his history of the Theatre Royal, Drury Lane, went further, writing (quite inaccurately): 'One of his best and wisest actions was to restore Shakespeare's own text to his mutilated plays. [. . .] Garrick threw overboard all the "improvers".'[23]

It is doubtful whether any of these writers had closely studied Garrick's alterations of Shakespeare. For example, his major biographer of the mid-twentieth century, the historian Carola Oman, pays them scarcely any attention.[24] Indeed, had they wished to do so, they would have found it difficult to obtain either texts to consult or reliable data on performances. All this was to change when Garrick found his Boswell in the person of George Winchester Stone, whose doctoral thesis[25] marked the beginning of a long career as Garrick's devoted champion, in which he returned again and again to the defence of Garrick's alterations of Shakespeare. Garrick is Stone's hero, who

> found God's plenty in the tragic vein in the great plays of England's past, largely (but not exclusively) in Shakespeare. His genius lay not in imitating those plays (as a number of writers had tried to do), but in making their texts live anew on stage by restoring them in many ways to their authors.[26]

Stone was one of the editorial team employed on *The London Stage*, a 'calendar of plays, entertainments and afterpieces, together with casts, box-receipts and contemporary comment, compiled from the playbills, newspapers and theatrical diaries of the period'. This remarkable work of reference appeared in five parts between 1960 and 1968, Stone being responsible for the critical introduction and editing of part 4, covering Garrick's period of management. It was now easy to find out what had been performed at any of the London playhouses on any night in any theatrical season between 1660 and 1800. Casts, and changes of cast, were noted and, where known, the takings from each evening were itemised.[27]

The London Stage also made it possible to check the validity of Garrick's reputation as the great restorer of Shakespeare to the playhouse. Robert D. Hume, writing in 1997, exposed it as a fable. He showed that in 1747, at the beginning of Garrick's managerial career, Drury Lane was offering twenty-two plays by Shakespeare. Only thirteen were in the repertoire by the mid-1770s, when Garrick retired.[28] Myths, it seems, are difficult to dispel. For, as Hume himself points out, Arthur Scouten, editor of the third part of *The London Stage* (1729–1747), had demonstrated as early as 1956 that Garrick could not have been the initiator of the eighteenth-century Shakespeare boom, since there had been a series of revivals prior to his debut.[29] Stone was, of course, aware of Scouten's revelation, which had originally appeared as early as 1944. But Stone continued to maintain 'a broader view'[30] of his hero's influence, and to press Garrick's claim to be the primary restorer of Shakespeare.

Another powerful advocate of the case against Garrick is Brian Vickers:

> He certainly cashed in on the vogue for Shakespeare, and undoubtedly increased the audience for his plays. But it would be wholly false to present him as in any way the 'restorer' of Shakespeare. In all his adaptations, from the 1740s to the 1770s, he expresses the values of D'Avenant, Dryden, Tate and Shadwell.[31]

Whereas Stone had championed a Garrick intent upon driving his theatre ever closer to textual fidelity to Shakespeare, Vickers accuses Garrick of lacking the courage and the inclination to revive Shakespeare as written. He 'enjoyed a position of eminence that would have enabled him to make the decisive break with the adapters, had he wished', but was not prepared to risk alienating conservative audiences by presenting the unfamiliar. Vickers identifies as 'desperate special pleading by his modern admirers' the claim that Garrick's 'was "the most accurate" or "the most complete" *Lear* or *Hamlet*' but, in attempting to strike a better balance, Vickers is certainly less than fair to Garrick and makes little allowance for the economic exigencies of competitive theatre management in a system of duopoly.

It is time to recognise that caricatures of Garrick either as rescuer or as false priest of Shakespeare are equally distorted. The reality is both more complicated and more interesting. Many scholars now examine how Shakespeare has been appropriated to accommodate, not only the changing tastes of audiences, but also the wider cultural and national concerns, while critics such as Dobson and Jean Marsden pay our ancestors the compliment of assuming that they had what seemed to them good reasons for the changes they made to Shakespeare's plays, and study their alterations with respect.[32] Furthermore, unlike the editors of Garrick's day, we are now less confident that a definitive 'authorised version' of what Shakespeare actually wrote (or actually intended) is achievable – or even desirable. Stephen Orgel, for example, has argued that scripts for performance were meant to be fluid and were constantly adapted by the actors, authorial authenticity in a single text becoming an issue only when plays were to be published.[33] Meanwhile Peter Holland praises Garrick for continually reviewing, revising and restoring the acting-texts of *Lear* and *Hamlet*.[34] The starting point of this book, therefore, is the recognition that Davenant, Tate and Garrick in their alterations were only doing what acting companies (including Shakespeare's) have always done, and some still continue to do.

Bernard Shaw's coinage 'Bardolatry', with its connotations of a quasi-religious worship of Shakespeare and his writings, though it dates from 1900, is too useful an anachronism not to employ in the context of Garrick's alterations. The term is particularly pertinent because Shaw's original targets were ignorant actor-managers, from Cibber and Garrick to Irving and Tree, who, though claiming to adore the Bard, had mounted mangled versions of his plays:

> It was the age of gross ignorance of Shakespear and incapacity for his works that produced the indiscriminate eulogies with which we are familiar. It was the revival of serious attention to those works that coincided with the movement for giving genuine instead of spurious representations of his plays. So much for Bardolatry![35]

But the chapters that follow will show that, in the age of Garrick, eulogising the national Bard and paying 'serious attention' to his works was not thought by actors, critics or editors to be incompatible with altering his plays to suit the cultural preferences of the period. They will demonstrate that when, across the dark backward and abyss of time, Garrick is seen in a literary as well as a theatrical context, our understanding of a period in Shakespeare studies prior to 'the divorce of stage and page' will be enhanced. Several of the alterations of Shakespeare's plays made by Garrick will be closely examined in order to show that, during the period of his professional career (1741–1776), the processes of altering and editing were more closely allied than they were to become by the end of the eighteenth century. By looking at his extensive involvement with several of the period's editors of Shakespeare, the book will explore the hypothesis that Garrick's very centrality in all matters Shakespearean, and in particular his sense of a 'special relationship' with Shakespeare, actually held back the separation of stage and page. As Stanley Wells has said: 'Few Shakespearian activities in Garrick's lifetime do not, in one way or another, impinge upon him.'[36]

Garrick's career straddles the middle decades of a century in which attitudes to altering themselves underwent rapid alteration. While the term 'alteration' today carries mainly negative overtones, Hume suggests that for potential purchasers of play texts in the early years of the eighteenth century, the word could well have had positive connotations of helpful improvement.[37] In 1745, Eliza Haywood commented on *Caius Marius* (Otway's version of *Romeo and Juliet)* that 'it is not to be doubted but that the admirable Author, had he lived to see the Alteration, would have been highly thankful and satisfied with it'.[38] Yet, by the end of the century alteration in the sense of rewriting had virtually ceased. How Garrick both accelerated and retarded this change will be explored below.

CHAPTER 2

The contexts of Garrick's alterations of Shakespeare

It was Garrick's good fortune that his career in the theatre (1741–1776) took place before editors and actors went their separate ways. While squabbling editors pursued their illusory goal of establishing once and for all precisely what Shakespeare had written, they nevertheless agreed in accepting the need to adapt the plays for performance. Lewis Theobald had made an alteration of *Richard II* in 1720 and had claimed that his *Double Falsehood* (1728) was based on the lost *Cardenio*. William Warburton warmly commended Garrick's 'Reformed Winter's Tale',[1] and Edward Capell collaborated on an alteration of *Antony and Cleopatra* for Drury Lane. George Steevens encouraged Garrick to ditch the final act of *Hamlet* and re-write the play's dénouement, while Samuel Johnson, famously, supported Tate's happy ending for *King Lear*.[2] Indeed, it was still possible at this period for a publisher to claim that the plays could be best understood and appreciated in performance. In 1734 Jacob Tonson had included in his cheap edition of the plays an advertisement from W. Chetwood, the Drury Lane prompter, indignantly denying a claim by Walker, Tonson's rival, that Walker had published plays 'printed from Copies made use of at the Theatres'.[3] Walker's 'Editions', he says, are 'Useless, Pirated and Maim'd'; Chetwood has never allowed Walker access to Drury Lane's scripts. Tonson, speaking through Chetwood, thus implies that the most authoritative source for editions of the plays is the playhouse; the authority of Garrick's performances could only reinforce this view.

Though the word 'editor' had wider connotations in the eighteenth century than it does in the twenty-first, the essential difference between an editor and an alterer remains that the former is preparing a text to be read, while the outcome of the latter's efforts is a script to be performed. However, this simple distinction does not seem quite adequate for 'acting editions'. While the publishing of individual plays 'as perform'd' by well-known acting companies has a long history, the first of the *collected* acting editions was Bell's *Shakespeare's Plays as They Are Now Performed at the*

Theatres Royal in London, issued in nine volumes in 1773 and 1774. Bell offered readers, and amateur actors too, transcriptions of the Drury Lane and Covent Garden prompt-books – the work of alterers, in fact. It seems that in the eighteenth century the boundaries between categories were much more fluid, since the role of an editor of Shakespeare had yet to be fully defined. Ought an editor to reproduce in full the prefaces, glosses and notes of his predecessors, agreeing or disagreeing with them as he thought necessary? Was an editor at liberty to substitute modern for obsolete words? Should he (as Pope had done) highlight 'beauties' while downgrading to footnotes passages he judged unworthy? In addressing such questions, editors from Rowe (1709) onwards were progressively making up the rules of the game as they went along. It was not until more than a decade after Garrick's death that the role of editor was codified into what is essentially its modern form by the publication in 1790 of Edmond Malone's ten-volume *Plays and Poems of William Shakspeare*.

This chapter contextualises Garrick's alterations of Shakespeare's plays by first looking briefly at the phenomenon of the eighteenth-century literary club, where members' social and professional lives inter-mingled, and which provides an image of the London that Garrick inhabited. Next, the characteristics of the theatre in which he worked will be explored. Then, in order to throw light upon the principles that informed Garrick's practice as an alterer, and following a general survey of the practical and cultural constraints upon him as actor-manager and dramaturge, the chapter ends with a brief examination of his alteration of a play by a contemporary of Shakespeare: Ben Jonson's *Every Man in His Humour* (1751). A non-Shakespearean text has deliberately been chosen as exemplar of Garrick's principles for alteration, as carrying less editorial 'baggage'. As altered by Garrick, the play was a huge success. His own role, Kitely, the jealous husband, was one of the most popular of his career, and he appeared in it no fewer than eighty-one times between 1751 and his retirement in 1776.[4] The changes Garrick made are instructive and illuminate his theatre's response to the drama of Shakespeare and his contemporaries.

Garrick's celebrity gave him entrance into every social circle, while his dominant position in the theatre gave him huge power and influence over the lives of others; he was both courted and reviled. Many contemporaries sought to advance their careers through him; many fell out with him. Obvious examples are his early biographers: Arthur Murphy, playwright and for many years Garrick's 'house dramatist', and Thomas Davies, theatrical historian, scholar, bookseller and Drury Lane actor. Davies's multi-faceted career in itself demonstrates the permeability of the barrier between stage and page in the small world of literary London where the club, among its other benefits, provided a way to manage the tensions that arise when professional and private lives overlap.

The online *Oxford English Dictionary* reproduces Johnson's famous definition of a club as 'an assembly of good fellows, meeting under certain conditions'. It also credits him with the coinages 'unclubable' (c. 1764) and 'clubable' (1783). Although this chapter concentrates on that most famous of the eighteenth-century clubs, The Club (later the Literary Club) founded by Johnson and Joshua Reynolds in 1764, which met at the Turk's Head, Gerrard Street, it should be remembered that this was a period when many clubs flourished. There may have been as many as 2000 clubs and other societies in early Georgian London, some social, some debating and some artistic.[5] Johnson loved clubs; he founded the Ivy Lane Club as early as 1748, and another within a year of his death, at the Essex Head in December 1783. Clubs had developed from the coffee houses, those centres of social, business and cultural life open to all men.[6] Once a group of good fellows had begun to meet regularly for conversation in a coffee house or tavern, it was a natural next step to ask the proprietor to reserve a private room for their exclusive use at pre-arranged times. For example, Davies mentions 'a respectable society called the Shakespeare Club, which had been chiefly brought together by Mr. Garrick and his most intimate friends'.[7] Members would club together to share the costs. If they then proceeded to formalise their exclusivity by restricting membership and instituting a system of electing new members, a club in the modern sense had been formed.

Though much of their attraction lay in the pleasures of conversation in a relaxed, woman-free atmosphere, where smoking was permitted, and where eating and drinking were part of the entertainment, clubs had more serious functions. They were, of course, ideal places for 'networking': advancing one's professional career through social contacts. But some aimed higher, seeking to patronise the arts through sponsorship and publication.[8] Clubs of this kind represented a counter-force to the system of aristocratic patronage that had dominated the sixteenth and seventeenth century and against which Johnson himself had struggled so painfully. The club of which Thomas Davies was a member certainly served as a stimulus to creativity: it was here that Johnson's *Lives of the Poets* (1779–1781) and Davies's *Memoirs of the Life of Mr. Garrick* (1780) originated. Davies himself told Boswell that it had been Johnson who in 1779 gave 'the key-note to the performance' by writing the first sentence of the *Memoirs*.

One of the things that made The Club remarkable was the wide range of professions to which its members belonged. When first set up in 1764, it was essentially a circle of nine friends. They came from the worlds of letters (Oliver Goldsmith, Sir John Hawkins, Johnson himself and two Oxford gentlemen, Topham Beauclerk and Bennet Langton); the law and politics (Edmund Burke); medicine (Dr Christopher Nugent, Burke's father-in-law); stock-broking (Anthony Chamier) and of course the fine arts (Reynolds himself). Later this tight little group was expanded to twelve (in 1768) and then, in 1773, to sixteen. It was through this second expansion that Garrick and Boswell became members. In 1775, when Steevens and Gibbon were elected (election had to be unanimous), the membership stood at twenty, and in 1778, the year before Garrick died, it was increased again to a total of thirty.[9] Each avocation represented among the membership had its own separate structures for professional and social intercourse; The Club brought them together. Like a Venn diagram of intersecting circles, The Club provided a forum for the stimulation of cross-cultural ideas, in which members could co-operate to influence and shape developments, especially in the field of literature. As early as 1766, Johnson could write to Langton: 'Mr. Lye is printing his Saxon and Gothick dictionary; all THE CLUB subscribes.' Brewer lists the diverse fields of literature in which members of The Club were active: aesthetics and art, biography, literary criticism, medicine and science, oriental languages and literature, political economy, botany and travel, theology, history and the history of music. 'Much of this work', he adds, 'codified and ordered the sprawling, diverse and heterogeneous creative activity of previous generations'.[10] This comment seems particularly apt when applied to the editing of Shakespeare during the period of The Club's greatest power and influence, the later decades of the eighteenth century.

Garrick's own election to The Club was in no sense a walkover, though he seems to have made the bad mistake of assuming that it would be. There are three versions of what happened, all recorded by Boswell, who goes out of his way to correct the misrepresentations of the two sources that reflect badly upon Johnson.[11] The first, Sir John Hawkins, had claimed that Johnson had objected to Garrick's 'buffoonery', the second, Mrs Piozzi, to his being an actor. Boswell's preferred account has Johnson affronted by Garrick's presumption in assuming that he would be welcome. Garrick was so busy and so sought after, both professionally and socially, that this setback is unlikely to have caused him much grief. But he might have felt some chagrin at the news of the election to The Club in 1768 of

George Colman, co-author with him of *The Clandestine Marriage* (1766), who had become manager of Covent Garden in 1767. Boswell does not explain why so many years were allowed to pass before Garrick's election. Johnson's well-known touchiness about his former pupil was undoubtedly one factor. Reynolds famously remarked that 'Dr. Johnson considered Garrick as his property, and would never suffer any one to praise or abuse him but himself'.[12] Probably, too, members were afraid that Garrick's compulsion to perform offstage as well as on, his hunger for applause and his need to dominate any social gathering would distort their meetings. The Club had a heady and distinctly macho atmosphere, in which many strong personalities competed to exhibit their wit and learning.

It was Garrick the manager and man of letters, rather than Garrick the player, who was finally welcomed to meetings of The Club in March 1773. Indeed, for nearly a century, he remained the only actor to be elected to membership. Opposition from Goldsmith was another reason for the delay in electing him. Goldsmith had been unable to persuade Colman at Covent Garden to stage his new comedy, *She Stoops to Conquer.* But he was reluctant to offer it to Drury Lane, whose manager he regarded with hostility. (Garrick had rejected Goldsmith's *The Good Natur'd Man* in 1767.) Garrick actually became a member of The Club at precisely this point in its history. Within its convivial circle professional conflicts had to be suppressed. For example, Walpole describes a ludicrous party piece performed that winter. Goldsmith sat in Garrick's lap, both covered by a cloak, 'and while Goldsmith spoke [a speech from Addison's *Cato*], Garrick's arms that embraced him, made foolish actions'.[13] This suggests some level of intimacy but there was always tension between them, a tension that gives added bite to the mock epitaphs that each produced of the other within the close-knit yet competitive atmosphere of The Club.

Garrick's clever yet cruel improvisation 'Here lies NOLLY Goldsmith, for shortness call'd Noll, / Who wrote like an angel, but talk'd like poor Poll' demanded a response. Goldsmith was still working on his 'Retaliation' when he died; it was published fifteen days later. It comprises mock epitaphs of several members of his circle. All, except the unfinished tribute to Joshua Reynolds, are more or less barbed, and much of the epitaph for Garrick, in particular, is extremely cutting. But it ends kindly:

> But peace to his spirit, wherever it flies,
> To act as an angel, and mix with the skies:
> Those poets, who owe their best fame to his skill,

> Shall still be his flatterers, go where he will.
> Old Shakespeare, receive him, with praise and with love,
> And Beaumonts and Bens be his Kellys above.[14]

From a founder member of The Club who had absolutely no wish to be counted among Garrick's flatterers, this is generous and represents a valuable contemporary estimate of the relative standing of Garrick and Shakespeare. First, it acknowledges that Shakespeare's ever-rising reputation owes much to Garrick. Furthermore, it is reasonable to read the lines as tribute to Garrick's skills as adapter as well as performer and publicist, since plays by 'Beaumont' (or at any rate Fletcher), 'Ben' and 'Kelly' had all undergone alteration by Garrick for production at Drury Lane.[15] The lines also demonstrate the special status that Shakespeare had achieved by the 1770s. By linking the name of the despised Kelly with those of Shakespeare's contemporaries, Goldsmith firmly dismisses Beaumont and Jonson to the second rank.

To have enjoyed continuing access to The Club's stimulating environment must have eased Garrick's transition to retirement in 1776. In 1775 members began to dine together regularly in addition to their weekly evening meetings, but Club records show Garrick as an infrequent diner, despite the fine of five shillings for each dinner missed. For him, The Club provided a convivial setting for exchanging ideas and gossip, for influencing events and, above all, for what Boswell called 'shining'. By the time of Garrick's death in 1779, The Club, of which he was a member of the inner circle, had become very powerful, as members worked hard to subscribe to, praise and promote one another's works. Of the thirty-three coaches carrying mourners to his funeral in Westminster Abbey, four were allocated to members of The Club. 'I saw old Samuel Johnson standing beside his grave, at the foot of Shakespeare's monument, and bathed in tears,' recalled an onlooker.[16] According to Boswell, it was at Garrick's funeral that the decision was taken to adopt the name 'the Literary Club'.[17] With Garrick's status as actor-playwright no longer a complication, members felt free to clarify where their main interest lay. Though many applications were made to fill Garrick's vacant place, Johnson, in a remarkable tribute to his old friend, decreed that no worthy successor could be found. He insisted that there should be a year's 'widowhood', and Club records confirm that no fresh election was held until November 1780. One of those anxious to succeed to Garrick's place in such an influential literary circle was Edmond Malone. After several unsuccessful efforts, he was eventually elected on 5 February 1782 and served as treasurer until his death in 1812.

Garrick enjoyed membership during The Club's most creative phase, when sparkling conversation and the cross-fertilization of ideas from many disciplines characterised its meetings. In a society seemingly obsessed with the privileges of rank, The Club was remarkable in valuing members primarily for personal brilliance. In later years it became more settled, more expensive, more rule based and more respectable. Soon, bishops and peers outnumbered writers among its members, and reputation rather than promise became the key to election.

That the social and intellectual pleasures of the clubs of the mid-eighteenth century were confined to males was a cause of chagrin to literary ladies like Garrick's friend, Mrs Elizabeth Montagu, society hostess and author of the *Essay on the Writings and Genius of Shakespeare* (1769). The theatres, on the other hand, welcomed women as well as men, both as performers and as spectators. Ensuring that the language used and situations depicted in the plays he offered to a mixed public did not cross an ever-more strictly drawn line of 'indelicacy' was just one of the constant pressures on a manager – and indeed upon an alterer. Before any of Garrick's alterations of Shakespeare's plays are considered in detail, this chapter reveals his general principles for alteration by examining the changes he made to a play by another Renaissance dramatist: Ben Jonson. First, however, will come a brief contextual sketch of theatrical conditions and constraints during Garrick's years of management (1747–1776). This highlights some of the developments during Garrick's reign at Drury Lane that impinged upon his work as alterer, as well as some differences between his theatre and today's, and draws largely upon many historical accounts of the English theatre in the eighteenth century.[18]

Whatever elevated aims managers might lay claim to, running a London theatre in the mid-eighteenth century was primarily a commercial and competitive enterprise. Since the Stage Licensing Act of 1737, the two patent houses, the theatres royal in Covent Garden and Drury Lane, had been the only legal providers of dramatic entertainment in London; they directly competed for audiences. At first, the managers of several minor theatres found ways round the act, and it was at one of these (in Goodman's Fields) that Garrick made his London debut in 1741 in the role of King Richard III. Ironically, his very success there led to calls from the patent houses for the act to be strictly enforced. In each season thereafter, from September to June, the duopoly were the sole providers of theatrical entertainment in the capital, although from 1766 the Haymarket Theatre was permitted to stage plays during the unfashionable summer months.

The situation was closely analogous to the period in Britain after 1955 when two television channels (BBC Television and the ITV companies) contended for viewers. Popular performers and writers discovered their market value. Some were induced to change sides by generous financial incentives, others attempted to play one employer off against another. Managers kept a close eye on each other's audience figures, imitated each other's successes and became expert in 'spoiling' rival productions by shrewd counter-scheduling. This competition to secure and retain the greater market share worked against innovation and experiment. Rather, it promoted a tendency to offer works in genres that had proved their popularity.

There were other reasons for the growing conservatism of the London stage in the mid-eighteenth century. The fact that the texts of all new plays had to be approved prior to production contributed to the caution of the managers when commissioning new writing. The censor was primarily concerned to prevent the expression of undesirable political views, but in their plots and language plays had also to conform to contemporary standards of decency and morality. Over the course of his managerial career, Garrick grew increasingly conservative in planning the repertory and was much criticised by would-be playwrights and their patrons for mounting so few new plays. For just one example, see the huffy exchange of letters between him and Sir Joshua Reynolds in 1774.[19] Reynolds's nephew had submitted a play to Garrick. Garrick had replied politely, regretting that there were no slots available for new plays for two seasons ahead. Reynolds took this as both an outright rejection and a personal slight, but subsequently apologised when he found out that Garrick's statement had been true. Garrick's defence to the charge of failing to champion unknown playwrights was the obligation upon the management to minimise financial risk: if audiences stayed away, the company would not eat. In any case, he believed that he knew from experience what would please his audiences, and that his duty was to give them what they wanted.

What the Drury Lane audiences wanted above all, of course, was to be entertained. In a book that concentrates upon Shakespeare it is easy to overlook the fact that the theatre's repertoire was far from exclusively devoted to the national Bard. Michael Booth has shown that the popularity with audiences of pantomime and farce far outstripped that of comedy and, in particular, tragedy, though in both the latter genres Shakespeare predominated over any other single author.[20] Pedicord's analysis of the Drury Lane repertoire between 1747 and 1776 confirms

Booth's findings.[21] In terms of numbers of performances, he shows that the 'top ten' most popular offerings during Garrick's management were four pantomimes, three written by Henry Woodward, one by Garrick himself (259, 207, 171 and 158 performances, respectively); two farces: Edward Ravenscroft's *Anatomist* (157) and Garrick's *Lethe* (154); Garrick's entertainment *The Jubilee* (153); Charles Coffey's ballad opera *The Devil to Pay* (143); while Garrick's alteration of Shakespeare's *Romeo and Juliet* (142), tied for ninth place with *The Padlock*, a comic opera (142). Along with the preference for comedy went a growing demand for new and elaborate scenery and costumes, not merely in the traditionally lavishly staged pantomimes, but also in main pieces (the first production for which Garrick ordered entirely new scenery and dresses was Johnson's *Irene*, first performed on 6 February 1749). These costly innovations were assisted by the improvements in stage lighting that Garrick introduced in 1765 on his return from his European tour, and by the skilled scene painters whom he employed, most notably (from 1771) De Loutherbourg.

While new plays were, of course, staged from time to time, it would be impossible to claim that 1747–1776 was a period of great dramatic writing in the English theatre. None of the new tragedies in which Garrick starred has survived. Of new comedies, only those of Sheridan and Goldsmith (in which he did not appear) are still performed, though Garrick's and Colman's *The Clandestine Marriage* (1766) is occasionally given, and there is evidence for a recent revival of interest in the comedies of Suzanna Centlivre. (Garrick played Don Felix in Centlivre's *The Wonder* seventy times and chose this role for his final appearance.) The status of the performer rose as the level of dramatic writing fell, and the actor, not the writer, increasingly came to dominate the stage. Thus, when Thomas Davies in his *Life of Garrick* begins 'to review the state of our playhouses' at the start of his subject's career, the 'review' consists of two chapters of biographical sketches of the leading actors of the time. Drury Lane was far from being a one man band; Garrick knew the vital importance of building a strong company of established favourites and rising stars. Among the pleasures of theatre-going at that time was that of comparing different actors in the same part, much as opera-goers at, say, the New York Metropolitan today enjoy assessing the merits of rival sopranos in *Traviata* or *Turandot*. This predilection was tested to the limit during 'the battle of the Romeos' at the opening of the 1750–1751 season, when for twelve successive performances both the patent houses presented *Romeo and Juliet*. Barry played Romeo at Covent Garden, Garrick at

Drury Lane. Thomas Davies records an epigram printed during 'this struggle for theatrical pre-eminence':

> Well, what's to-night, says angry Ned,
> As up from bed he rouses?
> Romeo again! and shakes his head;
> Ah! pox on both your houses![22]

The stratification of Georgian society was reflected in the design of the theatres, in their pricing policies and in the timing and construction of the programmes of entertainment they offered. In fact, Garrick had not one audience, but several. In many of the prologues that have survived, the speaker recognises this fact by separately addressing each part of the house. For example, in the prologue that Garrick wrote to Bickerstaffe's comedy *'Tis Well it's no Worse* (1770), the speaker appeared as an Irish sea captain, asking for indulgence for his nervous cousin, the author. Metaphorically, the theatre was transformed into a warship, similarly structured on hierarchical principles, where the space occupied by each rank was kept strictly separate.[23] The topmost crew members in the upper gallery had paid one shilling each, a price beyond the means of the very poorest, but not too much for genuine seamen on leave and looking for a good night out. This was the cheapest and the rowdiest part of the house; in 1768 it held 100 paying customers, as well as some 'free servants'.[24] If the entertainment did not please them, they were quite capable of 'firing' (line 34) missiles such as fruit onto the stage. Seven hundred seats at one shilling and sixpence were available in the first gallery and slips ('the quarter-deck', line 35), which was mainly frequented by respectable tradespeople and their families. Another noisy area was the pit ('between decks', line 37), where seats cost two shillings and sixpence. This held 500, and was the preferred area for middle-class men-about-town, especially the *literati*, who prided themselves on their critical 'broadsides' (line 38). At this period it was still unusual for women to sit in the pit. Fashionable ladies ('sweet craters, who sit in the cabin', line 39) occupied the side and front boxes, while prostitutes were expected to confine themselves to an upper range of green boxes and to behave with decorum. Altogether, some 600 places were available in the boxes. The price of a box seat was four shillings, beyond the reach of all but the very well-to-do. This was the section of the public whose approbation in the long term was of most value to the managers; hence flattery of the ladies in the boxes was a very frequent feature of contemporary prologues.

Each section of the house had its prejudices and preferences. To keep the different audiences happy – or at any rate quiet – required the skills of a ringmaster controlling a four-ringed circus. The risk of disruption, even of riot, was always present. Twice during Garrick's period of management, in 1755 and 1763, his theatre was almost destroyed by rioters. A claque determined to ensure that a new piece be not heard, as happened on the first night of Kelly's *Word to the Wise* in 1770, could disrupt the playhouse for days. The struggle for dominance between management and audience was in itself something of a public entertainment. The knowledge of its potential to disrupt and destroy gave a dangerous edge to the audience's enjoyment, and both sides knew that, ultimately, the house always had the upper hand. The actor-manager had to be lion tamer as well as ringmaster. His chief weapons were music, spectacle and the collective power and charm of his company's personalities and performances.

The structure of the evening's entertainment reflected the social differences within the audience. The main piece, a five-act tragedy or comedy, usually began at 6.00 p.m. The timing was primarily designed to suit the more leisured patrons, who would have dined in the afternoon. This was rather too early a start for tradespeople, shopkeepers and apprentices, who customarily worked long hours. Usually, therefore, the main piece was followed by a farce or afterpiece of a comic or musical nature, designed to have particular appeal to this second category. To encourage their attendance, it was the practice at both the patent houses to charge half price for admission after the end of the third act of the main piece. The only exception to this rule was during the first season of a new pantomime when, in recognition of the extraordinary production costs, the bills would announce 'nothing under full price will be taken'. However prestigious the main offering, it was often the takings from the second half of the bill (the 'after money') that determined the financial success of the evening. The attempts in 1763 of first Drury Lane and then Covent Garden to withdraw the half price concession on grounds of rising recurrent costs ended in complete failure. For Garrick, the price of the two-day riot, which had included attempts at arson by members of the audience, was personal mortification, the public humiliation of certain of his actors who had displeased the mob, and the expense of rebuilding benches and replacing chandeliers. Indeed, though not quite in the sense that Johnson meant it, 'The drama's laws the drama's patrons give'.[25]

One of the most significant cultural changes that impinged on British drama and its patrons during Garrick's period of management was the increasingly overt patriotism of the period of the Seven Years War with France, which began in 1755. The xenophobia of some sections of the audience in that year gave rise to the most serious disruptions ever known at Drury Lane. The struggle went on for six days, as the rioters protested against attempts to perform a lavishly staged ballet, *The Chinese Festival*, on the grounds that the dancers were French. (Actually the choreographer Noverre was Swiss, and many of the dancers German.) The aristocrats in the boxes, on the other hand, insisted that the ballet should go ahead. Swords were drawn, bloodshed ensued, two men died, the theatre was trashed and the windows of Garrick's house were broken by the mob. Reluctantly, Garrick withdrew the ballet; Noverre and his hundred dancers were paid off and sent back to France. Garrick, of Huguenot descent and married to an Austrian, had learnt his lesson: in wartime, the belief that art transcends national boundaries must give place to a narrower patriotism. Since the anxious days of 1745, the orchestra at Drury Lane had played 'God Save the King' at all performances. Garrick had to find new ways to demonstrate the theatre's loyalty, and Shakespeare was his trump card. In 1756 he presented an opera based on *The Tempest*. Though often attributed to him, he denied that he was responsible for the libretto, writing on 7 December 1756 to James Murphy French:

> if you mean that *I* was the person who altered the *Midsummer's Night Dream*, and the *Tempest*, into operas, you are much mistaken. – However, as old Cibber said in his last epilogue,
>
> But right or wrong, or true or false – 'tis pleasant.[26]

To serve as a prologue to the operatic *Tempest*, Garrick wrote a brief dialogue between a critic (Wormwood) and an actor (Heartly).[27] Wormwood deeply disapproves of any tinkering with the Bard, and claims to hate music: 'What! Are we to be quivered and quavered out of our senses? Give me Shakespear in all his force, rigor, and spirit!' Heartly does not attempt to defend directly the principle of altering Shakespeare; his major object is to speak up for English music. He quotes *The Merchant of Venice* to make the point that those who, like Wormwood, do not love music are 'fit for treason'. By demonstrating the patriotic power of music, Heartly immediately induces a total reversal of view in his opponent. Suppose, he suggests, that 10,000 French had invaded:

> HEARTLY Why, then I say, let but 'Britons strike home!' or 'God save the King' be sounded in the ears of five thousand brave Englishmen with a Protestant Prince at the head of 'em, and they'll drive every Monsieur into the sea and make 'em food for sprats and mackrell.
>
> WORMWOOD Huzza! And so they will! 'Egad, you're in the right.[28]

By linking Shakespeare with English music and English bravery, Garrick implies that attending a performance of *The Tempest, An Opera* is an act of patriotism.

Three years later, with the Seven Years War at its height, Drury Lane staged the only pantomime Garrick wrote. This was *Harlequin's Invasion*, in which a country headed by King Shakespear (Britain) faces invasion by Monsieur Harlequin and his troops (the French). The natives, represented by a 'Dad's army' of stock comedy types, are roused to resistance by Mercury, who sings:

> To arms, you brave mortals, to arms,
> The road to renown is before you.
> The name of King Shakespear has charms,
> To rouse you to actions of glory.[29]

In the spectacular finale, Shakespear rises in triumph as Harlequin sinks defeated through the front trap. At the climax, as he was to do ten years later in *The Jubilee*, Garrick introduces a procession of Shakespearean characters who join in the chorus ('Come away, come away, come away. / His genius calls and you must obey') and in the grand dance that brings down the curtain. By staging Shakespeare as a national icon, Garrick had found a lucrative means of controlling his audience through their patriotism.[30]

While it is true that, for almost the entirety of Garrick's reign at Drury Lane (1747–1776), his theatre was essentially the building that had been designed by Wren in 1674, changes made over the period, on stage and off, brought about a reduction in the intimacy in the relationship between actors and audience. Pedicord says that when Garrick and his partner James Lacy were granted half-shares in the patent in 1747, they immediately enlarged the seating capacity from about 1000 to an estimated 1268, which increased the takings by more than £40 a night to over £190.[31] A further enlargement in 1762 provided for an estimated audience of 2362 (Pedicord's figure) and a potential increase in the gross of £90 per night. Thus, the theatre in which Garrick had first appeared in 1742 had more than doubled its capacity by the time of his retirement in 1776. But an even more significant change directly associated with this enlargement – and which marks a break point in the evolution of theatrical practice from Shakespeare's day to Garrick's – was the enforcement, with effect from the 1762–1763 season, of a ban on spectators backstage, including the practice of permitting seats on stage on benefit nights. (The increase in capacity of 1762 had been needed in order to ensure that the actors would not suffer financially.) The announcement on the front page of the *Public Advertiser* on 21 February 1763 suggested that the change was made in response to complaints and 'for the sake of rendering the Representation more agreeable to the Public', but in fact Garrick had been struggling to achieve it ever since his first days in charge of Drury Lane. 'Order, decency, and decorum, were the first objects which our young manager kept constantly in his eye at the commencement of his administration', says Thomas Davies.[32] The epilogue that Garrick composed for his leading actress, Peg Woffington, to speak on the opening night of his first managerial season makes the same point with a lighter touch. The verse is fluent, colloquial and perfectly adapted to the speaker's personality. It begins:

> SWEET doings truly! We are finely fobb'd!
> And at one stroke of all our pleasures robb'd!
> *No beaux behind the scenes*! 'tis innovation!
> Under the specious name of reformation!
> *Public complaint*, forsooth, is made a puff,
> Sense, order, decency, and such like stuff.[33]

Garrick was much praised by biographers for his efforts to introduce 'order, decency and such like stuff' into the raffish and morally ambiguous world of the playhouse. Confining the audience to the public areas brought the theatre closer towards the respectability he sought for it. But it was also a significant step away from the intimacy of the early playhouses, where actors had been all but surrounded by their audience. The trend towards total physical separation of entertainers and entertained had begun. Nevertheless, as a glance at any engraving of the interior of an eighteenth-century theatre will show, a Georgian audience was still much closer to the actors than in the Victorian theatre, where the picture frame of the proscenium arch kept them apart. At Garrick's Drury Lane, at Covent Garden, and at the growing number of provincial theatres modelled upon London's patent houses, the stage boxes abutted or surmounted the performers' entrance doors on either side of the forestage. Until the improvements in stage lighting that Garrick introduced late in his career, most action, in order to be visible, had to take place on the forestage. Actors positioned there would have been aware of the audience on three sides of them, and some spectators would have been close enough to touch. Eye contact would have been almost unavoidable since, just as in the open air playhouses of Shakespeare's day, performers and spectators shared the same light. By raising or lowering the rings of candles (girandoles) that hung above the stage it was possible to make the acting area lighter or darker, but the candles in the sconces around the auditorium stayed lit throughout the evening. Though actors were sometimes criticised for coming out of character and gazing round the house,[34] the fashionable sector of the audience attended as much to observe one another and chat as to enjoy the performance. For this a constantly illuminated auditorium was essential. An example from fiction is the fop, Mr Lovel, in Frances Burney's *Evelina*. ' "For my part", said Mr Lovel, "I confess I seldom listen to the players: one has so much to do, in looking about, and finding out one's acquaintance, that, really, one has no time to mind the stage. Pray, – (most affectedly fixing his eyes upon a diamond ring on his little finger) pray – what was the play tonight?" '[35] This need for shared light is one of the most important ways in which the conditions of Garrick's theatre differ from our own. We are polite spectators in a darkened auditorium. If we approve, we clap; if we disapprove, we keep quiet. But our ancestors were much more actively involved in the performance.

The more one reads about Garrick's theatre, the more alien, and the more fraught with contradictions, it appears. It was a theatre that prided itself on its good taste, and frequently re-wrote the indecent comedies of the Restoration to suit a more delicate age. For example, Garrick's *The Country Girl* (1766) was a cleaned-up, prettified adaptation of Wycherley's *The County Wife* (1675). What was objectionable about the old plays, it seemed, was not so much the subject matter itself – the perennial themes were sex, class and money – but the crudity of the language used to refer to staple plot elements such as cuckoldry and seduction. Sexual frankness was thought to be offensive to female ears, especially those of young ladies. Evelina's response to a performance of Congreve's comedy of 1695, *Love for Love*, is exemplary:

> The play was Love for Love, and tho' it is fraught with wit and entertainment, I hope I shall never see it represented again; for it is extremely indelicate, – to use the softest word I can, – that Miss Mirvan and I were perpetually out of countenance, and could neither make any observations ourselves, nor venture to listen to those of others.[36]

Her admirer, the cultured and correct Lord Orville, concurs: 'I am sure this is not a play that can be honoured with their [ladies'] approbation.'

Actors expected, and received, a highly emotional response from their audience. Tears were a sign of sensibility and even of moral worth.[37] The young Boswell knew how to prepare himself for the impact of Garrick's Lear:

> I went to Drury Lane and saw Mr. Garrick play *King Lear*. So very high is his reputation, even after playing so long, that the pit was full in ten minutes after four, although the play did not begin till half an hour after six. I kept myself at a distance from all acquaintances, and got into a proper frame. Mr. Garrick gave me the most perfect satisfaction. I was fully moved, and I shed abundance of tears.[38]

It is almost as if Boswell is preparing through self-denial for a religious experience. Yet his next sentence is a reminder of another striking difference between Garrick's theatre and today's: the mixture of genres in a single night's entertainment. Boswell's evening concluded with a comic afterpiece: 'The farce was Polly Honeycomb, at which I laughed a good deal.' Those who stayed for the entire programme certainly had value for their money. Musicians played before the main piece and between the acts, and dancers would entertain between the main piece and the afterpiece.

Thomas Davies considered the theatre of his age to be in an 'almost perfect' state,[39] yet it tolerated audience behaviour that would nowadays merit eviction, if not prosecution. Boswell claimed that one evening, while sitting in the pit at Drury Lane, 'in a wild freak of youthful extravagance, I entertained the audience prodigiously, by imitating the lowing of a cow'.[40] And theatre-going could actually be dangerous. There was no system of advance booking; tickets were allocated on a first-come-first-served basis, often leading to an unseemly scramble for seats. Pickpockets made the most of the opportunities provided by the scrum, and playgoers could not count themselves safe even when seats had been secured. On 15 February 1755 Drury Lane offered a reward of ten guineas in the *Public Advertiser* for the discovery of 'who it was that flung a hard Piece of Cheese, of near half a Pound Weight, from one of the Galleries last Tuesday Night, and greatly hurt a young Lady in the Pit'.

All in all, then, whether writing, commissioning or altering plays, Garrick had to bear in mind Whitehead's exhortation:

> A nation's taste depends on you.
> – Perhaps a nation's virtue too.[41]

He needed to be alive to the prejudices and preferences of a volatile and voluble audience made up of very different social elements, all of whom tended to regard him and his company as their personal servants. This audience was emotional and as noisy in its approbation as in its disapproval; it favoured star performers in showy roles; it believed itself to be superior in taste and delicacy to barbarous previous ages; it relished comedy as long as the language was not too offensive, and it had a growing taste for lavish staging, though little interest in historical accuracy. The other major constraint on managers was the censorship exercised by the Lord Chamberlain's office. A theatre holding a royal patent was expected to do its part in upholding the established church and the Hanoverian succession; challenging the *status quo* was no part of its remit.

The preceding paragraphs have described the context for Garrick's professional activities – the social life of the clubs, the organisation of the theatre, the make-up and prejudices of its audience – all greatly different from those of the world of 1600. Just as Davenant and Dryden had done, Garrick in his day saw it as inevitable that old plays needed to be altered to make them fit for performance. Against this background, Garrick's principles of alteration will be demonstrated by an examination of his version of *Every Man in His Humour*.

What factors influenced Garrick's decision to revive Jonson's *Every Man in His Humour*? In 1750 he had been manager of Drury Lane for two full seasons. To keep his theatre prospering and the competition at bay it was essential to find plays, whether new or in revival, that would suit the preferences of his audience and show popular performers to advantage. Jonson was not an obvious choice. In the mid-eighteenth century, his plays were only slightly better known to London audiences than they are today and then, as now, only a small percentage of his dramatic output was ever staged. In March 1743, however, Drury Lane had revived *The Alchemist*. It had proved a huge success, thanks mainly to the acclaim heaped on Garrick, not yet a manager but the company's star actor, in the small but showy part of Abel Drugger. By the time he retired from Drury Lane in 1776, Garrick had played Drugger eighty times. He had himself altered the text, mainly by cutting, to make it into a suitable main piece. Probably, then, it was the continuing success of his version of *The Alchemist* that caused Garrick to browse Jonson's *Works* in his on-going search for additions to the repertoire. *Every Man in His Humour* would be a novelty. *The London Stage* records for the first half of the eighteenth century just one revival: a three-night run at Lincoln's Inn Fields in January 1725. The cast list for that production indicates that the play was significantly altered, with the low-life characters, Cob and Tib, totally omitted, and two new female roles, Clara and Lucinda, introduced. Of course, dead authors came cheap. Garrick decided to make the alteration himself, having since *The Alchemist* gained further experience in doctoring old plays. His partial restoration of *Macbeth* (1744) and his alteration of *Romeo and Juliet* (1748) were continuing to be highly profitable to Drury Lane.[42]

As Garrick would quickly have discovered, *Every Man in His Humour* is a genial city comedy. The social status of Jonson's characters is carefully gradated and ranges from gentleman down to water carrier, taking in two students-about-town, a justice of the peace, a squire, a merchant, a clerk and a wily servant. It is the last, in a series of disguises, who mainly keeps the action moving. A second group of characters, which includes the gulls, is less socially secure. One is a foolish country cousin constantly harping on his gentility; another, the son of a shopkeeper, has achieved a foothold among the *literati* without realising that his new companions enjoy mocking his ridiculous and derivative verses. Also in this group is the well-known stock character, the boastful ex-soldier surviving on his wits, who will inevitably be shown up as a coward. Jonson is not so much interested in exploring in depth the mediaeval theory of humours as in adapting stock characters and situations, drawn ultimately from ancient Roman comedy, in order to satirise contemporary London.[43] In line with the 'theory of humours' – the belief that the biases of our physiological make-up compel us to behave in certain ways[44] – each of the male personages has his dominant characteristic. The merchant is jealous, the well-born student is mischievous, the squire is irascible. There is no leading part as such. None of the principal characters (all male) dominates, but each is provided with ample comic opportunities, including the 'old merry magistrate' who finally disentangles the complications of the plot and brings the play to an end by arbitrarily doling out 'justice' in his very own personal style. The women's parts are very lightly sketched in; as the title and the prologue to the play make clear, this is essentially a play about men. True to his classical principles, Jonson observes the unities. The tightly plotted action takes place over the course of a single day and, as that day progresses, moves from the outskirts to the centre of the city. His prologue boasts that Jonson would not purchase his audience's delight at the cost of neglecting those unities – for example:

> To make a child now swaddled to proceed
> Man, and then shoot up in one beard and weed
> Past threescore years; or, with three rusty swords,
> And help of some few foot and half-foot words,
> Fight over York and Lancaster's long jars . . . (F. Prologue, lines 7 – 11)

The audience will not be wafted 'o'er the seas' by Chorus (line 15); there will be no elaborate scenic or sound effects. No, his play will exhibit 'deeds and language such as men do use' (line 21) and 'sport with human follies, not with crimes' (line 24). If the audience will acknowledge 'popular errors' (line 26) by laughing at them, he concludes:

> . . . there's hope left then
> You that have so grac'd monsters may like men. (lines 29–30)

Clearly the play had the potential to provide plenty of opportunities for the many Drury Lane actors who excelled in comedy. But in order to turn it into a text acceptable to a contemporary audience, Garrick was faced with the same four main tasks as confronted him when altering a play by Shakespeare. Two were relatively straightforward, two more problematical. First, he had to shorten the play to serve as a main piece in a full evening's entertainment; second, he had to make adjustments to language and staging because of differences between the playhouses of Jonson's day and his own. Third, because his public wanted to see leading players in leading parts, he needed to build up at least one character into an unequivocally starring role. Fourth, he had to take care that the overall moral message of the play would be acceptable, not only to his audience but also to the Lord Chamberlain's office. It would not have taken Garrick long to discover that Jonson had, in a sense, begun the task of revision for him. There are in fact two versions of *Every Man in His Humour*. The earlier was first acted in 1598 by the Lord Chamberlain's men and was published in quarto in 1601. There is a copy among the collection of old English plays bequeathed by Garrick to the British Museum. This might be the actual volume mentioned by his friend Warburton in a letter of May 1756: 'I have the first Edition of Jonson's "Every Man in his Humour", (if it be not lost,) where the names and scene are Italian; this is much at your service, if you have it not.'[45] Jonson revised the play early in the seventeenth century – perhaps in response to the Act to Restrain Abuses of Players (1606) which forbade blasphemy on stage – and this amended version was the first play to be included in Jonson's folio of his *Works* in 1616. A copy of the second edition (1640) was among the contents of Garrick's library auctioned in 1823.[46] Comparison of the quarto with the folio text reveals that, whereas the play was originally set in Florence, in his revision Jonson makes overt the London setting that was merely implicit in the original. He 'Englishes' the names of the characters – the ingenious servant Musco becomes Brainworm, Lorenzo Senior and Junior are now Kno'well and his son Edward Kno'well, and Thorello, the jealous husband, is renamed Kitely. Only the low-life characters, Cob and Tib, retain their original names. Jonson also pruned many of the long speeches and modified the academic tone of certain scenes, particularly those in which the student wits, Prospero/Wellbred and Lorenzo Junior/Edward Kno'well, featured.

Garrick's first task was to keep his alteration of *Every Man in His Humour* to a maximum of two hours' playing time. His version is thus shorter than Jonson's folio text by some 500 lines, despite the addition of 'a whole new scene in the fourth act'.[47] With this exception, every scene is shorter than in the original, though cutting is heavier towards the end. The easiest and most obvious cuts to make would have been local references – to customs, places, clothes or catchphrases – no longer current. Typical of Garrick's many such excisions are Edward Kno'well's lines sarcastically exhorting his foolish cousin Stephen not to hide his light under a bushel:

> to conceal such real ornaments as these, and shadow their glory as a milliner's wife does her wrought stomacher, with a smoky lawn or a black cyprus? Oh coz, it cannot be answer'd; go not about it; Drake's old ship at Deptford may sooner circle the world again. (F.I.ii.99–104)

Dated literary references were also obvious candidates for cutting. In revising his quarto Jonson had begun the process. In the final scene (Q.V. iii/F.V.i), in particular, he had accelerated the action by shortening the mocking and burning of Matheo/Matthew's verses, and by deleting a thirty-line speech of Lorenzo Junior's in praise of 'poesy' (Q.V.iii.294–325). Garrick cut the entire episode, along with much of the students' mockery of Matthew's plagiarised verses in F.I.iii and F.IV.i. There was little point in retaining Matthew's clumsy borrowings from *The Spanish Tragedy* and *Hero and Leander* if the Drury Lane audience could not recognise those works. Garrick pruned some speeches of all the main characters – even Bobadill's glorification of 'most divine' tobacco (F.III. ii.272–290) is trimmed – but Matthew's part suffers especially.

A further set of cuts reflects a major shift in what Garrick believed audiences would find appealing. They amount to the virtual elimination of two broad comedy roles: Cob, the clown, and Tib, his much put-upon wife. In spite of the new prologue's advice:

> With no false niceness this performance view,
> Nor damn for *low* whate'er is just and true. (lines 24–25)[48]

Garrick cut so much of the 'low' Cob and Tib that their parts were reduced almost to vanishing point. In Jonson's original, they might have been at the bottom of the social scale, but they were part of the fabric of London society and had their fair share of comic scenes. Martin Butler has pointed out the important unifying function of Cob the water-bearer who has access to all households.[49] But in Garrick's alteration Cob's part undergoes heavy blue-pencilling. Almost all his fooling, puns, *double entendres* and wordplay disappear. To take just one example out of many, Cob's stand-up comedy routine on the theme of fasting days (Cash acting as 'feed'), at F.III.ii.146–208, has nothing to do with the plot. His puns on choler/collar, malapropisms ('Hannibal' for 'cannibal') and ruderies about red herrings and stockfish were there to entertain the groundlings of what Garrick's audience considered a barbarous era. He cut them all. Out, too, went the entire scene in which Justice Clement pretends to send Cob to prison for speaking against tobacco (F.III.iii.56–139). Garrick completely removed the episode in which Cob beats his wife (F.IV.viii.65–83); he knew that his audience would never tolerate such open violence. In the original, Cob and Tib have the resilience of Punch and Judy. They always bounce back, and Jonson makes sure that Tib has the last word, in a delicious final exchange also sacrificed by Garrick:

COB Why now I see thou art honest, Tib, I receive thee as my dear and mortal wife again.
TIB And I you, as my loving and obedient husband. (F.V.i.258–260)

From Garrick's point of view, the clown's part – crude and rude, with language offensively obscene where it was not obscure – was obviously the prime candidate for shortening the play. He had treated those 'low' characters, the Porter in *Macbeth* and Peter in *Romeo and Juliet*, in exactly the same way. The effect in this case was to undermine Jonson's care to spread the comedy through a wide range of social levels, and instead to concentrate the audience's interest on a rather more 'polite', and smaller, circle of characters.

To make adjustments to language and staging to prepare the play for Drury Lane in 1751 was Garrick's second task. Profanity had to be purged from the text. Helpfully, Jonson in his revision had already toned down or cut many oaths, and had generally soft-pedalled on swearing. To take two random examples, 'By the faith I bear unto God', (Q.II.ii.43) had become 'By the faith I bear unto truth' (F.II.iii.73), and ' 'Sblood' (Q.III.iv.61) had been altered to ' 'Slight' (F.IV.i.64). Garrick's audience was far less tolerant than Jonson's of verbal crudity. 'Indecencies' in the original, particularly when spoken by female characters, had to be either cut or bowdlerised. Thus, for example, Squire Downright's vigorous farmyard language:

Well, go to, I say little: but by this good day – God forgive me I should swear – if I put it up so, say I am the rankest cow that ever piss'd. (F.II.i.137–139)

The above was weakened to 'I am the rankest coward ever lived' (G.II.i.136–137). And Garrick cuts most of the dialogue playing on the word 'tricks' in F.IV.i.95–104, ensuring that neither of the remaining *double entendres* is assigned to Dame Kitely or her sister. Obsolete words are removed, so that 'Oh, that villain dors me' (F.IV.vi.128) becomes 'Oh, that villain cheats me' (G.IV.iii.235), and 'leystalls' (F.II.iii.64) are changed to 'brothels' (G.II.ii.136).

Some changes were needed because the Elizabethan and Georgian stages were differently configured. Garrick was forced to cut a comic episode when one of the posts holding up the canopy suddenly becomes part of the action. In F.III.ii.330–338, Stephen practises what he believes to be gentlemanly discourse by addressing flowery phrases such as 'As I have somewhat to be saved, I protest –' (line 333) and 'Upon my reputation –' (line 336) to a post. A delightful stage direction is also lost:

(*Master* Stephen *is practicing to the post.*) (F.III.ii.331)

Occasionally Garrick had to invent a line to cover an exit, such as Edward's 'Come, let's in. Come, cousin' at the end of F.III.ii.356/G.III.ii.243. Garrick's usual method for this was to repeat a key word from earlier in the scene; with luck this reminder might procure a round of applause for the departing actor. Downright's exit line at G.II.i.158 – 'I will. – Scavenger, scavenger!' – seems to have been created for just this purpose.

The text had also to take account of the fact that the Georgian theatre used moveable scenery, drop cloths and a front curtain. The absence of these features from Jonson's playhouse meant that the action of the play could flow briskly on a clear stage, with the whereabouts of scenes being conveyed through dialogue, if necessary. The scene headings in the printed quarto and folio versions do not include locations. At Garrick's Drury Lane, however, elaborate sets were employed for major scenes, and other episodes would be played before a drop cloth. The 1752 published text indicates the location of each scene, for example:

ACT II.
SCENE I, *a warehouse belonging to* Kitely.

ACT V.
SCENE I, *Stocksmarket.*
SCENE II, *the street before* Cob's *house.*

The third scene of Jonson's first act is long (247 lines in the folio revision). It begins outside Cob's house, with Matthew knocking for admittance to visit Bobadill. Tib lets him in (F.I.iii.57), and at line 88 'Bobadill *is discovered lying on his bench.*' The action has flowed seamlessly from outside to indoors. Garrick had no option but to split this scene into two. The first (G.I.iii) is located in '*the street before* Cob's *house*', the second (G.I.iv) in '*a room in* Cob's *house*', where Bobadill is '*discovered upon a bench*'. Conversely, Garrick ran the second and third scenes of the folio's Act II into one, with the single location of '*Moorfields*' (G.II.ii). The need to allow time for scene changes gave an added reason for shortening the dialogue.

Garrick's third task was to create at least one star part. He knew that a revival of *Every Man in His Humour* would have a greatly enhanced chance of success if he himself appeared in it. On the precedent of his impact as Abel Drugger, he might have selected a cameo part such as Formal, the naïve young servant, whose comic entrance, drunk and trying to conceal his nakedness within an old suit of armour, is a high point of the final scene (F.V.i.177–190). However, the actor-manager judged that his audience would wish to see him in a major role – but which? Jonson had distributed the comedy very fairly; there was no obvious leading part, though probably Bobadill was the showiest. But Garrick was not tall enough for the braggart soldier. Had any indication survived of the distribution of parts among the original cast, Garrick would surely have earmarked for himself the role played by Shakespeare.[50] Why he decided to build up for himself the part of Kitely, the jealous husband, is unknown, but it is at least possible that his decision was prompted by the echoes of *Othello* in some of Kitely's lines. Lever, in his introduction to his parallel-text edition, lists several, including

> They would give out, because my wife is fair,
> Myself but lately married, and my sister
> Here sojourning a virgin in my house,
> That I were jealous! (F.II.i.108–111)

and

DAME KITELY What ail you, sweetheart? Are you not well? Speak, good muss.
KITELY Troth, my head aches extremely, on a sudden. (F.II.i.206–207)[51]

Lever here speculates that Shakespeare 'borrowed a number of Othello's attitudes and turns of speech from Jonson's character', and even conjectures that the name Thorello (the Kitely character in the 1601 quarto) 'suggested to Shakespeare the near-anagram Othello for a character with no name in the source-story'. Garrick's performance as Othello in 1745 had been one of his few failures. Possibly, he fixed on Kitely as a second chance to show that passionate jealousy was within his range (later he was to play Posthumus in his own alteration of *Cymbeline*). Whatever his reasons for selecting the part, Garrick's decision to play Kitely led to significant alterations to Jonson's original.

The enhancements Garrick made to the part of Kitely are most easily demonstrated in, though not confined to, the new scene that he composed for the fourth act (G.IV.iii.1–210). Its whole purpose is to build up the role of Kitely into a star part. Garrick had great respect for Jonson as a writer,[52] but the original Kitely was too one-dimensional. Garrick's merchant has much more light and shade than Jonson's. The part, as altered, provides maximum opportunity to demonstrate the dazzling turns that audiences looked for in Garrick's performances: 'the sudden transitions from hot impetuous rage to the most sedate and temperate calmness, arising from the natural feelings of the heart', as Davies put it.[53] Take, for instance, the rapid shifts of emotion, from anxiety through suspicion modulating into indignation and then into anger, in this short speech added by Garrick to Act III:

Laughing within.

KITELY Hark! hark! Dost thou not hear? What think'st thou now? Are they not laughing at me? – They are, they are; they have deceived the wittol, and thus they triumph in their infamy. – This aggravation is not to be borne. (G.IV.iii.35–38)

Though Garrick was certainly capable of a passable pastiche of Jonson, in both prose and verse, throughout the interpolated scene Kitely's speeches are increasingly couched in the language of the eighteenth-century stage. As the merchant's efforts to conceal his jealousy almost overwhelm him, anxiety becomes stress, and stress yields to hysteria in the chopped and broken rhythms of a showy speech carefully organised to provoke applause. Dame Kitely innocently asks whether her husband has ever been jealous.

KITELY What! Ha! never, never – ha, ha, ha!
(*Aside.*) She stabs me home. – Jealous of thee!
No, do not believe it. – (Speak low, my love,
Thy brother will o'erhear us.) – No, no, my dear,
It could not be, it could not be – for – for –
What is the time now? – I shall be too late. –
No, no, thou may'st be satisfied
There's not the smallest spark remaining. –
Remaining? What do I say? There never was,
Nor can, nor ever shall, be. So, be satisfied. –
Is Cob within there? – Give me a kiss,
My dear; there, there, now we are reconciled.
I'll be back immediately. Good-bye, good-bye. –
Ha! ha! jealous! I shall burst my sides with laughing.
Ha! ha! – Cob, where are you, Cob? – Ha! ha! *Exit.* (G.IV.iii.146–160)

The passage is printed as verse, but it is doubtful whether it would be heard as such. What audiences would remember would be the ever-shifting turns and counterturns of a bravura performer.

Reynolds's famous portrait of Garrick as Kitely shows him dressed as an aristocrat. He wears a richly embroidered cinnamon-coloured silk coat and cloak, adorned with an exquisite falling lace collar and matching cuffs, and looks far more like a melancholy Caroline court poet than a busy Elizabethan city merchant. The pose is hard to read. One hand is concealed, the other clenched, while the large and beautiful eyes gaze fixedly to the spectator's left. Responses to the question 'What sort of man does this portrait depict?' have ranged from 'kind' and 'caring' to 'creepy' and 'shy'. Garrick's Kitely is certainly a much more complex individual than Jonson had depicted and, moreover, one with whom the audience is expected to feel some sympathy. Garrick deliberately cuts the most ridiculous episode arising from Kitely's jealousy: the merchant's sudden conviction that his wife is trying to poison him (F.IV.vi.15–43). Instead, he composes a new scene between husband and wife (G.IV.iii.115–144), where Kitely is given an opportunity to show tender and very un-Jonsonian affection to his wife. In the farcical confrontation scene outside Cob's house (F.IV.viii and G.V.ii), where husband and wife each believe that they have caught their spouse in an assignation, Garrick inserts several new lines for Kitely to ensure that *his* feelings are foregrounded. For example: 'I tremble so, I scarce have power to do the justice / Her infamy demands' (G.V.ii.33–34). At this late stage in the play, Garrick seems to have given up trying to write like Jonson; this is entirely the language of eighteenth-century comedy. Garrick's version of the final scene makes Justice Clement send the Kitelys off-stage to 'think coolly of matters' (G.V.iv.37). In their absence, Clement unravels at top speed, thanks to heavy cutting, the remaining complications of the plot. In the closing moments of the play, the Kitelys re-enter just in time for the wedding junketings (G.V.iv.177). But Jonson had kept them on stage throughout the final denouement scene, along with all the other fools and knaves whose foibles had given rise to the action of the play. Garrick's alteration gives Kitely special status as most favoured character.

In deciding to make Kitely the single leading part, Garrick chose not to benefit from one major advantage that his theatre enjoyed over Jonson's: the presence of female actors in the company. It is disappointing not only to see good lines for female characters cut, but also to recognise that Garrick made no efforts to build up the sketchy women's roles. None is expanded to any degree, though Mrs Kitely gains a few lines to underscore

Figure 1 Garrick in the role of Kitely, in his own alteration of Ben Jonson's *Every Man in His Humour*. After Sir Joshua Reynolds, oil on canvas (1768). National Portrait Gallery, London.

her desire to pay back her jealous husband in kind. The part was not worthy of a Mrs Pritchard or a Mrs Clive; instead it was assigned, in the first season, to Mrs Ward. When the beautiful Susanna Davies, wife of Thomas, joined the company in September 1752, the role of Mrs Kitely became hers, and she played it regularly for eleven seasons. As altered by Garrick, the part would have been well within her apparently limited capabilities.[54]

Garrick's final task as alterer was to ensure that his revision of *Every Man in His Humour* would not offend either the censors of the Lord Chamberlain's office or the moral sensibilities of the Drury Lane audience. McIntyre says that 'on the whole he made few concessions to eighteenth-century susceptibilities',[55] but this is debatable. The advertisement to the edition of Garrick's version published by Tonson and Draper in 1752, though slightly apologetic in tone, gives a clue:

It is hoped the liberty that is taken with this celebrated play of Ben Jonson, in leaving out some scenes, with several speeches and parts of speeches in other places and in adding what was necessary for connection, and a whole scene in the Fourth Act, will be excused, as the distance of 150 years from the time of writing it had occasioned some of the humour to be too obsolete and dangerous to be ventured in the representation at present.[56]

This raises the interesting question of what Garrick could have found 'dangerous' in Jonson's humour. The prologue, written by William Whitehead, does not help. In it, Jonson is simultaneously praised, patronised and misquoted. He is 'immortal Ben, / A rough old Bard' (lines 4–5). The critical discrimination of the audience is subtly flattered. They are not to 'slight the gold, because not quite refined' (line 23), but to remember

Nature was Nature then, and still survives;
The garb may alter, but the substance lives –
Lives in this play – here each may find complete
His pictured self. Then favor the deceit –
Kindly forget the hundred years between;
Become *old* Britons, and admire *old* Ben. (lines 28–33)

Undoubtedly, the most profound difference between Jonson's *Every Man in His Humour* and Garrick's lies in their respective treatments of the magistrate, Justice Clement. Jonson had shown the ostensible upholder of the law to be a fantastical, capricious, 'mad, merry old fellow' (F.III.ii.253), upon whom little if any reliance for justice could be placed. He is introduced at the mid-point of the play, his whimsical sense of humour having first been signposted in dialogue between the young students-about-town:

WELLBRED He is a city magistrate; a justice here, an excellent good lawyer and a great scholar; but the only mad, merry old fellow in Europe!

EDWARD KNO'WELL [...] I have heard many of his jests i' the university. They say he will commit a man for taking the wall of his horse.

WELLBRED Ay, or wearing his cloak of one shoulder, or serving of God; anything indeed, if it come in the way of his humour. (F.III.ii.251–261)

In the following scene with Cob, Jonson demonstrates Clement's 'humour' and his quite arbitrary view of 'justice' by his apparently sending the water-carrier to jail simply for holding anti-smoking views. Jonson's Clement advises old Kno'well not to fuss over his son's behaviour (F.III.iii.131–139), but to drown all his cares in a cup of sack. Garrick felt obliged to make drastic changes. He retained the students' description of the justice, but minimised the opportunities for Clement to demonstrate his idiosyncrasies by holding back his entrance until the last scene of the play (G.V.iv). When at last he appears, Garrick's Clement is a far soberer justice than Jonson's. He drinks less sack, and most of his episodes of knock-about comedy – putting on full armour to meet Bobadill (F.V.i.43–47), the mock long-sword attack on Brainworm (F.V.i.103–117), the encounter with his half-naked drunken young servant, Formal (F.V.i.176–191) and the burning of Matthew's verses (F.V.i.200–249) – are deleted. Clearly, these are the humorous episodes that Garrick described as 'too obsolete and dangerous to be ventured in the representation at present'.

While retaining vestiges of Clement's sense of fun and love of hospitality, Garrick presented him as essentially the authoritative embodiment of conventional morality. Among the wits, gulls, obsessives and clowns, there had to be one trustworthy establishment figure. So Garrick composed new, totally un-Jonsonian, dialogue to underscore Clement's new persona as 'wise magistrate', and to spell out the moral of the play:

CLEMENT Did I not tell you there was a plot against you? Did I not smell it out, as a wise magistrate ought? Have not you traced, have you not found it, eh, Master Kitely?

KITELY I have. – I confess my folly and own I have deserved what I have suffered for it. The trial has been severe, but it is past. All I have to ask now is that, as my folly is cured and my persecutors forgiven, my shame may be forgotten.

CLEMENT That will depend upon yourself, Master Kitely. Do not you yourself create the food for mischief, and the mischievous will not prey upon you. – But come, let a general reconciliation go round, and let all discontents be laid aside. (G.V.iv.178–188)

Why did Garrick feel compelled to change Clement into a wise and just authority figure? It was one thing for Jonson, in the original quarto, to have made the representative of justice in far-away Florence a crazy buffoon, rather as the Venetian judges of Mosca and Volpone (1606) are shown to be as corrupt as the defendants. But in revising *Every Man in His Humour* to set it in contemporary London, Jonson had taken a big risk by keeping his authority figure as a comic *deus ex machina*. The London theatre at the turn of the sixteenth and seventeenth centuries was a dangerous place in which to work. Jonson twice went to prison because of the content of plays (*The Isle of Dogs*, 1597 and *Eastward Ho!* 1605) of which he was author or part-author. But his theatre was young, developing fast and, despite the 'thought police' of the time, as exciting as it was hazardous. The 'rules' were not fixed, no one knew how the emerging medium would mature, and experimentation flourished. Much trivia, but many undoubted masterpieces resulted. But risks such as Jonson took were unthinkable for Garrick. By the mid-eighteenth century the two London patent houses were part of the establishment. Garrick's was an essentially conservative, unchallenging, even prudish theatre, which was expected to play its part in reinforcing the values of the governing classes. The alarm caused by the Young Pretender's advance on London in 1745 was still fresh in the memory. The theatre could play its part in rebuilding confidence by providing reassurance that benevolent and competent authorities were in charge. Above all, it was expected to offer a clear-cut morality and to show that virtue would be rewarded and vice punished.

To state the obvious conclusion, the differences between the two versions of the play arise from the nature of the theatres for which they were designed. Jonson was working in a dramatists' theatre. His *Every Man in His Humour*, like all his major comedies, is an ensemble piece. It depicts a comic cross-section of London life in which every personage has some character flaw or obsession and each receives equally satiric treatment. By the time Garrick staged his alteration, he was working in an actors' theatre, where managers made money through presenting star performers in leading roles. The pre-eminence given by Garrick to Kitely seriously distorts Jonson's carefully balanced 'image of the times' (F. Prologue, lines 23). But it was Garrick, above all, whom audiences paid to see. As Davies put it: 'When Mr. Garrick acted a part in a play, his genius had raised him to that eminence, that he was considered by the greatest part of the spectators as the only object worthy of attention.'[57] However, it would be wrong to conclude that the 1751 *Every Man in His Humour* was designed simply as a vehicle for 'Garrick-as-Kitely', and that Garrick wanted to diminish the comic opportunities afforded to his fellow actors. Davies confirms the care he took over casting the play, 'where all the personages were so exactly fitted to the look, voice, figure and talents of the actor, that no play which comprehends so many distinct peculiarities of humour, was ever perhaps so compleatly acted'.[58] Woodward, in particular, made the part of Bobadill his own. He often chose to play it on his benefit night, and when he joined Covent Garden in 1762 the play entered the repertoire there. But at the rival house, until Garrick's retirement in 1776, Kitely was without a doubt regarded as the play's leading role. Garrick's performance in the part was one of the greatest successes of his career and he played it on all but one of the eighty-two occasions on which it was revived during his reign at Drury Lane. In Garrick's 'theatre of reassurance', revivals of classics such as this were a safe and profitable choice for a manager, provided that they offered – or could be altered to offer – opportunities for star performances within a reassuring moral framework. This formula suggests a reason why, for example, Tate's *King Lear* held the stage for so long. Succeeding chapters will examine the extent to which such a policy could serve as an adequate guide to altering Shakespeare, as Garrick continued to shorten, adjust and re-present, in both small and large ways, his idol's plays.

CHAPTER 3

'To give the actor more eclat' – Garrick's earliest alterations of Shakespeare

This chapter explores Garrick's treatment, early in his career, of two of Shakespeare's plays previously familiar to eighteenth-century audiences only in the form of alterations: *Macbeth* (1744) and *Romeo and Juliet* (1748). The London stage was increasingly becoming an actor's theatre, and Garrick's own success was itself accelerating this trend. What drew audiences to attend the same plays over and over again was, above all, the powerful performances of popular actors. Both the alterations by Garrick discussed below are designed to show the principal male protagonist in as appealing as possible a light. In each play, additional lines are inserted prior to the death of that character to ensure that the way he meets his fate, rather than any more general theme, will predominate in the memory of the audience. Just like many directors nowadays, Garrick also cut and rearranged texts to meet the constraints of his theatre. Other actor-managers of his day likewise altered these plays. But only Garrick's versions had the power to dominate the stage after his death. Well into the nineteenth century, successor Macbeths expired on stage with Garrick's death speech on their lips. His alteration of *Romeo and Juliet*, which included a highly emotional final encounter in the Capulets' vault for the lovers, even if slightly revised, was essentially the only text played to London audiences for a hundred years.[1] Successive generations that wrote and spoke of Shakespeare actually had Garrick's words in mind. No other alterer since Garrick has achieved such influence and such permanency.

Garrick's right to the title of 'restorer of Shakespeare' often appears dubious when his alterations are compared with modern editions of the plays. Hume is one critic who takes a very severe view:

> David Garrick [. . .] who loudly and vigorously advertised his veneration for the Bard and did much to promote Bardolatry, was anything but a textual purist. Garrick's admirers have heaped praise upon him for his contributions to the Shakespeare boom and the return to 'pure' texts, but an unprejudiced examination of Garrick's handling of Shakespeare yields a very different picture. Early and late,

Garrick was an aggressive appropriator who spouted pieties and hacked the texts about any way he pleased . . .[2]

But this judgement is certainly too harsh if applied to Garrick's version of *Macbeth*, which has an undoubted claim to be called a restoration. First performed on 7 January 1744, though not published until 1773,[3] it is the earliest and arguably the bravest of all his alterations of Shakespeare. Significantly, it was made before he took on the financial responsibilities of management. The 1743–1744 season was Garrick's third as a star actor in the theatres of London and Dublin. Not yet 27 years old, he had already triumphed as Hamlet, King Lear and Richard III. To undertake yet another major tragic Shakespearean role would obviously be a good career move for Drury Lane's main attraction. Garrick's choice of Macbeth could be seen as a direct challenge to Quin, his senior and rival, who had more or less made the role his own. Between March 1737, when Garrick and his friend Samuel Johnson came to London, and January 1744, when Garrick's alteration had its first night, *Macbeth* was given thirty-nine times in London. Quin appeared in the title role on twenty of those occasions, so Garrick would have had plenty of opportunities to study his performance. In the 1742–1743 season immediately prior to Garrick's debut as Macbeth, Quin had played the part at Covent Garden no fewer than six times, and Drury Lane had not offered the play at all. But the text performed by Quin, although by now regularly advertised as 'written by Shakespear', was no such thing; it was the still popular alteration made by Davenant, probably for the 1663–1664 season of the Duke's Company, and published in 1674.[4]

It is not known for certain what prompted Garrick to look back at Shakespeare's text and to decide to make his own alteration. Whether he found difficulty in persuading the Drury Lane manager Fleetwood to take on the risk of its production is also unknown. But it seems highly likely that Johnson drew *Macbeth* to Garrick's attention, since before long he was to publish, anonymously, his *Miscellaneous Observations on Macbeth*.[5] Bate says in his biography[6] that Johnson began to work on *Macbeth* during the winter of 1744–1745, but the clear influence of *Miscellaneous Observations* on Garrick's alteration, which had its first performance in January 1744, suggests that Johnson was thinking about the play and discussing it with Garrick in 1743. Though short, *Miscellaneous Observations* demonstrates, at an early stage in Johnson's career, his broad and deep reading in history and in the classical authors, as well as his knowledge of French and Old English. It shows also his readiness to engage with the views of editors whom he respected (Pope and Theobald), while condemning those whom he did not (Hanmer). As the title page makes clear ('To which is affix'd, Proposals for a New Edition of Shakeshear *[sic]*, with a Specimen'), *Miscellaneous Observations* was intended as a 'taster' for the full edition that was eventually to appear, after many vicissitudes, twenty years later.

Stone has established that Garrick's starting point for making his alteration was Theobald's 1740 edition, which was, of course, also available to Johnson and to which Johnson in *Miscellaneous Observations* often alludes.[7] Although Garrick certainly adopted several of Johnson's suggested changes in wording and punctuation, a detailed comparison of his acting version with Johnson's recommendations reveals that Garrick rejected far more than he accepted. Of course, it is always possible that not all Johnson's proposed amendments were available to Garrick when he was preparing his alteration. He was probably working on the script during the autumn of 1743, a period when he was one of the leaders of a two-month walk-out from Drury Lane by some of its principal players, and hence a time of unusual leisure. Garrick's version of *Macbeth*, billed as 'written by Shakespeare', had its first night on 7 January 1744, more than a year before the publication date of *Miscellaneous Observations* (6 April 1745). But the main reason for the differences between Garrick's alteration and Johnson's 'Specimen' edition of *Macbeth* is certainly the differing objectives of the two friends. Johnson is primarily interested in producing a book, 'to correct what is corrupt, and to explain what is obscure'.[8] As well as being concerned with meaning, he is constantly on the lookout for breaches of the rules of grammar, punctuation and metrics that might be offensive to readers. Such solecisms are secondary for Garrick who, above all, wants to end up with a playable script. He knows that minor textual blemishes, provided that they are played with conviction, are not remarked in the speed of performance. Some of the relatively few of Johnson's amendments that Garrick chose to adopt were to clarify meaning, such as:

And Fortune, on his damned quarrel [Theobald had *quarry*] *smiling,* (G.I.ii.16);[9]
This castle hath a pleasant site. [Theobald had *seat*]. (G.I.vi.1);

Other changes offered enhanced opportunities for the actor:

It will have blood – they say blood will have blood. (G.III.v.140) [Theobald had a comma after the first *blood* and a semi-colon before the second. Johnson considered that the line lost 'much of its force by the present punctuation'.];

I have lived long enough. My May [Theobald had *way*] *of life / Is fallen into the sere, the yellow leaf;* (G.V.ii.20–21).

Evidence of how Garrick played the last line comes from a letter written to him on 19 April 1769 by the Revd Dr Scrope, who recollected that many years earlier he had heard Garrick say 'May of life' on stage. This he considered 'as happy a restoration of a passage as any one in the many late editions of the poet'.[10]

'We are all offended by low terms', wrote Johnson in a famous number of *The Rambler*, citing as particularly objectionable the words 'knife' and 'blanket' in I.v.51–52.[11] Davenant had taken the same view and had amended to 'my keen steel' and 'the Curtains of the dark'. But Garrick, recognizing the words' dramatic impact, restored them. Nor did he see any need to alter the 'forced and unnatural metaphors' of 'Here lay Duncan, / His silver skin laced with his golden blood' (II.iii.111–112), which Johnson had condemned ('No amendment can be made to this line of which every word is equally faulty but by a general blot').[12] It was rare for Johnson to comment upon the use of language to express character. Garrick the actor may have found useful in performance Johnson's suggestion in *Miscellaneous Observations* that this speech marks Macbeth's 'artifice and dissimulation, to show the difference between the studied language of hypocrisy, and the natural outcries of sudden passion'. Or perhaps, on the assumption that the friends went through Theobald's text together, this comment may be an instance where the actor influenced the editor?

Stone states that Garrick, in preparing his text of *Macbeth*, consulted Warburton, another future editor of Shakespeare,[13] and later critics have followed Stone. Although Warburton's edition did not appear until 1747, there is evidence that he was working on Shakespeare as early as the 1720s.[14] Stone cites the following 'Warburton emendations [of Theobald]' adopted by Garrick:

'And Fortune, on his damned *quarrel* [for *quarry*] smiling,' (G.I.ii.16);
'*weyward* [for *weird*] sisters' (G.II.i.21);
'And on *the blade o' th' dudgeon* [for *on thy blade and dugeon*] gouts of blood,' (G.II.i.51);
'Unmannerly *reech'd* [for *breech'd*] with gore.' (G.II.i.233).

As stated above, the first of these emendations was actually proposed by Johnson, who pointed out in his 1765 notes that Warburton had here followed him. As to the other three, it is highly unlikely that Johnson would have had access to Warburton's unpublished notes.[15] Johnson, absorbed in a hand-to-mouth struggle for survival in Grub Street, and

Warburton, at work in the comfort of his well-endowed Lincolnshire rectory, were not acquainted at this period. Therefore, if coincidence is ruled out, Warburton must have lent his notes to Garrick or, which is more likely, agreed to comment on Garrick's proposed script. It must be noted, however, that no direct evidence has yet emerged of their acquaintance prior to 1747, at which point Warburton presented Garrick with the eight volumes of his edition 'as a mark of regard due to the merit of a true genius excelling in his profession'. The volumes were retained by Mrs Garrick through the four long decades of her widowhood, and eventually sold by auction in 1823.

By the mid-1750s, the future bishop and the celebrated actor-manager had become close friends. This is demonstrated by the twenty-five letters from Warburton printed by Boaden, the earliest dated 1756. Unfortunately Garrick's replies have not survived. Boaden comments snidely: 'I cannot perceive, in any of Warburton's letters, that he attended his friend Garrick's theatre.'[16] But this was just what made Warburton's flattering notice so valuable to Garrick; Warburton treated him not as a mere actor, but as a literary colleague of equal standing to himself. The letters published by Boaden demonstrate that Warburton both lent and gave Garrick old plays from his own library. In 1756 Warburton called upon Garrick to 'reconcile' Johnson and Capell, who were in competition to bring out yet another edition of Shakespeare's plays.[17] Warburton at this stage strongly supported Johnson.

The following year Warburton loftily applauded Garrick's skilfulness in evading the pitfalls of the literary world:

> You have given me fresh occasion to commend and esteem you. I have been told you have carefully avoided the occasions of having the Poet Laureate's place offered to you. I will tell you my mind frankly: I think it as much below you, as some others, who have declined it, think it below them.

To have the approval of Warburton, eminent theologian and (however controversial) editor of Shakespeare, for his alterations of the plays, represented for Garrick valuable reassurance that he was not being too cavalier in his treatment of his idol's works. Warburton's response to reading the text of *Florizel and Perdita* in 1758 must have been particularly gratifying:

> As you know me to be less of an idolizer of Shakspeare than yourself, you will less suspect me of compliment when I tell you, that besides your giving an elegant form to a monstrous composition, you have in your additions written up to the best scenes in this play, so that you will easily imagine I read the 'Reformed Winter's Tale' with great pleasure.

In 1759 Warburton was equally civil in response to a copy of the Drury Lane *Antony and Cleopatra*, though critical of the 'conjectural readings' of Capell, Garrick's collaborator, which were appended to the volume. Throughout his career, Garrick valued Warburton's friendship; 'I have a great intimacy with ye Bishop of Gloucester' he boasted in 1771.[18] Warburton's last recorded letter to Garrick, dated February 1771, flatteringly equates Garrick's eminence with that of Shakespeare:

> Speaking of *eloquence*, I am naturally put in mind of you and Shakspeare. It may be a question who is most dishonoured; you by the idle boys called *spouters*; or Shakspeare by the idler men called critics and editors? Both of you are answerable for them. Your several excellencies have produced them . . .[19]

Garrick found a graceful way to return Warburton's compliments. In 1768 the Corporation of Stratford-upon-Avon, wishing to adorn their new town hall, invited him to present them with works of art that would link and commemorate both Shakespeare and himself. In addition to donating a statue of Shakespeare to the town, he arranged for the Corporation to commission a full-length portrait from Gainsborough. Garrick is shown in a garden, with one arm flung casually round a pedestal upon which stands a bust of Shakespeare. The setting has been identified as Prior Park, near Bath, the estate of Ralph Allen, Gainsborough's patron. Warburton made his home at Prior Park for many years, and his meetings with Garrick often took place there.[20] Thus, Garrick arranged for Warburton's implicit inclusion in the cosy and intimate circle of Shakespeare and friends.

To reach a fair assessment of Garrick's achievement in altering *Macbeth*, it is necessary first to compare his version, not with Theobald's 1740 edition, but with the Davenant text, which was all that most audiences and actors of the period knew of the play. Murphy records Quin's understandable puzzlement when Garrick's alteration was announced: 'What does he mean? [D]on't I play *Macbeth* as written by Shakespeare?'[21] Davenant's version of *Macbeth* is less a revision than a re-write. In the interests of clarity, much of the densest poetic language is emasculated. As just a single example out of the multitude available, take the complex passage in which Macbeth expresses his mental agony at the prospect of murdering Duncan. In the original lines, intricate syntax, hissing sibilants and battering plosives enact the tortured struggle ('if', 'but', 'if', 'but') within the speaker's soul:

> If it were done when 'tis done, then 'twere well
> It were done quickly. If th'assassination
> Could trammel up the consequence, and catch

With his surcease success: that but this blow
Might be the be-all and the end-all, here,
But here upon this bank and shoal of time,
We'd jump the life to come. But in these cases
We still have judgement here, that we but teach
Bloody instructions which, being taught, return
To plague th'inventor. (I.vii.1–10)

Any actor will feel challenged by the difficulty of attempting to convey to the audience the import of language as complex as this.[22] Davenant opts for straightforwardness and substitutes a much brisker and more succinct version:

If it were well when done; then it were well
It were done quickly; if his Death might be
Without the Death of nature in my self,
And killing my own rest; it wou'd suffice;
But deeds of this complexion still return
To plague the doer, and destroy his peace: (D.I.vii.1–6)

Throughout the play, Davenant smoothes Shakespeare's language and makes it less extreme. 'Their daggers / Unmannerly breeched with gore' (II.iii.115–116) becomes 'their Daggers / Being yet unwip'd, seem'd to own the deed' (D.II.iii.81) and, famously, 'The devil damn thee black, thou cream-faced loon! / Where gott'st thou that goose-look?' (V.iii.11–12) is softened into 'Now Friend, what means thy change of Countenance?' (D.V.iii.3–38). The impact on audiences in 1744 of hearing such unfamiliar lines must have been startling (although Garrick, always cautious, restored only part of the latter passage, leaving out the first five words).

At the time of the Restoration, the moral instruction offered by a tragedy was expected to be unambiguous. Davenant builds up the parts of Macduff and (in particular) Lady Macduff to create, symmetrically, a 'good' couple to counter-balance the wicked Macbeths. His Macduff, like Macbeth, is tempted to 'Assume the Scepter for my Countrey's good' (D.III.ii.24), but Lady Macduff successfully persuades him not to succumb to ambition. At the end of the play, Macduff presents Macbeth's sword to Malcolm – who is a much more kingly figure than Shakespeare depicted – 'to shew that Heaven appointed / Me to take Revenge for you, and all / That Suffered by his Power' (D.V.ix.11–13). Macbeth's brief final speech baldly restates the moral message: 'Farewell, vain World, and what's most vain in it, Ambition. [*Dies.*] (D.V.viii.41). Davenant also took care to maximise the opportunities for the female members of his company. He inserted a new scene for a remorseful Lady Macbeth, in which she blames Macbeth for accepting her advice to murder the king, and encounters the silent ghost of Duncan (D.IV.iv).

The chief reason for the long-lived popularity of Davenant's *Macbeth* is obvious from the reaction of Pepys, who saw the show – the word is chosen deliberately – no less than four times in a single year (1667): 'though I have seen it often, yet is it one of the best plays for a stage, and variety of dancing and music, that ever I saw.'[23] Altogether the *Diary* records nine visits to *Macbeth* between 1664 and 1669. Pepys usually adds an approving comment, for example: 'which though I saw it lately yet appears a most excellent play in all respects, but especially in divertisement [i.e., amusement or entertainment], though it be a deep tragedy; which is a strange perfection in a tragedy, it being most proper here and suitable'.

In the theatre, spectacle is often a key to success, and it was mainly the passages now attributed to Middleton that Davenant chose to expand. He built up the parts of the witches, inserting an entirely new scene for them (D.II.v) containing two dances and two songs, in the course of which they confront Macduff and his lady. In successive stagings the Duke's Company introduced progressively more elaborate effects. By 1674, when Davenant's text was published, the witches were flying on and off stage.[24] At the end of D.III.viii, Heccate *[sic]* makes a spectacular exit, ascending in a 'machine' accompanied by 'Musick and Song'. The next scene (D.IV.i) contains yet more thrills for the audience. The three weird sisters are joined by three 'singing witches' and Heccate; 'Musick and Song' precede Macbeth's entrance. The cauldron sinks, and then 'A shaddow of eight Kings, and Banquo's Ghost after them pass by'. Macbeth stands 'amazedly', and Heccate attempts to cheer him. Again there is 'Musick'; the witches 'Dance and Vanish'. Then comes the most spectacular effect of all: 'The Cave sinks' (D.IV.i.116). Clearly for Pepys this scene was the highlight of the piece, and it brought him back to the playhouse again and again.

Pepys's response to Davenant's version seems to have been typical of subsequent audiences. Addison in 1711 describes the behaviour of a woman of quality at *Macbeth*:

> A little before the rising of the Curtain, she broke out into a loud Soliloquy, *When will the dear Witches enter*; and immediately upon their first Appearance, asked a Lady that sat three Boxes from her, on her Right Hand, if those Witches were not charming Creatures.[25]

In the early eighteenth century the advance publicity for performances of *Macbeth* always laid emphasis on music and spectacle. Typical is the playbill for Lincoln's Inn Fields on 21 September 1730, with Quin as

Macbeth: 'With the Musick, both Vocal and Instrumental, incident to the Play [. . .] Written by Shakespeare. And all the Flyings, Sinkings, and usual Decorations.' Eight singers and six dancers are named on the bill. Throughout the late 1730s and into the 1740s, when Garrick, then a stage-struck young wine merchant, was haunting the London theatres, the playbills consistently highlighted as major attractions 'the Original Musick', along with 'Scenes, Machines, Dancing and other Decorations'. When Quin played Macbeth at Drury Lane on 19 May 1737, a performance which Garrick could well have seen, the 'Original Musick, carefully reviv'd' was sung by four women and five men. The dances between the acts advertised as part of the entertainment included '*two Pierrots*', '*Punch's Dance* by a Child of Six Years old that never performed on the Stage before' and a 'Wooden Shoe Dance'.[26] Thomas Davies, writing in 1784, recalled that '[d]ances of furies were invented for the incantation scene in the fourth act, and near fifty years since I saw our best dancers employed in the exhibition of infernal spirits'.[27] For a manager, choosing a composer must have been equally as important as casting Macbeth.

When discussing Garrick's bold restoration to the stage of what was essentially Shakespeare's *Macbeth*, it is important not to overlook or underestimate what he retained from Davenant. Stone, always so anxious to establish Garrick's fidelity to Shakespeare's words, gives examples of 'about a dozen places', all relatively minor, where Garrick stuck to Davenant's text.[28] He says that Garrick 'retained only two of the witches' songs, which he placed at the close of the second and third acts, and changed their words'. This seriously underestimates the extent to which the witches feature in Garrick's alteration. They may not fly, as in Davenant, but they 'sink' following their first appearance. They have a wholly un-Shakespearean and mainly Davenant scene (G.II.ii) after the discovery of Duncan's murder, in which they sing ('We should rejoice when good kings bleed': G.II.ii.23), and dance. Garrick retains almost all of Davenant's expansion of the witches' scene after the banquet (D.III. viii; G.III.vi), including Hecate's spectacular ascent. The Drury Lane stage direction reads: '*Symphony, whilst* Hecate *places herself in the machine*' (G.III.vi.53). Stone celebrates Garrick as a textual restorer and downplays the theatrical impact of his alteration. When Garrick's *Macbeth* is studied as a script, however, it is clear that he had no intention of disappointing those patrons who came primarily for what Pepys called the 'divertisement' associated with the witches. Indeed, he introduced additional and unfamiliar special effects by restoring to the cauldron scene (G.IV.i) the ascending and descending apparitions – the armed head, the bloody child and the crowned child with a tree in his hand – that had been cut by Davenant. In the mid-eighteenth century the witches, traditionally played by men and dressed like market women with aprons, mob caps and high crowned black hats, had in the absence of the porter become the light relief,[29] and Thomas Davies confirms that their parts were 'always distributed amongst the low comedians'.[30] While offering novelty in the form of Garrick's first appearance as Macbeth, new costumes and a text 'as written by Shakespeare', the Drury Lane management in January 1744 was careful to add to the playbill the reassuringly familiar formula: 'With the Songs, Dances and other Decorations'.

Why did Garrick follow Davenant in eliminating the porter? When he came across the scene in his copy of Theobald's edition, it is likely that he hesitated scarcely at all before blue-pencilling it entirely, and from much the same motives that led him all but to eliminate the part of Cob in *Every Man in His Humour*, and totally to remove the gravediggers from his 1772 alteration of *Hamlet*. The porter's language is 'low' – indeed gross – and full of baffling topical allusions. Had Garrick chosen to retain the scene, it would have to have been substantially sanitised. Instead, a servant admits Macduff and Lenox *[sic]* and, to give Macbeth time to alter his costume, Lenox's eight-line speech to Macbeth (II.iii.53–60) from later in the scene ('The night has been unruly') is brought forward and addressed to Macduff (G.II.i.156–163). Lenox's lines maintain the ominous atmosphere of fear and horror that the Macbeths' dialogue has created. To interpolate any abrupt change of mood into the high dramatic tension of the murder and its discovery was exactly what Garrick did *not* want. In his alteration of Act II, the entire sequence from Banquo's 'How goes the night, boy?' to the flight of Malcolm and Donaldbain on the morning after the murders, is presented as one terrific, continuous scene (G.II.ii). The focus remains intensely on the central characters, and above all on Macbeth himself and on his lady.

Paul Prescott has laid to rest the myth that Garrick was virtually the only great English actor to have successfully 'conquered' the role of Macbeth.[31] Nevertheless, his triumphant success has cast a long shadow, and much has been written, in Garrick's lifetime and since, about how he played the part. Because this book is concerned primarily with Garrick the writer, rather than with Garrick the actor, the temptation to quote at length from contemporary and later descriptions of his performance has to be resisted.[32] But mention must be made of a strange little sixpenny pamphlet, *An Essay on Acting*, which appeared when Garrick's alteration was in its first season at Drury Lane.[33] It was published anonymously, but Garrick's biographers from Murphy onwards seem unanimous that he was himself the author, and that it was written to fend off hostile criticism.[34] Bizarre behaviour perhaps, but during his managerial career Garrick often anonymously issued to the press slightly negative reviews of productions at Drury Lane, in the hope of heading off stronger condemnation and even perhaps of provoking positive rejoinders. The two mock quotations on the title page of *An Essay on Acting* reinforce this conclusion:

> – *So have I seen a Pygmie strut,*
> *Mouth and rant, in a Giant's Robe.* Tom Thumb
>
> – *Oh! Macbeth has murder'd G . . . k.* Shakespear

Garrick was always sensitive about his height, and a recurring theme in *An Essay on Acting* is his physical unsuitability for the part of Macbeth: for example: 'Mr. *G . . . k*, could he *Speak* the *Part*, is well form'd for *Fleance*, or one of the *Infant Shadows* in the Cauldron Scene' (p. 14). The pamphlet purports to be by a keen student of the stage who aims to undeceive the town as to Garrick's merits. Eight pages are devoted to a sensible and apparently serious 'Short Treatise upon Acting' (pp. 4–12), and this is followed by some tongue-in-cheek 'Critical Observations upon the Character of MACBETH, as it is at present Attempted at the Theatre-Royal in Drury Lane' (pp. 12–21). Here Garrick's novel approach to the role (in delivery, in gesture, even in costuming) is weighed against the familiar ponderous and stagy acting style of Quin, and found to be totally wanting. Thus, by exposing to a conservative audience the absurdities of his rival's performance, Garrick indirectly defends his own innovations.

Oddly, Garrick (if it is he) never mentions his greatest achievement: the restored text, 'As written by Shakespeare', heard by the Drury Lane audience for the first time on Saturday, 7 January 1744. Orgel calls it 'a significant moment in both theatrical and textual history'.[35] Yet he reproaches Garrick for making a claim 'not even approximately true', pointing out that 'he cut more than ten percent of the play, [. . .] retained some of Davenant's most popular bits for the witches, and wrote a whole new dying speech of his own for Macbeth'. Would it not be fairer to say that the claim was indeed 'approximately true', since so much of the language was Shakespeare's-via-Theobald? In any case, the claim was not Garrick's; he was not yet the manager of Drury Lane.

Towards the end of *An Essay on Acting* (p. 24) appears a paragraph in praise of Shakespeare, which some have taken at face value, McIntyre, for example, calling it 'a rapturous hymn of praise'[36]:

Shakespear was a Writer not to be confin'd by *Rule*; he had a *despotick Power* over all Nature; *Laws* would be an *Infringement* of his *Prerogative*; his *scepter'd Pen* wav'd Controul over every *Passion* and *Humour*; his *Royal Word* was not only *Absolute*, but *Creative*; *Ideas*, *Language*, and *Sentiment* were his *Slaves*, they were *chain'd* to the *Triumphal Car* of his *Genius*; and when he made his *Entry* into the *Temple of Fame*, all *Parnassus* rung with *Acclamations*; the *Muses* sung his *Conquests*, crown'd him with never-fading *Laurels*, and pronounc'd him *Immortal*. AMEN.

If for no other reason, the excessive use of italics for nouns and adjectives gives rise to doubts about the sincerity of this passage. Brian Vickers is probably right in believing that Garrick is satirising 'the crudities both of contemporary acting and of unthinking panegyrics on Shakespeare'.[37] Ironically, however, the sentiments and language are all too reminiscent of the ode to Shakespeare that Garrick was to perform at the Jubilee twenty-five years later, and which will be discussed in a later chapter. The pamphlet ends with an abrupt change of tone, from rhapsodic to coarse, from which biographers and critics have chosen to turn away in silence. In private, Garrick had a taste for vulgar schoolboy rudeness[38]; if he was indeed the author of *An Essay on Acting*, he certainly indulged it here under the cloak of anonymity. The unnamed author announces (pp. 26–27) that he will

in a very short Time lay before the Publick, another Pamphlet [. . .] which will be *a proper Appendix* to the *Essay on Acting*; and call'd *An Essay on the Common Sewers* vulgarly stil'd *Common Shores*, in which will be consider'd the *Use* and *Abuse* of *Bum-fodder*; with some curious Observations upon the *present State of Politicks, both at Home and Abroad.*

For a moment the reader seems to be in the world of *The Dunciad*.

Pedicord and Bergman calculate that Garrick's alteration of *Macbeth* is 269 lines shorter than Shakespeare's 2341. To keep the audience's attention primarily on Macbeth's personal struggles, Garrick sacrifices the larger political and historical context. Totally omitted is the scene (III.vi) when, in a sudden change of focus, Lennox and 'another Lord' grimly discuss the realities of life under a tyrant and hope for relief from England. The difficult 'England scene' loses about eighty lines, including much of Malcolm's self-accusation (IV.iii.61–101), the doctor's appearance and Malcolm's account of King Edward's curing of 'the Evil' (IV.iii.141–159). All the poignant dialogue between Lady Macduff and her 'poor monkey' (IV.ii.30–65) is omitted; the child becomes a silent role. In keeping with public taste, he is not killed on stage, and the murderers are never seen.[39] Thus, in the next scene, the news of the slaughter of Lady Macduff and her children is broken to her husband and to the audience simultaneously. Apart from the porter's scene, the other cuts are relatively light – just sufficient to reduce the play to the two-hour maximum for a main piece. Surprisingly perhaps, the role of Lady Macbeth is also trimmed. It might have been expected that Garrick would have sought to soften and feminise her, and even to follow Davenant by showing her grieving and remorseful about her crime (see D.IV.iv). On the contrary, as Rosenberg has pointed out, if the audience were to retain some sympathy for the hero of the tragedy, then it was necessary for Macbeth to be tempted or even forced into the role of murderer. But since the Restoration the witches had been presented as silly caricatures. Thus, it was essential to cast Lady Macbeth as her husband's evil genius, ruthless in cruelty, a figure of implacable malevolent power, who drives Macbeth into crime in order to fulfil her wicked ambition.[40] As *An Essay on Acting* (p. 13) puts it:

> He is an experienc'd General crown'd with Conquest, *innately Ambitious*, and religiously Humane, spurr'd on by *metaphysical* Prophecies and the *unconquerable Pride* of his *Wife*, to a Deed, *horrid* in *itself*, and *repugnant* to his Nature[.]

In the scenes up to and through the murder of Duncan, Lady Macbeth is at her most fiend-like, and Garrick leaves her part wholly intact. But he keeps her offstage during the discovery of the murder (II.iii), following a tradition that, according to Davies, was of long standing: 'The players have long since removed Lady Macbeth from this scene.'[41] Davies explains that the 'hypocrisy' of her 'surprise and fainting' was so intolerable to audiences that it provoked merriment from 'persons of a certain class'. 'Mr. Garrick thought, that even so favourable an actress as Mrs. Pritchard would not, in that situation, escape derision from the gentlemen in the upper regions.' Hannah Pritchard was, of course, Garrick's most famous, though not his first, Lady Macbeth. The huge dramatic impact of their performance together is well conveyed in several famous paintings, including one by Zoffany, and also Fuseli's watercolour of c. 1766 and his much later 'Lady Macbeth Seizing the Daggers' (c. 1812).[42] Johnson claimed that Mrs Pritchard had 'never read the tragedy of *Macbeth* all through',[43] and she may not even have realised that Garrick had also denied her another entrance: the scene where she greets Banquo on her first appearance as queen at III.i.10 (G.III.ii.10). Garrick thus confines Lady Macbeth to three widely separated sections of the play: first, the sequence at Inverness running from the letter scene to the accomplishment of Duncan's murder

Figure 2 ‘Infirm of purpose!/Give me the daggers.’ Garrick and Hannah Pritchard in Garrick’s alteration of *Macbeth*, by Zoffany. The Art Archive/Garrick Club.

(G.I.v–G.II.i.153); second, the dialogue between Macbeth and Lady Macbeth before the murder of Banquo (G.III.iii) leading to the banquet scene (G.III.v); finally the sleep-walking scene (G.V.i). In these scenes Shakespeare's lines for Lady Macbeth remained intact, and the gaps between her appearances would have served only to increase the audience's desire to shudder at her once again. As Johnson observed in his 1765 notes on the play, 'Lady Macbeth is merely detested'.[44]

Unsurprisingly, the part of Macbeth suffered very few cuts. With Lady Macbeth played throughout as irredeemably evil, attention focused on her husband as the more interesting, because still developing, character. Garrick would have welcomed the account of Macbeth's character given in 1748 by an anonymous contributor to *The Gentleman's Magazine*:

> In the person of *Macbeth* we behold a man possess'd of many noble qualities, actuated by a most violent ambition, which, after a severe conflict, gets the better of his virtues, in spite of the suggestions of a conscience naturally sensible and tender, and urges him on to the murder of his sovereign and benefactor. From this beginning of a vicious conduct, we find all the sentiments of gratitude, love, friendship, humanity, *&c.* by insensible degrees, give place to his violent lust of power, and the instigations of a wicked woman; 'till, from a generous, noble, and (bating his ambition) a good man, we find him transformed to perhaps as great a monster of wickedness, as human nature ever produced.[45]

It is hard to believe that the writer had not been influenced by Garrick's performance. Shakespeare depicts Macbeth at the end of the play as so mentally depleted and emotionally exhausted by the effects of the choices he has made that he is reduced to little more than a baited bear sustained only by a desperate and innate animal courage. Garrick could not leave matters there. While Johnson might have been justified in saying that 'every reader rejoices at his fall',[46] Garrick wanted every *playgoer* to regret the tragic end of a once noble man. Such a fallen hero, as Holland says, deserves to avoid the indignity of decapitation[47]; after the duel Macduff carries not Macbeth's head, but his sword, to Malcolm as evidence of the tyrant's death. Furthermore, he is entitled to – and the audience will expect – a dying speech, in which the moral instruction to be gained from the play will be explicitly spelt out. Since Shakespeare had omitted to provide such a speech, Garrick supplied eight lines of his own. Francis Gentleman, writing anonymously in 1770, praised the speech ('[N]othing could be more suitable, or striking'),[48] but no modern critic has anything to say in its favour. ' [O]verblown rhetoric', says Bartholomeusz[49]; 'claptrap', agrees Wells[50]; Burnim condemns the 'insipidness of the ridiculous farewell death rattle'[51] and McIntyre calls the addition a 'rather embarrassing piece of fustian'.[52]

Even Stone judges it 'a poor speech when compared with the poetry of Shakespeare', concluding, like all his successors, 'but evidently Garrick's acting made it acceptable'.[53]

Having condemned Garrick's dying speech for Macbeth, several critics proceed to quote an eye-witness's account of how he played the scene. Jean Georges Noverre was *maître de ballet* at the Paris Opéra Comique. In the previous chapter an account was given of how Garrick brought Noverre and his company to Drury Lane in 1755, and of the fiasco of their attempt to re-stage Noverre's ballet, *Les Fêtes Chinoises*. Noverre, himself a performer who aimed to convey human emotions truthfully and naturally through his expressive face and body, hugely admired Garrick, recognising him as a fellow artist:

> He was so natural, his expression was so lifelike, his gestures, features and glances were so eloquent and so convincing, that he made the action clear even to those who did not understand a word of English.[54]

Noverre says that he saw Garrick play 'a tyrant who [. . .] dies torn with remorse' in 'a tragedy which he had touched up'.[55] He does not name the play, but there can be little doubt that it is *Macbeth*. During his visits to London, Noverre would have had the opportunity to see Garrick as Macbeth at least twice. If Noverre's account is broken down into stage directions, and then interpolated into Garrick's lines, it becomes clear that the audience's attention was primarily directed to what they *saw*, not what they heard.

'Tis done! the scene of life will quickly close,
[The approach of death showed each instant on his face; his eyes became dim, his voice could not support the efforts he made to speak his thoughts.]
Ambition's vain delusive dreams are fled,
And now I wake to darkness, guilt and horror.
[His gestures, without losing their expression, revealed the approach of his last moment; his legs gave way under him, his face lengthened, his pale and livid features bore the signs of suffering and repentance.]
I cannot bear it! Let me shake it off. –
'Twa'not be; my soul is clogged with blood.
[At last, he fell; at that moment his crimes peopled his thoughts with the most horrible forms;]
I cannot rise! I dare not ask for mercy.
It is too late, hell drags me down. I sink,
[terrified at the hideous pictures which his past acts revealed to him, he struggled against death; nature seemed to make one supreme effort. His plight made the audience shudder, he clawed the ground and seemed to be digging his own grave,]

I sink – Oh! – my soul is lost forever!
[but the dread moment was nigh, one saw death in reality, everything expressed that instant which makes all equal.]
Oh! (*Dies.*)
[In the end he expired. The death-rattle and the convulsive movements of the features, arms and breast, gave the final touch to this terrible picture.] (G.V.vi.73–81)

This was the terrific visual climax to which the audience would have been looking forward from the moment that they saw the green carpet laid on the stage for the final scene.

No critic seems to have pointed out the similarities between Macbeth's death speech and the lines given by Cibber to King Richard as he awakes from his nightmare on the eve of the battle of Bosworth:

Rich. Give me a Horse: Bind up my wounds!
'Have mercy, Heaven. Ha! – soft! –'Twas but a dream:
But then so terrible, it shakes my Soul.
Cold drops of sweat hang on my trembling Flesh,
My blood grows chilly, and I freze with horror.
O Tyrant Conscience! how dost thou aflict me!
When I look back, 'tis terrible Retreating:
I cannot bear the thought, nor dare repent:
I am but Man, and Fate, do thou dispose me.[56]

It was as King Richard III two seasons earlier that Garrick had burst to fame, astonishing and thrilling audiences with his transitions from passion to passion, demonstrated not only by appropriate gesture and movement, but by his famously mobile features. Cibber's climax to the tent scene – as Richard's emotions shift rapidly from the horrors of nightmare, to momentary relief on waking, back to horror, then to the assault of conscience and finally to the rejection of repentance – provided exactly the showcase he needed. When in 1746, according to Desmond Shawe-Taylor, Hogarth attempted to paint Garrick in this scene, his sitter's constant changes of countenance forced him to alter the picture so often, that 'in the end he had to stick a fresh piece of canvas over the face and start again'.[57] What more natural than that Garrick should seek to achieve a similar effect at the climax of his *Macbeth*? As Thomas Davies put it: 'Garrick excelled in the expression of convulsive throes and dying agonies, and would not lose any opportunity that offered to show his skill in that part of his profession.'[58] However, fashions change and by 1773, when Gentleman came to write his notes to the first published edition of Garrick's alteration of *Macbeth,* he was beginning to have doubts about the final scene: 'a dying speech, and a very good one, has been furnished by Mr. *Garrick*, to give the actor more eclat; but as we are not fond of characters writhing and flouncing on carpets; and as from the desperate state of Macbeth's mind we think his *immediate* death most natural, we could wish it to take place'.[59]

In composing Macbeth's death scene Garrick was not attempting to write like Shakespeare, but to provide a vehicle through which to demonstrate his mastery of acting with the body and the face. Nevertheless, there is a ghost of a case to be made for the language of the dying speech. Several critics, including Stanley Wells,[60] have detected Marlovian echoes. The glimmers of self-knowledge gained too late, the recognition of sin, the swings from despair to resistance and back to despair and the final agony are indeed reminiscent of Faustus's last speech. Garrick's collection of 'old plays' eventually contained four seventeenth-century editions of *Doctor Faustus*,[61] but whether he had actually read the play at this early stage in his career is impossible to know. Whatever may be thought of the remainder of the speech, its first line does demonstrate some sensitivity to Shakespeare's language. ''Tis done' seems to be a deliberate link back to Macbeth's anguished soliloquy ('If it were done when 'tis done, then 'twere well / It were done quickly') at I.vii.1–10 quoted above. Russ McDonald has powerfully analysed the resonance of the single syllable 'done' throughout *Macbeth*.[62] Garrick, too, was aware of its force. When Charles Macklin criticised his employment of 'done' in the Jubilee Ode, Garrick's defence was robust:

> I stand by ye Expression because it is Shakespeare's, & a very favourite one of [h] is – *I've done the deed* – If it were *done* – I know no word more Emphatical, & Which Shakespeare has made use of more forcibly –[63]

The staging of Garrick's alteration of *Macbeth* by no means led to an immediate clean sweep of other versions. Quin continued to appear in Davenant's alteration at Covent Garden for the remainder of the 1743–1744 season, and in the following season also. From 1747, when Garrick entered into management, it was, of course, his own alteration that was performed at Drury Lane. But in 1753 another version, 'newly adapted to the Stage', was published anonymously in Edinburgh.[64] Since it contains in its entirety, with only tiny differences, the eight-line dying speech composed by Garrick for Macbeth, it would be easy to assume that the Edinburgh text represents a version of Garrick's alteration earlier than the one published by Bell in 1773. Closer scrutiny, however, shows major differences. Overall the play (though not the witches' scenes) is shorter; Lady Macduff's part has been totally deleted. The action takes place wholly in Scotland; Macduff and Malcolm are reunited in Birnam-wood, not in England. The restoration of Shakespeare's lines is less wholesale than in Garrick's version, and the Edinburgh text is more inclined to revert to Davenant, both in sense and in actual wording. This is particularly true towards the end, where all but a few lines of Shakespeare's final scene (V.xi.20 *et sec.*) are dropped in favour of Davenant's upbeat and morally uncomplicated conclusion (D.V.ix). Like Garrick's, the Edinburgh alteration is based on Theobald's 1740 edition, and in at least one aspect adheres more closely to it in retaining Theobald's mysterious practice – also followed by Warburton, Hanmer and Johnson, though not by Garrick – of occasionally italicising certain key words: 'If it were *done*, when 'tis done' (Theobald I.vii.1) and 'Might be the Be-all and the End-all *here* / But *here*' (Theobald I.vii.5–6). Indeed, the Edinburgh text, for good measure, gives *be-all* and *end-all* as well. The italics appear to indicate where the stresses should fall in performance or reading aloud: a rare example of stage influencing page.

The Edinburgh alteration appeared in print again in Dublin in 1761, claiming on its title page to be 'Now first Printed as performed at the Theatres in *London* and *Dublin*'.[65] Again, it was published anonymously, and again no credit was given to Garrick for Macbeth's death speech. The British Library catalogue attributes the Edinburgh text (though not the Dublin one) to 'J. Lee', and the actor John Lee (1725–1781) indeed appears to be the link between the two publications and Garrick's alteration. Lee was a useful if not brilliant member of the Drury Lane company under Garrick's management in the 1747–1748 and 1748–1749 seasons; among his parts was Rosse in *Macbeth*.[66] In October 1749 he broke his articles and defected to Covent Garden, where he played some leading roles, including Romeo. But Garrick forced him to return to complete his contract at Drury Lane. The ambitious Lee must have resented Garrick, feeling that under him his genius was rebuked. In 1752 he arrived in Edinburgh to manage the Canongate Playhouse for four years. His roles there tended to be those in which Garrick excelled and included Lear, Romeo, Benedick and, of course, Macbeth in his own alteration.[67] Garrick's dying speech for Macbeth was too good an acting opportunity for Lee to miss. Though it had not been published, he would have known the lines by heart from hearing them in the wings at Drury Lane as he waited for his final entrance as Rosse. Thus, the speech became incorporated into Lee's published version of 1753, incidentally providing a textbook example of memorial reconstruction.

Following the collapse of his Edinburgh venture, Lee moved in 1756 to Dublin to play leading roles at the theatre in Smock Alley, but soon fell out with the manager, Thomas Sheridan. If Macbeth was among Lee's roles in Dublin, this may account for the publication of his alteration there in 1761. Lee's career is marked by financial difficulties, legal entanglements and acrimonious disputes with patrons and managers. It is perhaps surprising that Garrick took him back into the Drury Lane company for the four seasons 1762–1763 to 1765–1766, albeit mainly in supporting roles. Towards the end of Lee's career he had two periods managing the Theatre Royal in Bath: from 1768–1769 to 1770–1771, and again in the season of 1778–1779. Under Lee's management, *Macbeth* was frequently performed there. It is virtually certain that the text played was Lee's own alteration, since the very full cast lists announced in advance in the *Bath Chronicle* never include Lady Macduff, a character omitted from the Edinburgh/Dublin version.[68] Lee's entire career was overshadowed by Garrick. He outlived his rival by two years, making his final stage appearance in Bristol on 14 July 1780; the role was Macbeth. Ironically, therefore, the last words Lee spoke on stage were Garrick's. Whether Lee asked Garrick's permission to include his dying speech for Macbeth in his own alteration is unknown, but the balance of probabilities is against it.

Garrick relinquished the part of Macbeth well before Lee did. Mrs Pritchard, his partner of greatness, left the stage in 1768; her final performance, on 25 April 1768, was as Lady Macbeth opposite Garrick. Thereafter, Garrick played Macbeth only once more. The occasion was a command performance for the king of Denmark on 22 September 1768; Mrs Barry played Lady Macbeth. In middle age, with declining health, Garrick found the role of Macbeth an immense physical strain. He called it 'the most violent part I have', and made excuses for not reviving it, claiming, for example, to be unprepared with costumes, 'for I have a design to exhibit y[e] Characters in y[e] old dresses'.[69] Shakespeare in modern dress was going out of style. Before Garrick's retirement, his old rival Macklin had re-staged and re-costumed *Macbeth*, locating it historically in ancient Scotland.[70] But though Garrick had missed a trick, the success of his alteration was assured. By the end of the eighteenth century, according to Pedicord and Bergmann, it had been given 284 times in the two patent houses and at Goodman's Fields, and their figures, of course, exclude performances in the provinces, Scotland, Ireland and English-speaking communities abroad.[71] Bate has shown that, well into the nineteenth century, Kemble and Kean continued to perform Garrick's dying speech for Macbeth in whole or part.[72] That his successors in the role continued to acknowledge his influence as writer, as well as actor, would have greatly gratified Garrick.

Four years after his *Macbeth*, Garrick, now manager of Drury Lane, made and staged an alteration of *Romeo and Juliet*. Unlike *Macbeth*, which had to wait thirty years for publication, it appeared in print immediately. This first edition of 1748 was followed by two published revisions, in 1750 and 1753, reflecting the changes that Garrick continued to make in performance. There were to be eight other re-printings before both *Macbeth* and *Romeo and Juliet* were included in John Bell's *Shakespeare's Plays. As They Are Now Performed at the Theatres Royal in London* in 1773–1774.[73] In the preliminary matter of the editions of 1748, 1750 and 1753, Garrick set out very clearly his approach to the task of altering *Romeo and Juliet*, and his reasons for the changes that he successively introduced.[74] These editorial introductions provide a rare glimpse into the actual process of alteration, behind which lies the complex network of considerations, both professional and personal, that influence the alterer's decisions. In no other advertisement to an alteration of Shakespeare did Garrick go into so much detail. Therefore, this discussion of his *Romeo and Juliet* will be structured on those introductory remarks: the information he thought it necessary for a reader (rather than a playgoer) to have in advance before turning to Act I.

Romeo and Juliet, in various guises, were familiar figures to audiences in the mid-eighteenth century, and their tragedy was already good box office when Garrick took up the task of alteration. As early as 1680, Thomas Otway, in his drama set in ancient Rome, *The History and Fall of Caius Marius*, had combined veiled comment on the politics of his day with a love story lifted from *Romeo and Juliet*. His borrowing was disarmingly acknowledged in the prologue:

> Like greedy Beggars that steal Sheaves away,
> You'll find h' has rifled him of half a Play.
> Amidst this baser Dross you'll see it shine
> Most beautifull, amazing, and Divine.[75]

Caius Marius was not performed in London after 1735, but Garrick was familiar with the play. This is clear from his reaction to a performance of an alteration of *Romeo and Juliet* made by Theophilus Cibber and produced at the Haymarket in September 1744. While Cibber had certainly gone back to Shakespeare – indeed, he had thrown in eight lines from *The Two Gentlemen of Verona* (III.i.178–184) for good measure – Garrick recognised that aspects of the plot and much of the language were actually Otway's.[76] Like Otway's young couple, Marius Junior and Lavinia, Cibber's are already in love at the beginning of the play; there is no Rosaline, and no ball scene at the home of the Capulets. Making only slight changes to their wording, Cibber incorporates from Otway several emotional speeches for the lovers, both separately and together, in which they express their determination to be faithful.[77] Most significantly, Cibber includes the whole of Otway's tomb scene, in which Lavinia wakes in time for a passionate final duet, and Marius Junior dies transported with joy.[78] Cibber was not the only contemporary of Garrick to adapt *Romeo and Juliet*. According to an article in *The Prompter*, Thomas Sheridan in Dublin and, later, John Lee in Edinburgh, as well as a certain Mr Marsh, all made alterations, though none of these actually appeared in print.[79] But for Garrick's to be successful, Cibber's version, 'tolerable enough' though he thought it, was the one that he had to supersede.

Garrick's starting point was a modern edition of Shakespeare. According to Copeland, he almost certainly worked from Pope's 1723 or Hanmer's 1744 text.[80] She shows that Pope's version was shorter than other editions of the play because of his reduction of the figurative language, and his excision from the text of passages he considered 'nonsense'; it was thus a particularly suitable basis from which to adapt a main piece. Whether Garrick sought assistance from Warburton, Pope's literary executor, is unknown; certainly, no correspondence between them on the subject has survived. No direct influence by Johnson can be seen in Garrick's alteration, which omits most of the passages that Johnson queried in his notes on the play.[81] Neither does Garrick incorporate any of Johnson's proposed re-writings: for example, 'It is an *hour* [for *honour*] that I dream not of' (I.iii.68). But Johnson surely would have supported, and may even have influenced, the clear statement of objectives that begins Garrick's introduction to the 1748 text:

> The Alterations in the following Play are few and trifling, except in the last Act; the Design was to clear the Original, as much as possible, from the Jingle and Quibble, which were always thought the great Objections to reviving it.[82]

In his Dictionary of 1755 Johnson defined a quibble as a 'low conceit depending on the sound of words; a pun'. His strong disapproval of Shakespeare's delight in puns is most famously expressed in his 1765 preface: 'A quibble was to him the fatal Cleopatra for which he lost the world, and was content to lose it.'[83] As Vickers has shown, Johnson was far from alone; the great majority of the critics of the eighteenth century deplored Shakespeare's wordplay.[84] Removing the much-frowned-upon puns provided Garrick with a straightforward way to begin his task of reducing the play to a maximum of two hours' traffic on Drury Lane's stage. As a result, the serving-men's dialogue in the opening scene is cut to the bone, and the young men's contest of wit in II.iii almost totally disappears, thus conveniently removing some of the bawdiest passages. Even Mercutio's 'Ask for me tomorrow, and you shall find me a grave man' (III.i.98–99) is sacrificed. There are other cuts, of course. The prologue and the chorus linking Acts I and II are omitted. So are the 'low' scenes involving Capulet's house servants and musicians, though Peter still carries the nurse's fan to her encounter with Romeo in G.II.4. Lady Montague never appears and Lady Capulet's part is trimmed, along with those of other supporting characters. Pedicord and Bergmann estimate that altogether some 830 lines are deleted; probably not much greater than the number cut in modern stage productions.[85]

As to Shakespeare's use of rhyme, contemporary opinion was almost unanimously hostile. As he shortened the play, Garrick simultaneously reduced the 'jingle' by numerous small changes as, for example, in the following lines:

> Then plainly know my heart's dear love is set
> On the fair daughter of rich Capulet.
> As mine on hers, so hers is set on mine,
> And all combined save what thou must combine
> By holy marriage. (II.ii.57–61)

At some (possibly deliberate) cost to the metre, Garrick alters and compresses this passage to:

> Then plainly know my heart's dear love is set
> On Juliet, Capulet's fair daughter.
> As mine on hers, so hers is set on mine. (G.II.iii.41–43)

Though Garrick is careful throughout the play to keep 'jingle' to a minimum, he does not attempt to remove the rhymes from Friar Lawrence's initial speech (II.ii.1–30, *cf.* G.II.iii.1–22). In Garrick's theatre, rhymed couplets were the standard form for humorous prologues; the Friar's language on his first entrance may be an indication that Garrick saw the part as containing some elements of comedy.

The next paragraph of Garrick's 1748 note to the reader shows him slightly on the defensive about his decision to stick, at least in one respect, to Shakespeare:

> Many People have imagin'd that the sudden Change of Romeo's Love from Rosaline to Juliet was a blemish in his Character, but an Alteration of that kind was thought too bold to be attempted; Shakespear has dwelt particularly upon it, and so great a Judge of Human Nature, knew that to be young and inconstant was extremely natural[.]

Garrick was taking a slight gamble here. 'Many People' wished to see leading characters behave as exemplars: quintessential 'types' who perfectly embodied particular virtues. Whether or not Romeo's behaviour was 'extremely natural' was to them beside the point. In their view, he ought to appear as the spotless, ever-faithful lover. Aware of this, Otway and Cibber had removed all references to Rosaline. Garrick knew that Romeo's prior attachment would surprise, perhaps shock, the Drury Lane audience. Prudently, he left himself a way out: 'However, we shall leave this to the Decision of abler Criticks; those, I am sure, who see the Play will very readily excuse his leaving twenty Rosalines for a Juliet.'

Garrick ends his 1748 introduction with a modest reference to his alteration's greatest departure from Shakespeare, the seventy-five lines he added to Act V to allow the lovers a final encounter before their deaths:

> The favorable Reception the new Scene in the fifth Act has met with, induc'd the Writer to print it, and if he may be excus'd for daring to add to Shakespear, he shall think himself well rewarded in having given Romeo and Juliet an Opportunity of shewing their great Merit.

This, no doubt, was the innovation that gave rise to a pained comment from Stone, always so anxious to demonstrate Garrick's fidelity to Shakespeare: '[h]ere he worked with a freer hand than his closest admirers of late years might wish.'[86] Garrick actually saw no reason to apologise. His liebestod for Romeo and Juliet was just what an audience familiar with *Caius Marius* or with Cibber's alteration would be expecting. To this day, romantics still hanker for that final encounter and Loehlin gives several very recent examples of early awakenings for Juliet in the tomb scene.[87] The 'Opportunity' that Garrick provides for Romeo and Juliet in his tomb scene is, in fact, a chance for some bravura acting, especially for Romeo. (It should be noted that when Garrick's alteration was first staged, in 1748, it was not Garrick himself but Spranger Barry who played Romeo.) Admittedly the words are cliché-ridden, but when performed by

Figure 3 Garrick and George Anne Bellamy in the tomb scene of Garrick's alteration of *Romeo and Juliet*. Engraving by R. S. Ravenet after Benjamin Wilson. Artist unknown. The Art Archive/Garrick Club.

Barry and Cibber and later by Garrick and Bellamy, their effect on the audience was deeply affecting. Copeland has carefully analysed the extent to which Garrick's tomb scene reflects, and where it deviates from, Otway's, calling Garrick's more extended version an example of 'pathetic prolongation'.[88] Just as in Macbeth's dying speech, the aim is to engage the sympathies of the audience in the swiftly changing emotions of the characters. Romeo shifts rapidly from ecstasy ('It is thy Romeo, love; raised from despair / To joys unutterable!' G.V.iv.83–84), through struggles against his approaching death, into madness ('My powers are blasted, / Twixt death and love I'm torn, I am distracted!' – lines 124–125). After a brief moment of tear-provoking sententiousness ('Fathers have flinty hearts, no tears can melt 'em. / Nature pleads in vain. Children must be wretched' – lines 129–130), Romeo's distraction returns, and he dies struggling in imagination against Juliet's father and lover:

> Capulet forbear! Paris loose your hold!
> Pull not our heart-strings thus; they crack, they break.
> O! Juliet! Juliet! *(Dies).* (G.V.iv.133–135)

Pedicord and Bergmann have modernised Garrick's original punctuation as well as his spelling. But the eighteenth-century texts, with their lavish use of dashes, convey much more effectively than do modernised versions the characters' violent swings of emotion.

Juliet, meanwhile, moves swiftly from bewilderment and delusion, through delighted recognition of Romeo into horror at his look of death and then agonised realisation of the truth. Her short exclamations – 'And did I wake for this?' (G.V.iv.123); 'Thou ravest; lean on my breast.' (line 128); 'O! my breaking heart!' (line 131) – counterpoint Romeo's more extended outbursts, and provide yet further opportunities to move the audience's pity. 'Nothing was ever better calculated to draw Tears from an Audience, than the last Scene, when it is happily performed', wrote MacNamara Morgan in 1753.[89] Jay L. Halio is under the impression that Garrick ended the play with Juliet's death[90]; but this is emphatically not the case. Though in later editions Garrick further shortened the last scene, he was always careful to include the prince's confrontation of the two fathers with the consequences of their enmity. He composed a final pair of couplets to underline the moral message anticipated in the dying Romeo's reference to fathers' 'flinty hearts' (G.V.iv.129):

> Well may you mourn, my lords, now wise too late,
> These tragic issues of your mutual hate.

From private feuds, what dire misfortunes flow;
Whate'er the cause, the sure effect is woe. (G.V.iv.250–253)

Two years later, in 1750, Garrick published, still anonymously, a second edition of his *Romeo and Juliet*. Much had happened in the interim. The play, the plot of which springs from the conflict between two ancient houses, had itself become a battleground in the endless struggle for dominance between the two London patent houses, Drury Lane and Covent Garden. As performed at Garrick's Drury Lane in the 1748–1749 season, with Spranger Barry and Susanna Cibber ideally cast in the name parts, *Romeo and Juliet* had been an undoubted success, and had been offered on twenty occasions. Even in that first season, however, Garrick had deemed it necessary to introduce more spectacle. A new stage direction in the 1750 text, 'A dance here', between G.I.vi.60 and G.I.vi.61, reflects a masquerade dance which, so the playbills indicate, was added to the ball scene as early as the second performance (on 1 December 1748).

Because of Mrs Cibber's ill heath, *Romeo and Juliet* was not performed at Drury Lane during the 1749–1750 season. Barry grew restive, and eventually both Romeo (Barry) and Juliet (Cibber) signed up with Covent Garden for the 1750–1751 season.[91] Their appearance there as the tragic lovers would be an undoubted draw, and a direct challenge to Drury Lane. Garrick could not afford to give up the play to the rival house, and he took on the fight with gusto. He determined to play Romeo himself, and for his Juliet engaged George Anne Bellamy. '[W]e are like to have warm work', he wrote to his partner, Lacy.[92]

Many accounts have been written of the 'battle of the Romeos' that began when both houses offered *Romeo and Juliet* on 28 September 1750. The contest continued for twelve successive performance nights, on which each theatre simultaneously staged the play as its main piece. Meanwhile, an accompanying war of words between Garrick and Barry ('alternate squibs, / Compos'd of little wit – and some few fibs', as he later admitted[93]) grew ever more acrimonious. The contest ended, at least in Garrick's mind, with triumph for Drury Lane, as he reported to Lady Burlington:

'ye Battle is at last Ended, & in our favour – our Antagonists yielded last Thursday Night & we play'd ye Same Play (Romeo & Juliet) on ye Fryday to a very full house to very great applause; Mr Barry and Mrs Cibber came incog to see Us, & I am very well-assur'd they receive'd no little Mortification.[94]

He proclaimed a peace in a good-humoured epilogue, spoken by Mrs Clive, that poked fun at both the Romeos.

What were the effects of the conflict with Covent Garden upon the text of his alteration of *Romeo and Juliet* that Garrick published in 1750 to coincide with his new production? As with the 1748 edition, the advertisement serves as guide. After the now familiar disclaimer about clearing the original from 'the jingle and quibble which were always thought a great objection to performing it', Garrick abruptly announces a U-turn:

> When this play was revived two winters ago, it was generally thought, that the sudden change of Romeo's love from Rosaline to Juliet was a blemish in his character, and therefore it is to be hoped that an alteration in that particular will be excused; the only merit that is claimed from it is, that it is done with as little injury to the original as possible.

For cautious Garrick, as with the prejudice against 'jingle' and 'quibble', what is 'generally thought' must determine policy. In Johnson's words, 'the publick ha[d] decided'.[95] (It seems, incidentally, that for Johnson, as for Garrick, those whose critical opinions are worth deferring to will be found in the theatre as well as the study.) Garrick gives no other explanation for the change, but the letter to Lacy referred to above shows that Garrick saw the removal of Rosaline as part of his 'well layed regular plan' to outdo Covent Garden after the defection there of Barry and Cibber.

In the summer of 1750, therefore, Garrick revised the text of G.I.iv and G.II.i, either excising all references to Romeo's prior attachment to Rosaline, or else altering them to make them apply to Juliet. Like Otway's and Cibber's, his revised version now had Romeo already in love with Juliet at the start of the play, and he composed new lines in very fair pastiche to make this clear. Unlike Otway and Cibber, however, he retained the ball scene (G.I.vi), and thus needed an explanation for Romeo's presence on Capulet territory. He added the following to the conclusion of G.I.iv:

> Lead, gallant friends;
> Let come what may, once more I will behold
> My Juliet's eyes, drink deeper of affliction.
> I'll watch the time, and mask'd from observation
> Make known my sufferings, but conceal my name.
> Tho' hate and discord 'twixt our sires increase,
> Let in our hearts dwell love and endless peace.

The ball scene also needed some minor alterations, since Romeo already loved Juliet secretly and knew her to be a Capulet. So Benvolio, not Romeo, asks the Nurse 'What is her mother?' (G.I.vi.69). In his 1748 alteration, Garrick had reduced the eighteen lines of the lovers' first encounter (I.v.92–109) to just seven. The spectacular masquerade dance preceding their dialogue, introduced early in the play's first season and now included in the published text, would have been particularly helpful to the actress playing Juliet, since it provided a more extended opportunity to show, if only in dumb show, the sudden onset of love.[96] Garrick had also to adjust Friar Lawrence's strictures on Romeo's fickleness (G.II.iii.48–59), substituting new dialogue that included eight lines of more generalised admonition. Probably by accident, Garrick did not cut Mercutio's comment at G.II.iv.4–5: 'Why, that same pale hard-hearted wench, that Rosaline, / Torments him so, that he will sure run mad.' No doubt the error was corrected in performance.

Branam is one of several critics who disapproves the removal of Rosaline, considering that it creates 'distortions', and reduces the force and intensity of the ball scene. Among Garrick's contemporaries, Murphy thought that 'by representing ROMEO so much enamour'd of JULIET before they actually meet on the stage, half the *pathos* is lost',[97] while Fennell was more concerned about the loss of a moral lesson:

> Garrick, in one alteration, was very injudicious; we allude to the poetical justice, which exists in Shakespeare, and which he destroys. In the present work [Garrick's 1750 alteration] Romeo and Juliet fall victims without any fault on their side: whereas, in the original, Romeo deserts Rosalind *[sic]* for Juliet; and is therefore punished for his inconstancy to a prior attachment.[98]

Stone, Garrick's stoutest defender, is silent on this point, neither condemning nor approving the loss of Rosaline.

Detailed comparison of the 1748 and 1750 texts reveals a few additional cuts in the latter, mainly reducing the garrulousness of the Nurse (e.g., at G.I.v.53–61 and G.III.viii.103–110) and the Friar (e.g., at G.III.v.88–97). Almost certainly, these and other minor trimmings were made to create time for Garrick's final and most spectacular addition: Juliet's funeral procession, inserted between the fourth and fifth acts. Once again, competition with Rich, the manager of Covent Garden, was the driving force. The managers strove to outdo each other in the pageantry of their rival funeral processions, contemptuously described by Arthur Murphy as 'the grand raree-show, at the end of the fourth act'.[99] Garrick's seems to have been very splendid, and the details closely reflect those prescribed by Capulet at IV.iv.111117. An impressed Hanoverian visitor wrote of tolling bells, a choir singing, Juliet on a state bed with a splendid canopy over her, girls strewing flowers, torch-bearers, robed choristers and clergy walking in front, with the mourning parents and friends following behind.[100] Garrick's lyrics for the dirge sung during the procession are unimpressive. The chorus runs:

Rise, rise!
Heart-breaking sighs
The woe-fraught bosom swell;
For sighs alone,
And dismal moan,
Should echo Juliet's *knell.*

The three verses are couched in highly conventional terms, reminiscent of the language used in eighteenth-century memorial tablets. For example:

She's gone, she's gone, nor leaves behind
So fair a form, so pure a mind;
How could'st thou, Death, at once destroy,
The Lover's *hope, the* Parent's *joy?*

But in this scene, as in opera, what mattered most was William Boyce's music; Garrick's role as librettist was secondary. Loehlin points out that the dirges composed by Boyce for Drury Lane and by Dr Arne for Covent Garden were important events in London's musical life. In a revealing insight into the high status afforded to theatre music and musicians in Garrick's day and beyond, he continues: 'The funeral dirge remained an important part of productions through the nineteenth century, and was often more prominent on playbills than the names of the actors.'[101]

When in 1753 Garrick brought out a new edition of his 1750 alteration of *Romeo and* Juliet, he made only minor changes to the play itself. The unsigned advertisement, however, he almost completely re-wrote, and much extended. He now identified himself as a member of the *literati,* 'the present editor', invoking scholarship and comparative criticism to defend the changes he had made to the play. First came a brief restatement of the now familiar basic principles on which he had worked to produce a text acceptable to the Drury Lane (and indeed the Covent Garden) audience, for it is clear from the quotations in Morgan's *Letter to Miss Nossiter* that by 1753 Garrick's text was also being played at the rival house:

The chief design of the alterations in the following play was to clear the original as much as possible from the jingle and quibble which were always the objections to the reviving it.

Then Garrick succinctly disposes of the Rosaline issue. The apologetic tone of 1750 is banished, and he cleverly positions himself as simultaneously the servant of the public and of the Bard:

The sudden change of Romeo's love from Rosaline to Juliet, was thought by many, at the first revival of the play, to be a blemish in his character; an alteration in that particular has been made more in compliance to that opinion, than from a conviction that Shakespeare, the best judge of human nature, was faulty.

It seems that some time in the five years since making his alteration Garrick had learned an important fact about the source of *Romeo and Juliet* that supported his decision to provide a final scene together for the lovers. His next paragraph tells the tale modestly, but his satisfaction is nonetheless evident:

Bandello, the Italian novelist, from whom Shakespeare has borrowed the subject of this play, has made Juliet to wake in the tomb before Romeo dies: this circumstance Shakespeare has omitted, not perhaps from judgment, but from reading the story in the French or English translation, both which have injudiciously left out this addition to the catastrophe.

How did Garrick learn about Bandello's tale, and discover that neither Boaistuau's version in French (1559) nor Brooke's translation of Boaistuau into English verse (1562) had included the reunion in the tomb?[102] Warburton had made no mention of Bandello. Theobald had cited him as a source for *Romeo and Juliet*, but had given no details that would suggest that he had read the Italian tale. Possibly Johnson (whose knowledge was vast) enlightened Garrick, but it seems most likely that the information reached him, directly or indirectly, from Johnson's friend, Charlotte Lennox. Johnson wrote the dedication for her study of Shakespeare's sources, *Shakespear Illustrated*,[103] and Baretti, friend of both Johnson and Garrick and a member of their literary circle, helped her translate Italian sources into English. Lennox includes a translation of Bandello's *novella* and, in her subsequent 'Observations' on the use Shakespeare made of it, makes exactly the same point as Garrick in his 1753 advertisement:

[H]e never saw, and did not understand the Original, but copied from a *French* translation extant in his Time; or, what is equally probable, from an *English* translation of that *French* one, both very bad . . .

She goes on to cite a large number of instances, including the tomb scene, where Shakespeare followed a deficient translation rather than Bandello's novel. Whether or not Lennox was the source of Garrick's information, the knowledge enabled him to present himself both as a scholar who could speak with authority about Shakespeare's education and working methods, and as a collaborator, providing 'improvements' that Shakespeare would surely have wished to have made, had he only had Garrick's advantages.

Finally, Garrick used the 1753 advertisement to defend his ability as a playwright. MacNamara Morgan, in his *Letter to Miss Nossiter*, had doubted that a mere actor could be capable of composing 'so happy an Alteration', and had asserted that the tomb scene was actually Otway's:

> I have heard it attributed to one of the Players; and it passes current, that his Knowledge of the Stage enabled him to do it. But that we may not learn to set too small a Value on the tragic Genius, by imagining, that every little Smatterer can, with such Delicacy, touch the human Heart; know, none but that Genius, who comes next to SHAKESPEAR's self, cou'd draw so fine a Stroke. It was OTWAY altered it. Compare the Tomb-Scene in ROMEO and JULIET with that in CAIUS MARIUS, which is but another Alteration of the same Play, and there you will find this noble Incident, and the very Words of the whole Scene, with very little Alteration.

Murphy had made the same allegation in 1750, claiming that Garrick had been 'little more than a bare transcriber' of Otway. The remainder of the 1753 advertisement is Garrick's defence against the serious charge of plagiarism:

> Mr. Otway in his *Caius Marius*, a tragedy taken from *Romeo and Juliet*, has made use of this affecting circumstance, but it is a matter of wonder that so great a dramatic genius did not work up a scene from it of more nature, terror and distress. – Such a scene was attempted at the revival of this play, and it is hoped, that an endeavor to supply the failure of so great a master will not be deemed arrogant, or the making use of two or three of his introductory lines, be accounted a plagiarism.

Garrick's response is somewhat short on sincerity, since in fact the first half of his tomb scene is clearly based on *Caius Marius*, and in at least six instances the actual words are Otway's[104] But the final forty lines, in which he piles on the 'terror and distress' if not the 'nature', are entirely Garrick's. As Copeland rightly points out, his language in 'this orgy of pathos' is 'functional rather than poetic', and its object is to wring from the audience every last drop of sympathetic emotion.[105] In this it succeeded triumphantly, and the advertisement ends on a smilingly sarcastic note:

> The persons who from their great good nature and love of justice have endeavored to take away from the present editor the little merit of this scene by

ascribing it to Otway, have unwittingly, from the nature of the accusation, paid him a compliment which he believes they never intended him.

Garrick's alteration of *Romeo and Juliet*, like his *Macbeth*, turns inward, away from the wider social and political world, to concentrate on characters' feelings and interactions at the personal and family level. Marsden places it within a mid-eighteenth-century trend towards domesticating and sentimentalising Shakespeare, and identifies the factors that made for its success as 'the shift from the pathetic to the tender female and the emotive rather than heroic hero, and the appeal these characters made to audience sympathy'.[106] These are exactly the elements that are built up in Garrick's additional scene. He was now a master at devising acting opportunities that would provoke emotion in the spectator. To effect this, the facial expressions, gestures and movements of the actors were equally as important as words they uttered.

Garrick played Romeo sixty times. Though he gave up the role in 1760, his version of the play continued to be hugely popular. The kudos afforded by displaying Garrick's name on the title page from as early as 1753 contributed to the decline of the convention of anonymity. In the second half of the eighteenth century, as the indexes of *The London Stage* demonstrate, *Romeo and Juliet* was given more frequently than any other play by Shakespeare except *Hamlet*. Garrick's alteration, with its spectacle and its tear-wrenching duet for dying lovers, survived for a century and remained unchallenged on both sides of the Atlantic until the 1840s.

Though Garrick proclaimed Drury Lane under his management to be a site 'sacred to Shakespeare', the context for the prologue in which he made this boast is instructive. It was prompted by the desertion of Barry and Mrs Cibber to the rival company, and takes the form of a defiant though humorous declaration of war against Covent Garden. Sometimes Garrick made apologetic noises about 'daring to add to Shakespear': for example, 'it is hoped that the alterations have not been made with great impropriety' in the advertisement to his version of *Cymbeline*. But in practice he did not hesitate to make whatever changes to the plays he considered were needed to maintain Drury Lane's ascendancy in this latter-day 'war of the theatres'. Rather than literal adherence to any printed text or indeed to any absolute principles of alteration, the best service that Shakespeare's self-selected high priest believed he could offer to his idol was to bring forward his plays in forms acceptable to contemporary audiences. The following chapter demonstrates how very far he was prepared to go in pursuit of this goal.

CHAPTER 4

'Re-bottling' Shakespeare – Garrick in mid-career (1753–1768)

When looking back at the practice of alteration in the mid-eighteenth century, it is essential to remember that the reverence later accorded to Shakespeare's language was not yet common in Garrick's day. Shakespeare was admired, even idolised, for his fidelity to nature and command of 'the passions'; he was also beginning to be seen as the Bard of the nation, a focus for patriotic fervour.[1] But a generally shared, quasi-religious veneration for his very words had not yet emerged among the public. In 1753, an agreed 'authorised version' of Shakespeare seemed as far away as ever. Rowe's, Pope's, Theobald's, Hanmer's and Warburton's editions were all in the public domain competing for attention, and Capell's was on the horizon. Nor were those involved in the search for a definitive text confined to the world of professional scholarship.

Speculating learnedly upon Shakespeare's meanings was still a favourite activity for the leisured amateur. Johnson, in his proposals of 1756 for yet another edition, acknowledged that in correcting the text he would have the advantage of the labours of preceding editors. However, he also intended to make use of his encyclopaedic erudition to give more attention than they had done to 'the elucidation of passages obscured by accident or time',[2] and in this endeavour he had other assistants upon whom to draw. When in 1765 his *Plays of William Shakespeare* finally appeared, Johnson gave credit in the appendix to the numerous individuals, scholars, gentlemen and one unnamed learned lady, who had helped him by contributing notes. Among these were all but three of the original members of The Club, including Reynolds, Hawkins and Goldsmith.[3] Garrick, however (and that perhaps grudgingly), was credited with only one contribution.[4]

Garrick at the mid-century was at the peak of three careers: as actor, manager and writer. He was developing a reputation as a man of letters and a collector of old plays of Shakespeare's period. Despite Johnson's disdain, he was increasingly widely perceived, not simply as an authority on all matters Shakespearean, but as the holder of power, inherited from

Shakespeare himself, to grant or withhold approval of projects relating to his idol. Yet he did not regard his public image as Shakespeare's spokesperson as any sort of impediment to changing the plays to make them acceptable to the Drury Lane audience.

The fifteen-year period, which this chapter covers, was marked by great diversity in Garrick's approaches to altering Shakespeare for performance at Drury Lane. It would be an error to assume that, as time went on, his versions became steadily more faithful to the texts from which they derived. Two of the plays, *A Midsummer Night's Dream* and *The Tempest*, were transformed into operas in the English language, although it is not known for certain who made the alterations. Garrick definitely wrote their prologues. These demonstrate that both productions were deliberate attempts to confront the challenge of competition from Italian opera at the King's Theatre, patronised by the aristocracy, by invoking the patriotism of a more socially diverse audience in favour of the English language.[5] Neither opera had any lasting success. Garrick continued to feel free to use Shakespeare's plays as a resource from which to develop performable texts, sometimes by radical alteration, sometimes with minimal changes. Included in the latter category are slightly shortened versions of *The Tempest* (first performed 20 October 1757),[6] *Antony and Cleopatra* (3 January 1759) to be discussed below and *Cymbeline* (28 November 1761).[7]

The freedom felt by Garrick and his contemporaries, despite their respect and admiration for Shakespeare, to move away from his texts and then return to them, to adapt and re-adapt, is well illustrated by their treatment of *A Midsummer Night's Dream* at the mid-century. Drury Lane's operatic version, *The Fairies*, survived for only two months beyond its debut season (1754–1755). But Garrick recycled a number of its songs into the alteration of the play that he prepared for performance in the 1763–1764 season. These were serious vocal interludes, mainly for the lovers; they reduced the comedy and slowed down the action. Overall, however, and despite extensive cutting, Garrick was faithful to the tripartite structure of the play, balancing fairies, lovers and mechanicals more or less equally, although he omitted the final fairy scene. His collaborator was George Colman the Elder, to whom was entrusted the management of Drury Lane, including the mounting of *A Midsummer Night's Dream*, when in September 1763 Mr and Mrs Garrick embarked on their two-year grand tour of Europe. During rehearsals Colman made further changes to Garrick's script, all designed to give prominence to the court characters and to downplay the clowns and fairies. He cut *Pyramus* and *Thisbe* altogether and ended the play with a grand procession to the temple for a triple marriage ceremony, and a hymn to Hymen. The first night – which was the only night – was a disaster, a nightmare rather than a dream. '[N]ever was a piece so murdered as this was by the singing speakers', wrote Hopkins, the prompter, in his diary.[8] Seeking to retrieve something from this expensive wreck, Colman, in Hopkins's words, 'luckily thought of turning it into a farce'. Transformed into a short comic vehicle for singers and dancers, the new afterpiece had its first performance three nights later, under the title of *A Fairy Tale*. In this guise it met with some success and was retained in the Drury Lane repertoire for four seasons; by this time it bore only the slightest resemblance to *A Midsummer Night's Dream*.[9]

Among the plays of Shakespeare subjected to the most extensive alteration at this period was Garrick's version of *The Taming of the Shrew* (1754). This much-abbreviated alteration in three short acts succeeded at least three other versions of the play performed earlier in the century. Garrick turned Shakespeare's comedy into *Catharine and Petruchio*, a farcical afterpiece. The Christopher Sly induction and the Bianca subplot were deleted, nine of the twenty-five characters were cut, bawdy lines blue-pencilled, other speeches shortened or broken up and more stage business introduced. Much of Katherine's famous advice to wives at the end of the play was re-assigned to Petruchio. According to Ann Thompson, 'Garrick's version [. . .] proved so popular that the full text had to wait for performance until 1844 in England and 1887 in the United States'.[10] But large-scale changes did not necessarily indicate less respect for the original. On the contrary, they were often made with the precise intention of rescuing a work of flawed genius from neglect. This concept is demonstrated most clearly in Garrick's wholesale re-working of *The Winter's Tale* (1756).

For none of his statements about Shakespeare has Garrick been more severely taken to task than for the prologue he spoke before the first performance (on 21 January 1756) of his alteration of *The Winter's Tale*.[11] Garrick presents his theatre as 'a tavern', the 'Shakespear's Head' (lines 1–9), and develops the metaphor in the next couplet (lines 10–11): 'From this same head, this fountainhead divine, / For different palates springs a different wine!' Each element in the audience, he claims, from boxes to upper gallery, will find in Shakespeare some 'liquor' to their taste – all but 'the learned critics' (line 30), who are '[s]o blindly thoughtful and so darkly read' (lines 34) that they cannot tell the difference between

Shakespeare's imitators ('Perry') and the real thing ('the best Champaign') (line 37). The prologue ends:

> In this night's various and enchanted cup
> Some little Perry's mixed for filling up.
> The five long acts from which our three are taken,
> Stretch'd out to sixteen years, lay by, forsaken.
> Lest then this precious liquor run to waste,
> 'Tis now confined and bottled for your taste.
> 'Tis my chief wish, my joy, my only plan,
> To lose no drop of that immortal man! (lines 50–55)

Using such a final couplet to introduce a version of the play that completely eliminates Shakespeare's first three acts has seemed to many little short of brazen hypocrisy. To a Victorian biographer, Knight, it represented 'effrontery' that 'cannot easily be surpassed'. Vickers calls Garrick 'high-handed'.[12] He quotes the harsh verdict of a rival actor and alterer, Theophilus Cibber: '*The Winter's Tale*, mammoc'd into a Droll'.[13] Garrick's 'marketing claims', says Taylor, 'were misleading, if not deliberately dishonest. Shakespeare did not need Garrick to rescue him from any looming oblivion'.[14] Furness, more kindly, blames the deplorable taste of the audience: 'It is not the author [. . .] who deserves the ferule, but the hands that applauded it.'[15] Stone, in his doctoral thesis, took the same line and, unusually, never subsequently published any defence of this alteration.[16]

When seen in its historical context, however, Garrick's prologue to *The Winter's Tale* requires no defence. There was nothing original about a writer's claiming to have rescued a play of Shakespeare from oblivion; audiences were used to hearing such assertions. Branam gives many examples from the period 1681 to 1770, including the prologues to alterations by Tate, Theobald, Johnson, Colley Cibber and Hawkins. He comments:

> The general assumption is the same in all: Shakespeare is uneven, and the adapter is doing a service by saving the good in Shakespeare – whether it be by separating his gold from his dross, pruning his garden, rebottling his liquor, tuning his lyre, or rebuilding his ships.[17]

Garrick was working in an established tradition. His originality lay in the trope he chose – himself as vintner of Shakespeare's wine – and the brilliance with which he worked and re-worked this core idea throughout the prologue's fifty-five lines. Neither he nor his contemporaries would have seen a conflict, as later critics have done, between confining the 'precious liquor' lest it 'run to waste', while at the same time losing 'no drop' of it. What mattered most was that the re-bottling should be done to suit the palate of a contemporary audience: if the play did not please, it would fail and be forgotten. 'For your taste' is thus the key phrase of the entire prologue.

On the page, Shakespeare's *Winter's Tale* flagrantly transgressed many of the eighteenth century's conventions about what constituted a well-made play; yet it had its appeal. Johnson, following Warburton, thought it 'with all its absurdities, very entertaining'.[18] Alterers were simultaneously attracted and repulsed by it, and continued to seek ways to bring it – at least in part – to the stage. Garrick's was, then, far from being the only attempt at an alteration; over the thirty years from 1747 to 1777 at least four others were made. Among the most obvious challenges presented by the play was its neglect of the neoclassical unities.[19] 'The author was himself aware of the impropriety of lengthening his plot to the immoderate space of sixteen years', wrote Thomas Davies, with Time's introduction to the fourth act in mind.[20] The shifts in location between Sicily and Bohemia (or Bithynia, if Hanmer's edition were taken as the base text) constituted a further blemish. The play was obviously far too long to be performed in full. Worse, its world was thoroughly old fashioned, shot through with fairy tale and magic, not to say superstition, where oracles were consulted and man-eating bears could suddenly appear.[21] Still worse, Shakespeare seemed to have been unconcerned about spelling out the moral lessons to be drawn by the audience, while the final family reunion contained some uncomfortable silences.

Even more of a problem was the embarrassing behaviour of some of the characters. Theobald had been shocked by Paulina's 'gross and blunt' language to Leontes; to call her king 'a fool' (III.ii.185) was undoubtedly going too far. He changed the offending word to 'soul'. The notes supplied by Francis Gentleman, an actor himself, to Bell's 1774 edition are highly critical of the unroyal behaviour of Leontes, Polixenes and Hermione in the opening scenes. For him, kings and queens on stage should be dignified and, as far as possible, noble. But Leontes's sudden and bizarre descent into jealousy shows him as 'little better than a bedlamite'. Gentleman, who commends Covent Garden for omitting these speeches in performance, reveals in his introduction a further difficulty. After the play has been 'prun'd and regulated' to conform to the eighteenth-century norms for tragedy, the resulting alteration still requires 'very good actors, who find too small a scope for impressive, creditable exertion'.[22] In other words, what ought to be the leading parts, once emasculated, become insufficiently attractive to leading players. Gentleman rightly excepts the roles of Florizel, Perdita and Autolycus. In all the eighteenth-century alterations of *The Winter's Tale* the parts of the young lovers are often expanded and Autolycus, the primary source of comedy – 'very naturally conceived, and strongly represented', said Johnson in his notes to the play – features strongly.

Garrick's re-working of *The Winter's Tale* to suit the taste of the times was drastic; there were to be no half measures about this re-bottling. Pedicord and Bergmann estimate (see *Plays of Garrick*, III. 434) that, as well as dropping Shakespeare's first three acts, he cut a further 600 lines from Acts IV and V, and added over 400 of his own. The result is a main piece in three acts, often, though not invariably, played as a double bill with *Catharine and Petruchio*, Garrick's three-act farcical afterpiece based on *The Taming of the Shrew*. It is probable that for convenience and ease of handling he worked from a copy of the 12mo text separately printed by Tonson in 1735 rather than from any version bound in with other plays, but changes made by several editors can be found in his alteration. For example, in Perdita's 'flowers o' th' spring' speech (IV.iv.110–129, *cf.* G.II. i.100–114), Garrick altered Tonson's 'my fairest friends' to Theobald's (and the First Folio's) 'my fairest friend' (line 112), to make clear that Perdita is here addressing only Florizel. In the same passage (line 125), he adopted Warburton's 'gold oxlips', whereas Theobald's and Tonson's oxlips had been 'bold', following the First Folio. As usual, Garrick made his own amendments for reasons of delicacy or clarity. For instance, in the same speech, 'Your maidenheads' (line 116) becomes 'Your maiden honors'.

To solve the problems of length, timescale and widespread locations, Garrick decided to begin the play sixteen years after Shakespeare, when Perdita has reached the age of sixteen, and to set it entirely in Bohemia. This necessitated the composition of extensive introductory dialogue between Camillo and a gentleman, to explain not only the 'back story' of Leontes's jealousy, and the infant Perdita's exposure, but also that Paulina had fled to the court of Polixenes after Hermione's supposed death. The entire first scene is essentially Garrick's, except for a brief exchange between Polixenes and Camillo about Florizel's mysterious retirement from court (G.I.i.80–105), and a few residual phrases that perhaps Garrick thought too good to lose. Examples of these are 'the innocent milk yet in her innocent mouth' (G.I.i.43–44) and 'the child-bed privilege denied, which belongs to women of all fashion' (G.I.i.49–50). The new scene sets up the absent Leontes, Garrick's own role, as a basically sympathetic figure, grieving and penitent. In any case, this Leontes has less to repent than Shakespeare's: there is no mention of Mamilius. Camillo tells the audience that Leontes's penitence is now 'as extreme as his suspicions had been fatal. In the course of his sorrows he has, as we are informed, twice attempted on his life' (G.I.i.62–64), and he is now en route to Bohemia 'to make all possible atonement to his injured brother'. Polixenes enters with Paulina, and in his very first line establishes the *leitmotiv* of the piece as fitted for the sentimental taste of the mid-eighteenth century: 'Weep not now, Paulina' (G.I.i.68).

In the popular literature, and to some extent in the drama, of the mid-eighteenth century, sensibility was the dominant mode.[23] The more readily and copiously characters wept, the more they demonstrated their capacity for sincere feelings of love, compassion, tender-heartedness and repentance. Shakespeare's *Winter's Tale* takes a sharply contrasting approach. The word 'weep' appears in the text only four times, 'weeping' and 'wept' three times each, whereas 'tears' are mentioned in all just seven times.[24] It is striking how anti-sentimental, how resistant to the whole concept of tears as an index of sensibility, many of these references are. Hermione, on trial, claims not to be 'prone to weeping' (II.i.110); her 'honourable grief [. . .] burns / Worse than tears drown' (lines 113–114). She proudly exhorts her attendants:

> Do not weep, good fools.
> There is no cause. When you shall know your mistress
> Has deserved prison, then abound in tears
> As I come out. (II.i.120–123)

Antigonus recalls the instructions of Hermione's apparition to name her baby Perdita and leave it in Bohemia: 'There weep, and leave it crying' (III.iii.31). Obeying, he comments: 'Weep I cannot, / But my heart bleeds' (III.iii.50–51). Sometimes Shakespeare's characters use tears in the painting of sentimental fantasies. Perdita resolves to 'queen it no inch farther, / But milk my ewes and weep' (IV.iv.448–449). Camillo, encouraging Florizel and Perdita to flee to Sicily, envisages 'Leontes opening his free arms and weeping / His welcomes forth' (IV.iv.548–549), while Florizel embellishes his fiction that Perdita is the child of Smalus, ruler of Libya, by describing an emotional leave-taking: 'from him whose daughter / His tears proclaimed his, parting with her' (V.i.158–159). Not one of these examples is retained in Garrick's text.

Shakespeare's economy gives force to the very few occasions when his characters do actually weep, and even then as often as not he finds ways to divert the audience from any temptation to take out their handkerchiefs.

When the Clown, now dressed as a gentleman, tells Autolycus about the great family reunion between himself, the Old Shepherd, the two kings, Florizel and Perdita, he describes a frankly comic 'group hug', culminating in 'and so we wept; and there was the first gentleman-like tears that ever we shed' (V.ii.141–143). A more significant distancing effect is achieved with the emotional reunion of Polixenes and Leontes. The encounter takes place offstage and is reported by Third Gentleman (Paulina's steward) in exaggerated language, more affected than pathetic. To take just one example:

> One of the prettiest touches of all, and that which angled for mine eyes – caught the water, though not the fish – was when at the relation of the Queen's death, with the manner how she came to't bravely confessed and lamented by the King, how attentiveness wounded his daughter till from one sign of dolour to another she did, with an 'Alas', I would fain say bleed tears; for I am sure my heart wept blood.(V.ii.81–88)

Here the Third Gentleman's foregrounding of his own emotions prevents the audience from vicariously entering into Perdita's.[25] Time after time, throughout the play, Shakespeare dares his audience to cry.

How different was the cultural climate of Garrick's theatre, where playwrights, actors and audience all strove to demonstrate their sensitivity by the engendering of tears. While Garrick sometimes had his doubts about the place of sensibility in comedy,[26] his Bohemia of 1756 was certainly saturated with feeling. Some of the passages he added could have been lifted intact from a sentimental novel. Take, for example, the description, given to Paulina by 'a gentleman', of the offstage meeting between the repentant Leontes and the wronged Polixenes:

> True, I have wronged you, cried Leontes; but if penitence can atone for guilt, behold these eyes, wept dry with honest sorrow; this breast, rent with honest anguish; and if you can suspect that my heart yet harbors those passions which once infested it, here I offer it to your sword. Lay it open to the day! (G.III.ii.25–30)

To which account, like a Richardsonian heroine, Paulina fervently responds: 'O, the force, the charm of returning virtue!'[27]

Analysis of Garrick's additions to what was left of Shakespeare's text shows that most were designed to set Leontes, the character he himself played, in a more sympathetic light. After his shipwreck on the coast of Bohemia – 'ye gods, Bohemia!' (G.I.ii.63) – Garrick inserts highly emotional speeches in which the penitent king lashes himself with self-reproach. As usual in Garrick's alterations, exclamations and broken-off sentences mark the rapid shifts of mood that were his trademark as an actor; in Steevens's words, 'those sharp turns, and that coachmanship in which you excel all others'[28]:

> Did I not
> Upon this coast expose my harmless infant –
> Bid Polixenes (falsely deemed the father)
> To take his child – O hell-born jealousy!
> All but myself most innocent – and now
> Upon this coast – Pardon, Hermione!
> 'Twas this that sped thee to thy proper heav'n; (G.I.ii.67–73)

Following a lachrymose appeal to Hermione, in her 'sainted seat above the clouds' (line 74) to look down on him with pity, Leontes segues simultaneously into despair and into an almost exact return to Shakespeare's words from an earlier episode (III.2.209–213):

> a thousand knees
> Ten thousand years together, naked, fasting,
> Upon a barren mountain, and still winter,
> In storms perpetual, could not move the gods
> To look this way upon me. (G.I.ii.83–87)

Ironically, these were once Paulina's lines, except for line 87, which originally read 'To look that way thou wert' (III.ii.213). Garrick clearly thought that they were too good to lose and appropriated them for his own part. Leontes is in tears again when, in disguise at the sheep-shearing feast, he admires the unknown Perdita: 'each salt dropt / That trickles down my cheek relieves my heart, / Which else would burst with anguish' (G.II.i.342–344). After Polixenes's confrontation with his son and furious exit, Leontes, not Camillo, offers help to the young couple. Yet again he weeps uncontrollably ('cease foolish tears') as he promises to intervene with Polixenes (G.ii.i.533). In the statue scene that ends the play Garrick inserts for Leontes not only a new direction at G.III.iv.75 '(*Bursts into tears*)', but a new speech to reflect the audience's assumption that true feeling will validate itself in weeping:

> O masterpiece of art! nature's deceiv'd
> By thy perfection, and at every look
> My penitence is all afloat again. (*Weeps.*) (G.III.iv.84–86)

Jean Marsden sees Garrick's version of *The Winter's Tale* as portraying bourgeois family values, with the emphasis on domestic happiness: 'its plot depicts the restoration not of a monarch, but of a husband and father'.[29] Certainly, Garrick's additions to the final scene combine to produce a situation not dissimilar from the happy ending of a sentimental novel. The virtuous family is reunited and its members show their gratitude, their sensibility and their mutual love through joyful tears. As Hermione comes down from the pedestal and moves into her husband's arms, the audience is told that tears choke her voice. Meanwhile, Perdita collapses with emotion onto Florizel's bosom. 'My princely shepherdess!' he murmurs, '[t]his is too much for hearts of thy soft mold' (G.III.iv.177–178). In Shakespeare's statue scene, Hermione, though she embraces him, never speaks to Leontes; her single speech is addressed solely to Perdita. Is her silence significant? Does it perhaps suggest that the couple's reunion could never be perfect in the absence of Mamilius? Garrick has no truck with gaps and uncertainties; the additional lines he provides for Hermione are absolutely unambiguous. After a blessing upon the kneeling Perdita and her Prince Charming, Garrick's Hermione at first holds back the emotional climax by reminding the reunited family, as, curiously, Shakespeare had neglected to do, that its primary obligation is to give thanks:

> Before this swelling flood o'er-bear our reason,
> Let purer thoughts, unmix'd with earth's alloy,
> Flame up to heav'n, and for its mercy shown,
> Bow we our knees together. (G.III.iv.204–207)

Rapturously, Leontes concurs ('Leontes' tears have washed away his guilt'), and then Hermione gives the signal to open the emotional floodgates:

> This firstling duty paid, let transport loose,
> My lord, my king – there's distance in those names,
> My husband! (G.III.iv.214–216)

Here again, Garrick finds it necessary to fill one of the troubling gaps left in the original.[30] His Hermione explicitly bestows forgiveness upon Leontes: 'be all that's past / Forgot in this enfolding, and forgiven' (lines 219–220). Perdita completes the sentimental tableau by kneeling at her parents' feet to kiss Hermione's 'honored hand' (line 222).

It seems that Garrick saw the shortage of lines for the young couple, and the general lack of attention paid to Florizel, as further deficiencies. He makes both Paulina and Leontes introduce Florizel formally to Hermione; both emphasise his royal status. Immediately before Leontes's final speech, Garrick inserted a sentimental exchange between the lovers.

Perdita speaks in the tones of the humble Pamela, almost as if she really were a shepherdess rather than a princess born:

> I am all shame
> And ignorance itself, how to put on
> This novel garment of gentility,
> And yield a patched behavior, between
> My country level and my present fortunes,
> That ill becomes this presence. I shall learn,
> I trust I shall with meekness – but I feel
> (Ah, happy that I do) a love, an heart
> Unaltered to my prince, my Florizel. (G.III.iv.251–259)

Florizel's response is a direct reminder to the audience of the pastoral elements in the play that represented such a large part of its appeal: 'Be still my Queen of May, my shepherdess, / Rule in my heart; my wishes be thy subjects, / And harmless as thy sheep' (lines 260–262). Finally, Garrick has Leontes, the now pious and forgiven husband and father, end the play with a banal prayer somewhat reminiscent of Pericles, another shipwrecked monarch reunited with his family after much affliction:

> – then thank the righteous gods,
> Who, after tossing in a perilous sea,
> Guide us to port, and a kind beam display,
> To gild the happy evening of our day. (G.III.iv.267–270)

Garrick's drastic cutting and altering certainly achieved his aim of showing Leontes in a more favourable light, but it was gained at the expense of the strength, dignity and resilience shown by female characters in the first three acts. The sententious and watery Paulina of Drury Lane bears little resemblance to the fearless, mouthy defender of Hermione. The queen herself is depicted as a model wife and mother, selfless and pious, infinitely forgiving and infinitely loving. As Irene Dash says: 'Hermione's strength becomes unnecessary if there is no challenge, no contest, for her to face.'[31] But Dash's further statement that Garrick (and Macnamara Morgan, of whom more below) 'substituted weak women for strong, and strong men for weak' is open to question. She argues that 'Leontes' passion-wracked passages, his intense spurts of jealousy, and his arrogance' are removed along with the first three acts. True, but this does not render him a stronger character. Garrick's Leontes is still 'passion-wracked', though now by remorse; he is constantly on the verge of breaking down. In line with the cultural preferences of the period, he is shown, above all, as a man of feeling, not a man of strength.

The account so far given of Garrick's transformation of *The Winter's Tale* into a lachrymose family drama is less than complete because it scarcely mentions the major selling point of his alteration: its pastoral aspect. It is clear from the pages of *The London Stage* that idealised portrayals of the life, and particularly the love life, of shepherds and shepherdesses in song and in dance were as popular as ever at this time. The dances performed between the acts of main pieces in the 1740s often had titles such as 'Shepherds and Shepherdesses', 'The Shepherd's Holiday' or 'The Shepherd's Wedding'. The grand ballet from Handel's opera, *Il Pastor Fido,* was also staged, and songs by or addressed to shepherdesses are frequently mentioned in the bills. An afterpiece, *The Shepherds' Lottery*, 'a new Musical Masque' written by Moses Mendez, with music by Boyce, was one of the big successes of the 1751–1752 season at Covent Garden, and had several subsequent revivals. In 1752, Allan Ramsey's *The Gentle Shepherd*, described as a 'Scots Pastoral Comedy', was revived for thirteen performances at the Haymarket. And *As You Like It* (at this period regarded primarily as a vehicle for a popular actress such as Mrs Pritchard) was a staple in the repertoire of both the patent houses.

Garrick was not the first to see the appeal of *The Winter's Tale* for audiences who delighted in dancing shepherdesses and singing shepherds. Less than two years earlier, Covent Garden had staged a new afterpiece in two acts, *The Sheep-shearing*, very loosely based on Act IV of *The Winter's Tale*. The object of its author, Macnamara Morgan, was to showcase the charms of the beautiful Isabella Nossiter (the previous season's Juliet), and his alteration gives Perdita centre stage.[32] The Sicilian scenes are totally dispensed with. Leontes's repentance is briefly announced, though he does not appear; Hermione and Paulina are never mentioned. The entire piece takes place in Bithynia, where sheep-shearing festivities and the wedding of Florizel and Perdita are interrupted by the king (i.e., Polixenes) and Camillo. The part of Autolycus, a singing pedlar, is largely re-written, and includes the well-worn comedy device of a cheeky encounter with the disguised king early in the play, for which the pedlar has to seek pardon before the final curtain. Once the Old Shepherd has revealed Perdita's royal birth, and that he himself is none other than Antigonus in disguise, the wedding can continue, and the play ends with a celebratory chorus:

> Then let us all be blithe and gay
> Upon this joyful bridal day.
> Sing high, sing down, sing ding dong bell,
> For Perdita and Florizel.[33]

No doubt Arne's music (now lost) for the many songs and dances which are *The Sheep-shearing*'s primary *raisons d'être* brought to the play the quality that is so lacking in Morgan's banal book and lyrics. The overall effect upon the reader is of a pantomime script. The few passages retained from Shakespeare – some dialogue for the lovers and the disguised king's dramatic discovery of himself to his son – come almost as a shock. Essentially, the Morgan version was a pretty afterpiece enlivened with knock-about comedy, which provided a useful vehicle to exhibit the versatility of leading actors like Barry. Over the following seven years, Covent Garden continued to perform *The Sheep-shearing* approximately three times a season; later it was occasionally given at Drury Lane.

Garrick's alteration of *The Winter's Tale* needs to be seen in the context of the continuous struggle for supremacy between Covent Garden and Drury Lane. His aims were more ambitious than Morgan's. *The Sheep-shearing* had followed the established theatrical trend of keeping the pastoral as a separate genre, charming, sometimes amusing, and always undemanding. But Garrick wanted a Shakespearean main piece, not just a light entertainment with which to finish the evening agreeably, and it was his combining of the dramatic with the pastoral that made his version novel. When published two years after its first performance, the title page described the play as 'a dramatic pastoral',[34] and it is evident from the text that Garrick's aim was to produce a main piece that integrated, and did full justice to, both elements.

This alteration of *The Winter's Tale* is noteworthy for another reason. In proposing the moral superiority of the country over the town, Garrick sounds a new note in English comedy. The dream of rejecting the corruptions of the court and city in favour of a well-ordered country life in harmony with nature became ever more seductive as the towns expanded.[35] It is a familiar poetic theme from Jonson's 'Penshurst' onwards. By the mid-eighteenth century, the pastoral idyll was common in the arts. One thinks of Gainsborough's family groups in landscape settings, of which *Mr and Mrs Andrews* (c. 1750) is perhaps the best known, and of the Staffordshire pottery and Chelsea porcelain designs that show ladies and gentlemen in the guise of idealised country folk. Paradoxically, however, at the theatres patronised by the urban middle class at the mid-century, the disparaging view of country life and manners exhibited in the comedies of the Restoration and in their predecessors, the Jacobean city comedies, remained more or less unchanged. This latter point is confirmed by an analysis of the offerings at Drury Lane in the season 1755–1756, up to and including the week in which *The Winter's Tale* opened. Setting aside the special cases of Shakespeare (*As You Like It* and *Much Ado about Nothing*), Buckingham's burlesque of rhymed heroic drama, *The Rehearsal*, and a popular revival of Charles Shadwell's entertainment *The Fair Quaker of Deal or The Humours of the Navy*, which ran up to, through and beyond the Christmas season, none of the comedies staged diverges from the view that country folk are credulous innocents or rustic boobies, fair game for the sophisticates who reside, or wish that they resided, in town. Above all, these comedies share the assumption that London is the true seat of fashion, culture and pleasure. This is as true of the comedies set in the provinces (*The Beaux' Stratagem*, *The Drummer* and *The Recruiting Officer*) as of those with a London setting such as *The Alchemist*, *Every Man in His Humour* or *The Provok'd Wife*.[36] Physically and culturally the London theatres were located between, to the east, the moneyed city and, to the west, their royal and aristocratic patrons and the ever more influential prosperous middle classes. Flattering their audiences was an essential part of their business.

The song that Garrick wrote for Perdita, 'Come, come, my good shepherds' (G.II.i.149–168), challenged the long-prevailing scorn of country by town that had hitherto dominated English comedy. Its five stanzas extol the virtues of the 'guiltless and free' rustic community (line 3), who 'harbor no passions by luxury taught' (line 5). 'By mode and caprice are the city dames led, / But we as the children of nature are bred,' claims Perdita (lines 9–10). She continues:

> That giant, Ambition, we never can dread;
> Our roofs are too low for so lofty a head;
> Content and sweet cheerfulness open our door,
> They smile with the simple and feed with the poor. (lines 13–16)

Thomas Davies praised Perdita's song as 'very pleasing'.[37] As sung by Mrs Cibber, who had returned to Drury Lane after her defection to Covent Garden at the start of the 1750–1751 season, it was an instant hit, and the words were immediately reprinted in magazines.[38] In subsequent seasons, the bills frequently highlighted it as one of the main attractions of the play, and if an actress were not capable of singing it, another would be billed to do so. It even found its way to the rival house: a Covent Garden text of it has survived.[39] One city dame upon whom the words made a lasting impact was Hester Thrale. In 1769 Boswell recorded her praising 'Garrick's talent for light gay poetry' and dwelling 'with peculiar pleasure on this [slightly misquoted] line: "I'd smile with the simple, and feed with the poor" '.[40] The point of the anecdote is Johnson's riposte: 'Nay, my dear Lady, this will never do. Poor David! Smile with the simple! What folly is that! And who would feed with the poor that can help it? No, no; let me smile with the wise, and feed with the rich. ' Both Johnson and Mrs Thrale appear to equate the sentiments of the speaker with those of the author: an indicator of the poem's independent popularity.

Although Garrick's *Winter's Tale* received some pleasing reviews and had thirteen performances in its initial season (1755–1756), it never fully established itself as a mainstay of the Drury Lane repertoire. It was played there as a three-act main piece twice in each of the two succeeding seasons, and published, as *Florizel and Perdita*, in 1758. It is hard to avoid the conclusion that the change of name was a deliberate spoiler. The play enjoyed a mini-revival during the 1761–1762 season, when it was performed under its new title on five occasions.[41] The change in nomenclature directly challenged Covent Garden's own two-act afterpiece by Macnamara Morgan, originally billed as *The Sheep-shearing*, but which since 1758–1759 had been performed at least four times each season under its alternative title of *Florizel and Perdita*. Morgan's afterpiece was published as *The Sheep-shearing: or, Florizel and Perdita* in 1762, the year of its author's death. Whether coincidentally or not, 3 May 1762 was the date of its last performance at Covent Garden for nearly thirty years. This in theory left the field free for Drury Lane, and when Garrick's main piece was again revived for two performances in 1764–1765, the bills reverted to his original title of *The Winter's Tale*. But Garrick had appeared as Leontes for the last time on 29 March 1762; his successor in the part, Powell, did not have the same drawing power, and Garrick's alteration was seen no more at Drury Lane until Sheridan revived it there, 'with some farther improvements',[42] in 1779–1780 after Garrick's death.

The confusion arising from the many changes of title in published and performed versions of Garrick's and Morgan's alterations[43] is compounded by the existence of other mid-eighteenth-century versions of *The Winter's Tale*. Two days after its first night on 21 January 1756, the imminent publication of Garrick's alteration was (somewhat prematurely) announced; it eventually appeared in 1758. On the same day, a young Cambridge undergraduate, Charles Marsh, brought out his own five-act version, with a provocative challenge to Garrick in blank verse on the title page:

> Think'st thou, the *Swan* of *Avon* spreads her Wings,
> Her brooding Wings, for thee alone to plume,
> And nestle there, O *Garrick*? – Thou deserv'st
> Indeed, much cherishing: thy Melody
> Charms ev'ry Ear. But sure, it ill beseems
> One *Cygnet*, thus to stretch it's little Pinions,
> Ambitiously intent, to fill that Nest,
> Whose roomy Limits well may shelter Numbers.[44]

Such a piece of youthful cheek must have ensured that this little cygnet's chances of ever writing for Drury Lane in the future were nil. At this stage in his life, Marsh seems to have been an enthusiastic alterer of Shakespeare. He had one great advantage: his father, also Charles, was a London bookseller and in a position to publish his son's efforts. The younger Marsh's *Cymbeline*, intended for Covent Garden, had been published the year before; he is also known to have made an alteration, now lost, of *Romeo and Juliet*. Getting his work staged, however, was less easy. A later printing of *Cymbeline* is indignantly sub-titled: 'as it was agreed to be Acted at the Theatre-Royal in Covent Garden'.

Marsh's alteration of *The Winter's Tale* is a brave one, in that it attempts to deal with the entire spread of the play. Whereas Garrick's solution to the problem of the long time span was simply to omit the first three acts, Marsh set all his five acts sixteen years after Leontes's initial outburst of jealousy, with Hermione having been imprisoned, awaiting trial, ever since. Despite a great deal of re-writing in the first two acts, his text is far closer to Shakespeare than Garrick's. Marsh allows Leontes to appear in a highly unattractive light, and Paulina and Hermione are not deprived of their big scenes. But his primary interest is the pastoral scenes. They are set in Bithynia, which suggests that Marsh was working from Hanmer's edition. His particular focus is on the young lovers, for whom he composes additional dialogue in a very elevated strain, full of classical allusions, personifications and elaborate similes. Contemporary attitudes to alteration are illuminated by Valerie Edden's quotations from reviews that 'condemned Marsh not for what he altered but for what he left'.[45] There is no evidence that Marsh's *Winter's Tale* was ever staged.

Another fairly faithful though shorter version of the full *Winter's Tale* was staged as a main piece at Covent Garden on 24 April 1771. Advertised as 'As Originally Written By Shakespeare [. . .] not acted for 30 years', it had been pruned by 'the ingenious Mr. Hull', whose benefit night it

Figure 4 Shakespeare, Tragedy and Comedy advance to welcome Garrick to Parnassus, while fellow actors mourn his passing. 'Immortality [or Apotheosis] of Garrick', by James Caldwall and by S. Smith, after George Carter. Line engraving, published 1783. National Portrait Gallery, London.

was.[46] Hull played Camillo and Time (Chorus in Act III), and Mrs Hull was Paulina. In George Carter's faintly ludicrous painting, *The Apotheosis of Garrick* (1780), Hull appears in the group of grieving actors, all costumed in their favourite Shakespearean roles, who mourn Garrick's angel-borne ascent to Parnassus and Shakespeare's outstretched arms. Hull wears a hat with an enormous plume, as Pisanio in *Cymbeline*.

It was Hull's alteration of *The Winter's Tale* that Bell printed in 1774. The Bell *Shakespeare* is usually fulsome in its references to Garrick. However, Gentleman's introduction to *The Winter's Tale* makes clear that Garrick's alteration, admirable though it was, had been deemed too radical for inclusion; hence the selection of Hull's. Gentleman considered that Hull had certainly made *The Winter's Tale* 'more bearable than the author left it'. His strong objections to the play, described earlier in this chapter, may well have been shared by the audience, and only one other performance of Hull's abbreviation is recorded, on 4 May 1772. It would probably have been forgotten, had it not found its way into Bell's edition. The text has curious similarities with Marsh's never-performed alteration. Both (like Morgan's) refer to Bithynia, not Bohemia. In neither version does Perdita sing. And both end with a pæan to innocence spoken by Leontes. In 1756, Marsh had written:

> Thy Hand, *Hermione*: thou art a Proof
> That only *Innocence* can be our Guard
> Against the rude Assaults, and Shocks of Fortune.
> 'Tis that secures us the protecting Hand
> Of gracious Providence. Hence learn, ye Fair,
> That *Innocence* is Heaven's peculiar Care.
> F I N I S[47]

Hull's ending expresses the same message, in only slightly less florid terms:

> Stand forth, *Hermione*,
> A shining proof that innocence can bear
> Affliction's sharpest tortures, unimpair'd;
> And from the trial to the wond'ring sight,
> Come forth more pure, more amiably bright.[48]

Before Garrick's retirement in June 1776, it is almost certain that his own version of *The Winter's Tale* itself underwent alteration for the rival house at the hands of his friend and erstwhile collaborator, George Colman the elder. In 1773–1774 Colman was coming to the end of his period as manager of Covent Garden. The performance of *The Winter's Tale* mounted there on 12 March 1774 as a three-act main piece, and advertised as 'Never Performed there', was a benefit for the popular comedy actor Henry Woodward, in the role of Clown (Perdita's supposed brother). Woodward had been Garrick's original Clown at Drury Lane in 1756, and perhaps it was he who suggested *The Winter's Tale* to Colman. He made the same choice for his benefit the following season. In July 1777 Colman, then proprietor of the Haymarket, staged *The Sheep-shearing* for one performance, in tandem with *A Fairy Tale*. This seems to confirm that the text published anonymously in that year, 'as performed at the Theatre Royal in the Hay-Market', is in fact Colman's work, and it is highly likely that this was the version that had been played for Woodward's benefit in 1774.[49] Colman pared down Garrick's text still further, though he took care not to cut the comic scenes with Autolicus *[sic]* and Clown. The first scene was completely cut; so was the final statue scene.[50] Instead, Colman transferred some of Hermione's lines to Leontes – a part by now so reduced that Garrick himself would never have considered playing it – and ended the play with a general reconciliation and with the uniting of the lovers. The emphasis was on singing and dancing; the two new songs (perhaps by Garrick) provided for Florizel in the Folger prompt-book are included. Whether or not Garrick made these additions to his alteration some time after its first performance in 1756, there is no doubt that Colman subsequently altered the text further, perhaps for Covent Garden in 1774 and certainly for the Haymarket in 1777. The playbills for the performances of *Florizel and Perdita* at Drury Lane in the early months of 1762 include Mrs Pritchard as Hermione, but Hermione never appears in Colman's text. Like Morgan, Colman brought the curtain down with a final chorus, in words ('Come, let us all be blythe and gay, / Upon this happy wedding day [etc.]') virtually identical with Morgan's. In effect, Colman had reinvented Morgan's *Sheep-shearing*.

Tracing the various versions of *The Winter's Tale* performed and published in the 1740s, 1750s, 1760 and 1770s is a confusing task. In some cases, certainty over linking playbill with text is simply not achievable. Garrick's and Marsh's alterations were published with their names on the title pages; but Morgan's, Hull's and Colman's reflected the still prevalent convention of anonymity. It is clear that managers borrowed features of rivals' productions and that, in the absence of any stringent copyright laws, these borrowings found their way into the various published texts. The frequent use of alternative titles compounds the difficulties. Nevertheless, the factor that provides at least a partial explanation of these complexities is the prevailing climate of competition – artistic as well as commercial – in which all these alterations were made.

A further mystery about *The Winter's Tale* remains, however. There are major differences between the first printed version of Garrick's alteration and the manuscript submitted for approval to the Lord Chamberlain's Office on 14 January 1756, a week before the first performance. This manuscript, in the hand of Cross, the Drury Lane prompter, with emendations by Garrick, survives in the Larpent Collection held in the Huntington Library at San Marino, California, and Stone, in his doctoral dissertation, analysed how it differed from the version published by Tonson in 1758.[51] Like Morgan's, it is a version in two acts, whereas Garrick's printed text is in three acts; indeed, Cross's diary for the first night specifically mentions three acts. The setting is Bithynia, not Bohemia. Each version contains some 40–50 lines not included in the other. In the Larpent manuscript a character called Rogero is assigned speeches but not mentioned in the cast list. In the Drury Lane playbill of January 1756 Rogero is listed as to be played by Walker. The cast list that precedes the first edition of 1758 again assigns the part to Walker, but by now Rogero has become a ghost character. In this published version, Rogero has no entrances, and his speeches are given to Camillo. If Garrick had made further changes in performance to his alteration of *The Winter's Tale* between its licensing by the Lord Chamberlain's office (14 January 1756) and its first appearance in print (1758), it would hardly be surprising. However, it may well be that some part of the explanation for these discrepancies involves young Charles Marsh's alteration, published two days after Garrick's first night, of which Stone was not aware. Marsh also included among the Sicilian lords a Rogero who had plenty to say, and he set the pastoral scenes in Bithynia, not Bohemia. Furthermore, the tenor of some high-flown speeches for Perdita and Florizel reproduced in Stone's dissertation from the Larpent manuscript that are absent from the printed text are similar to, though not identical with, the equivalent passages in Marsh's version. One person who could almost certainly have thrown further light on these various re-bottlings of *The Winter's Tale* was the editor of Shakespeare who was deputy examiner of plays at the time, that very odd character Edward Capell. His professional relations with Garrick are explored in the next section.

The Stage Licensing Act of 1737 had established the Theatres Royal in Drury Lane and Covent Garden as the only two theatres currently authorised to perform legitimate drama in London. Furthermore, it had imposed a legal requirement that not only theatres, but also plays, be licensed.[52] Theatre managers were to submit the texts they proposed to perform at least fourteen days in advance. The act was extremely demanding; pre-censorship was to extend, not only to new works, but also to 'any new act, scene, or other part added to any old interlude, tragedy, comedy, opera, play, farce, or other entertainment of the stage, or any new prologue, or epilogue' (Clause III). If applied literally, the act would have prevented even the slightest deviation in performance from the script as licensed. For an actor-manager, therefore, good working relationships with the Lord Chamberlain, and with his examiner and deputy examiner of plays, were essential. The Lord Chamberlain himself – six aristocratic grandees successively held this office during the period (1741–1776) of Garrick's professional career – was involved only when an entire play was suppressed. The day-to-day tasks of censoring scripts prior to performance and of issuing licences were delegated to the examiner, Chetwynd, who in turn left much of the work to his deputy. In addition to their salaries, the examiners received fees for reading the plays, irrespective of whether they approved them for performance; these fees were paid by the theatres, not the authors.[53]

Exactly how much of the work of censorship was undertaken by the examiner himself is uncertain; Garrick's correspondence shows Chetwynd directly involved on at least one occasion. Capell passes on to his boss a letter from Garrick submitting Colman's *Polly Honeycomb*. In an annotation he tells Chetwynd how to respond: 'you will have no objection to it; but on the contrary will approve it, and, I think, like it'.[54] Perhaps the formal process of licensing remained in the examiner's hands. But undoubtedly it was Capell's role, as deputy, to scrutinise the plays submitted (usually in manuscript) and to censor politically sensitive, immoral or profane passages, as well as satire directed at prominent persons. Conolly states that no evidence exists in the Larpent manuscripts 'that Chetwynd was ever actively engaged in reading or censoring them, and after Edward Capell's appointment as deputy examiner in 1749 the corrections that appear in the manuscripts are unmistakably in Capell's hand'.[55] Capell therefore occupied a position of great influence. His emendations (made in his favourite red ink) may often have been, as Conolly suggests, silly, irrelevant or over-zealous. Nevertheless, without his approval of a new piece in rehearsal, or of changes to an old one, an advertised performance could not go ahead. Garrick needed Capell. Indeed, in the interests of the smooth running of Drury Lane, it was essential to co-operate with him.

Co-operation with the examiner of plays meant more than submitting clearly copied manuscripts bearing a minimum of subsequent corrections. Garrick was careful, cautious and conservative. Unlike his contemporary, the playwright and actor Samuel Foote, he would not attempt to challenge the censor or try to slip something past him. Garrick's way was to work with and not against the examiner – in effect to do his work for him by pre-censoring texts before submission. He was not alone. Conolly shows that the majority of managers and dramatists supported the examiner's efforts to keep plays and politics separate.[56] Neither was there much to censor on moral grounds; the theatre was already engaged in a largely audience-driven clean-up campaign to purge its language of indelicacy and its plots of immorality.[57] It would be misleading to conclude from this that Capell was more or less free to devote himself to his passion for Shakespeare and Elizabethan literature. Theatres frequently breached the rule requiring that scripts intended for performance be submitted at least fourteen days in advance. For example, it can be seen from the catalogue of the Larpent Collection that, of the four manuscripts submitted by Drury Lane for examination in the 1755–1756 season, not one met the minimum criterion of a fortnight's notice. While this fact may suggest a high degree of mutual trust between censor and manager, it also implies that Capell could not invariably give priority to his literary studies. It seems that often he had to make himself available for his examining duties more or less immediately, to suit the managers' schedules.

Garrick certainly needed Capell's co-operation, but Garrick had something that Capell and the other contemporary editors of Shakespeare needed just as much: his great collection of English plays of the Renaissance and Restoration periods. Why and when he began to collect them is uncertain. George M. Kahrl, in his full and fascinating account of the history of the collection, suggests that Robert Dodsley, Garrick's bookseller friend, may have assisted him until their falling out in 1758.[58] Nor is it known exactly when Capell and Garrick began to collaborate about the collection. Kahrl shows that they worked very closely together in searching for missing plays; both of course were particularly interested in acquiring early Shakespearean texts. Capell issued a leaflet listing the quartos they were seeking: 'any price, not greatly unreasonable, will be given; and for an edition, that is not in the list, a consideration extraordinary'. By the mid-1750s there were approximately 1300 plays in Garrick's collection; all the major English playwrights were included, along with many minor works. We know this because Capell catalogued the collection for Garrick in about the year 1756, and organised its binding into 242 volumes.

Garrick's enthusiasm for old English plays, and the scope of his collection, which also included some very early printed romances, became well known in literary circles. He was generous in making his library available to scholars, many of whom became his friends. Of the thirty-one items in the first edition of Bishop Percy's *Reliques of Ancient English Poetry* (1765), nine were sourced from Garrick's collection.[59] Four years later, Thomas Warton, working on his *History of English Poetry*, wrote: 'Among your old plays you have some metrical romances, namely in vol. k. 10, and vol. k.9. Will you be so good as to send them to me at Trinity College, Oxford, as soon as convenient? I see you have these by Percy's references'.[60] The gratified Garrick of course sent the volumes off to the professor of poetry and future laureate. Many other contemporaries made use of Garrick's books, including Whalley, editor of the works of Ben Jonson (1756), Hawkins in his *The Origin of the English Drama* (1773), and Steevens, who brought out his *Twenty of the Plays of Shakespeare* in 1766.[61]

The editor who had the best opportunities to make use of the Shakespearean material in Garrick's collection was Samuel Johnson. In his 'Proposals' of 1756 he had promised: 'The corruptions of the text will be corrected by a careful collation of the oldest copies, by which it is hoped that many restorations may yet be made.'[62] But when his edition at last emerged in 1765, he stated in the preface: 'I collated such copies as I could procure, and wished for more, but have not found the collectors of these rarities very communicative.'[63] As Boswell confirms, Garrick, rightly, assumed that this jibe was meant for him, and was greatly piqued.[64] What had gone wrong? Whereas Theobald, for instance, had made his own collection of 'the oldest copies' and Capell was assembling one, Johnson had none of his own and was dependent upon others' generosity. Surely he could have relied upon Garrick, his former pupil and close friend, to make available to him the texts he needed? Boswell sought an explanation from Johnson:

> I told him, that Garrick had complained to me of it, and had vindicated himself by assuring me, that Johnson was made welcome to the full use of his collection, and that he left the key of it with a servant, with orders to have a fire and every convenience for him. I found Johnson's notion was, that Garrick wanted to be courted for them, and that, on the contrary, Garrick should have courted him, and sent him the plays of his own accord. But, indeed, considering the slovenly and careless manner in which books were treated by Johnson, it could not be expected that scarce and valuable editions should have been lent to him.

Johnson's response seems less than reasonable but, where Garrick was concerned, Johnson could often be exceedingly touchy. The contrast in their fortunes following their arrival together in London in 1737 must often have caused him chagrin. For example, it cannot have been easy for Johnson to have had to seek Garrick's public endorsement of his first edition of Shakespeare in order to enhance its saleability.[65] Boswell gives example after example of Johnson denigrating Garrick, yet fiercely repudiating any criticism of his friend by others – a feature of their relationship also highlighted by Joshua Reynolds, co-founder of The Club. At bottom, however, the bond between them was immensely strong. Boswell's description of their encounter before a dinner that he gave in October 1769 demonstrates the strength of their relationship; only Garrick would have dared to tease Johnson. The passage also provides a metaphor for the success of their very different literary careers, Garrick's so dazzlingly rapid, Johnson's so hard-won and slow:

> Garrick played round him with a fond vivacity, taking hold of the breasts of his coat, and, looking up in his face with a lively archness, complimented him on the good health which he seemed then to enjoy; while the sage, shaking his head, beheld him with a gentle complacency.[66]

Garrick's possession of so many rare old plays certainly bolstered his reputation as a man of letters. One feature of the collection, however, was distinctly unhelpful: the catalogue made by Capell. Elegant in appearance, the catalogue was rendered virtually useless by Capell's decision to arrange the books in sequences according to the size of their pages. His personal collection of 256 early editions of Shakespeare and his contemporaries, which he donated to Trinity College Cambridge in 1779, was arranged on the same plan. Capell seems to have made a speciality of decreasing the effectiveness of a work through adopting a quirky principle of organisation. In preparing his edition of Shakespeare he did the ground work that Johnson had neglected, and patiently collated as many early texts as he could find. But when his edition appeared, anonymously, in 1767–1768,[67] its usefulness was much reduced by his insistence, on aesthetic grounds, that the notes should be published later and separately. The notes were very slow in coming; fifteen years elapsed before the last of them appeared in print, and by then Capell was dead.

Capell is often depicted as an unsociable recluse, eccentric and difficult to deal with. Garrick himself noted on one of Capell's last letters: 'an odd devil'.[68] From Johnson and Malone onwards, his editorial endeavours have been the subject of mainly adverse criticism. Yet, as deputy examiner of plays he must have been a pivotal figure for the London managers, and the most tangible evidence of his close involvement in their world is the alteration of *Antony and Cleopatra* on which he and Garrick collaborated. Normally, a decision to publish a play depended upon its success at the box office; very unusually, this one appeared in print two months before its first performance (3 January 1759).[69] Though Pedicord and Bergmann include the 1758 abridgement of *Antony and Cleopatra* among Garrick's *Plays*, neither collaborator's name appears on the original title page. The decision to revive the play was certainly Garrick's, and his letters show that preparations to stage it (e.g., the making of new Roman 'shapes', i.e., costumes) had begun during the previous season. According to Stone, his motives were two-fold: he needed 'a new sort of spectacle' to counter Covent Garden's successes in pantomime and opera, and he wanted to 'further his ideal of adding lustre to Shakespeare's name'.[70] Garrick would have discussed with Capell in some detail how the abridgement should be made, and what re-arrangement of scenes would be needed to facilitate the staging of this long and complicated drama. Undoubtedly, he would have retained the power of final script approval. But the basic work of preparing the text was Capell's. The Folger Shakespeare Library holds a copy of Tonson's 1734 printing of the play, marked up in Capell's beautiful copperplate hand with cuts and a few added stage directions. Garrick's hand appears nowhere. Though Pedicord and Bergmann say that the result differs scarcely at all from the version published in 1758,[71] there is one significant change that surely indicates Garrick's involvement at the rehearsal stage. Capell's draft retains in its original place the description of Cleopatra in her barge (II.ii.197–233); in the later version the lines have been moved to the first scene (G.I.i.66–95). The speaker is Thyreus, 'sent from Caesar'. No explanation is given as to how a follower of Caesar happened to have been present at Cydnus to witness the fateful meeting of queen and triumvir.

Judging from the text prepared by Capell for publication in October 1758, the collaborators added virtually nothing to *Antony and Cleopatra,* apart from five additional lines for the shipboard song at II.vii.110–115. However, they sometimes made small adjustments to a line in order to achieve greater metrical regularity. For example, 'The ostentation of our love' (III.vi.52) was clipped to 'The ostent of our love' (G.II.v.58), while 'How! Not dead? Not dead?' (IV.xvi.103) became 'How! Not yet dead? Not dead?' (G.IV.ix.123). Otherwise, the words the audience heard were Shakespeare unimproved. The collaborators shortened the play by about

600 lines, transposed others, re-arranged scenes to reduce the number of changes of location, and omitted or conflated some minor characters. Stone's detailed analysis of the alteration shows that cuts occur mainly in Acts I to IV, especially in the first three, and 'are made in general with a view to concentrating upon the tragedy of Love, and of minimizing the political and historical implications'.[72] As Garrick knew, this had also been the approach taken by Dryden in 1678 in his once popular, but by now less frequently staged, *All for Love*, written 'in imitation of Shakespeare's stile', which was all that most audience members of Garrick's day knew of *Antony and Cleopatra*. Dryden's stately lovers are dignified, and preoccupied with considerations of personal honour; Shakespeare's are far more complex. Capell and Garrick were daring enough to retain Cleopatra's part almost intact, though they did omit the description (II.ii.235–239) of the queen hopping forty paces through the public street, as well as the statement that 'the holy priests / Bless her when she is riggish' (II.ii.245–246). Antony is placed in a rather more rational, if not idealised, light by the omission of his furious outburst ('O, that I were / Upon the hill of Basan ...' III.xiii.127–132) and of his farewell scene with his servants, when he deliberately reduces them to tears (IV.ii). The strange episode (IV.iii) in which his soldiers hear divine music, indicating that the God Hercules is abandoning Antony, is also cut. Reducing the details of Roman power struggles and military campaigns also has the effect of slightly simplifying the audience's view of Antony. But these are no more than minor adjustments; the substance of the part, with all its dense and powerful poetry, is kept intact.

The roles that lose most by the cuts, textual re-arrangements and streamlining of locations – there are no scenes in Parthia or Athens – are Octavia and Enobarbus. She is reduced to little more than a walk-on; he is deprived of his best speech. Overall, however, this alteration is more remarkable for what it retains than what it omits. For example, most of the bawdy dialogue between Charmian, Iras and the Soothsayer at I.ii.1–72 is left in.[73] And the part of the Clown who brings Cleopatra the asp (V.ii.238–274) is uncut but for seven lines (lines 266–272). All in all, then, the version of *Antony and Cleopatra* published by Garrick and Capell in 1758 deserves the label 'respectful' – some might even call it brave.

The relatively uncut text of *Antony and Cleopatra* performed at Drury Lane in January 1759 represented a considerable risk to the management. Garrick spent freely, and the play was lavishly mounted, the bills announcing 'New Habits, Scenes, and Decorations'. Unlike with *Macbeth* and *Hamlet,* some attempt at historical costuming was made. Very unusually, there was no afterpiece. This could possibly have been for reasons of length, although *Hamlet*, which is even longer, was habitually followed by a farce. Probably, Garrick's decision to let *Antony and Cleopatra* stand alone was intended to signal to the public that here was something really special: a major play by Shakespeare that had not been revived since the author's death. After all, the occasion represented the first-ever recorded performance. Unfortunately, it failed. *The London Stage* quotes what Cross, the prompter, wrote in his diary after the first night: 'This Play tho' all new dress'd and had Fine Scenes did not seem to give ye Audience any great plasure *[sic]*, or draw any Applause.' Madelaine, who calls this production 'Garrick's important failure', speculates that it failed 'because of persistent, though more subdued, antagonism to the play's idiom'.[74] Certainly, some thought Garrick miscast as Antony; others held that his Cleopatra, Mrs Yates, was not ready for the part. Garrick withdrew the play after six performances, and never revived it. Many years later he admitted in a letter to Steevens that, had he had the energy to nurse it (he had been ill on the first night), he might have turned the play's fortunes around:

> An^y^ & Cleopatra I reviv'd Some Years ago, when I and Mrs Yates were Younger – it gain'd ground Every time it was play'd, but I grew tir'd, & gave it up – the part was laborious –[75]

In their different ways, the attitudes to Shakespeare exemplified in the careers of Garrick and Capell demonstrate exactly what is meant by the shorthand term 'before the divorce of stage and page'. Capell may have been a scholarly editor, but he was closely involved in the London theatre too. His wish to bring the experience of the reader at home closer to that of the spectator in the theatre is demonstrated by a remarkable feature of his editorial practice: his unique system of typographical marks. They appeared for the first time and without explanation in the first edition of the *Antony and Cleopatra* alteration (October 1758), and were elucidated at length in Capell's preface to *Prolusions*, dated the following July.[76] Briefly, Capell employed different symbols in his text (various crosses, inverted commas, dashes and so on) to indicate either a change of address within a speech, a thing pointed to, a thing delivered, an aside or the use of irony. Warburton, as well he might have been, was baffled by these unexplained 'mysterious marks' when he received a copy of *Antony and Cleopatra* from Garrick. Later commentators have been scornful of Capell's system. To introduce such a novel scheme without explaining it to the reader was undeniably yet another example of the lack of basic common sense demonstrated by Capell's system of cataloguing and, more seriously, by his insistence on decoupling the notes to his edition of Shakespeare from the plays themselves.[77] A contemporary commented: 'every trait of him, be it found where it may, betrays a fondness for singularity, which prevailed in him over everything'.[78] Whether Garrick was consulted about including Capell's system of marks in the published text of *Antony and Cleopatra* is unknown, but he would surely have given credit to his collaborator for wishing to bring the experience of encountering the play in a library closer to that enjoyed in a theatre, however inadequately it was realised in practice.

After *Antony and Cleopatra*, Garrick and Capell made no further alterations of Shakespeare together, but Garrick's 1762 version of *Cymbeline* demonstrates a similarly respectful, if not exactly minimalist, approach. Garrick cut approximately one-fifth of the play, including passages that assume belief in a supernatural or fairy world. His alteration foregrounds the three main roles (Posthumus, Imogen and Iachimo) at the expense of the other characters. Significantly, the material is shaped to reflect the audience's patriotic sentiments during the Seven Years War. Garrick plays down Britain's status as a tributary of Rome and omits Cymbeline's final pledge to submit to Caesar and to restore the payment of tribute. Thus, the play ends with a peace made between equals. Garrick himself played Posthumus for the first two seasons, and his version, lavishly staged and costumed, remained in the Drury Lane repertoire for nearly forty years.[79] Though the first edition was published anonymously, its advertisement strikes a characteristically Garrickian note:

> The admirers of Shakespear must not take it ill that there are some scenes, and consequently many fine passages, omitted in this edition of *Cymbeline*. It was impossible to retain more of the play and bring it within the compass of a night's entertainment. [. . .] As the play has met with so favourable a reception from the public, it is hoped that the alterations have not been made with great impropriety.[80]

Straddling both the literary and the theatrical worlds of the mid-century, the figure of Garrick personifies an attitude to Shakespeare studies that disappeared completely among professional editors of the nineteenth century and has yet fully to re-establish itself. As the advertisement to *Cymbeline* makes clear, Garrick saw public approbation as confirmation of artistic excellence. Even before the Stratford Jubilee of 1769, his own success had earned him the reputation, not only with theatregoers but also with the reading public, of being Shakespeare's spokesperson, whose endorsement of any project relating to Shakespeare it was essential to obtain. Thus, in 1766, Steevens, in an advertisement proposing a new edition and a glossary of difficult words, assured the public that his proposals had been seen by Mr Garrick and Mr Tonson, the respective guardians of Shakespeare's reputation on stage and page.[81] Two years later another gentleman amateur, the botanist Richard Warner, who later contributed eleven notes to the 1773 Johnson–Steevens *Shakespeare*, published a letter to Garrick, seeking his endorsement of a plan to publish a glossary to the plays.[82] His final paragraph, gushing in its flattery though it may be, shows how contemporaries regarded Garrick as a living link between library and theatre. Warner seeks Garrick's sanction for his project on the grounds of '[t]he intimate acquaintance you have had with his [Shakespeare's] writings, the very *minutiae* of which you have made your study; the obligations his admirers with the warmest sense of gratitude profess to owe to you for your repeated revivals on the Stage of most of his Plays; [and] the allow'd connexion of your name with that of our immortal Bard, as the Guardian of his Fame'.

Garrick's knowledge of what later editors would come to call 'the canon' was not quite as extensive as Warner supposed; it is not wholly accurate to say that he revived 'most' of the plays. Nor was the view that Garrick had become Shakespeare's representative on earth ever universally held; Johnson, for one, knew better, and Walpole consistently belittled any such pretensions on Garrick's part. Nevertheless by 1767, for the majority of the public the names of Shakespeare and Garrick had become virtually interchangeable. The following year the Corporation of Stratford-upon-Avon, conscious that Garrick had 'done so much Honour to Shakespear'[83] and anxious to adorn their new Town Hall, suggested that he might like to present them with 'some statue, bust or picture' of their local hero, together with a picture of himself, 'that the memory of both may be perpetuated together'.[84] Such a flattering invitation was of course irresistible.

At the mid-century, editors of Shakespeare were still far from accomplishing what Kastan calls 'the age's sustained editorial project of establishing Shakespeare's genuine text'.[85] Alterers still felt free to restructure the plays (and their colleagues' alterations) for performance, and to insert new material, albeit with less abandon than their predecessors of the Restoration had displayed. But attitudes were beginning to change and alteration was increasingly becoming a matter of abbreviation. As Marsden has shown, by the end of the eighteenth century, critical opinion was coming to regard Shakespeare's language as his greatest claim to fame; thus re-writing his words became unacceptable.[86] This chapter has shown

Garrick in mid-career making alterations that used a broad range of approaches: at one extreme the wholesale 're-bottling' of *The Winter's Tale*, at the other the respectful reducing of *Antony and Cleopatra*, *The Tempest* and *Cymbeline*. Though the last became the dominant mode of the last part of his career, his 1772 alteration of *Hamlet* (to be discussed in a later chapter) demonstrates that Garrick never ceased to believe himself entitled to make any changes he deemed necessary in order to render a play by Shakespeare acceptable to what he understood to be the taste of the Drury Lane audience.

CHAPTER 5

(Entr'acte): Celebrating Shakespeare on page and stage in 1769

Previous chapters have demonstrated the effect of competition between Covent Garden and Drury Lane upon Garrick's practice as alterer of Shakespeare's plays. That rivalry was nowhere more evident than in the contest that followed the Jubilee at Stratford in 1769, with possession of Shakespeare himself as the ground of battle. Before Garrick's handling of *King Lear* and *Hamlet* are examined below, this chapter, by way of divertissement, looks briefly at the Ode that Garrick performed and delivered at the Jubilee at Stratford,[1] and at his later dramatisation of the celebrations, *The Jubilee*, staged at Drury Lane for the first time on 14 October 1769.[2] Though the first was conceived as a tribute of high seriousness, and the second as a jolly entertainment, they represent equally valid aspects of the emergence in English culture of the myth of Shakespeare as national Bard. Together they demonstrate what mainstream opinion valued most about Shakespeare in the third quarter of the eighteenth century. When considered along with the multiple spin-offs of the Jubilee, they show the increasing potential of Shakespeare-related products to make money in the cultural market place. They also indicate something of the esteem in which Garrick was held; an esteem that made him confident that in altering Shakespeare's plays he was appropriately serving the Bard.

The Jubilee celebrations at Stratford were masterminded by Garrick and took place on 6–8 September 1769; they gave rise to huge public interest. They were widely reported in the press, and several contemporaries have left accounts, some admiring, others satirical.[3] Garrick's earliest biographer, Thomas Davies, is wholly positive in tone. The 'high festival', he says, was graced by 'many persons of the highest quality and rank', and marred only by the ridicule of George Steevens and the 'strange stupidity' of the 'more ignorant' inhabitants of Stratford.[4] The points of view of the many later writers on the Jubilee are as diverse as those of Garrick's contemporaries. Several histories of the event were published in 1964 to coincide with the 400th anniversary of Shakespeare's birth; of these, Johanne M. Stochholm's *Garrick's Folly* can be recommended as both full and sympathetic. More recently, Holland has provided a brief but helpful summary,[5] while McIntyre's chapter, 'Rain Stops Play', makes entertaining reading.[6] Other modern critics have sought to draw out the cultural implications of the Jubilee. Bate, for example, sees it as 'a fiasco in itself', which nevertheless 'set the seal on a number of developments', including the recognition of Shakespeare as '*the* National Poet and for many people not merely a poet but a god', of Stratford as a place of pilgrimage and of Garrick as 'Shakespeare's self-proclaimed representative on earth'.[7] Susan Green is scathing: 'Most scholars agree that English Bardolatry was affirmed when Garrick held his grandiose but hilariously tawdry deification of the Bard at his jubilee.'[8] Péter Dávidházi, on the other hand, is interested in the paradoxes inherent in the quasi-religious context of the event, given Garrick's Huguenot ancestry.[9] Gillian Russell highlights the importance of the Jubilee for Georgian cultural politics in general,[10] while Maria Cocco points to the Jubilee as a rare example of an occasion when 'the Shakespeare myth [. . .] absorbed and exploited' elements from both popular and high culture.[11]

The Ode, that ultimate *pièce d'occasion*, was performed in a temporary rotunda beside the rain-swollen Avon to a crowded and fashionable, if damp, audience at noon on 7 September 1769. Around Garrick were massed the choir and orchestra from Drury Lane, some 100 persons in all, conducted by the composer, Dr Arne. Dominating the platform was the statue of Shakespeare that Garrick was presenting to the town, and before it stood Garrick himself, ready to pay homage to his idol. The effects of his performance on the audience were electrifying, as many contemporary accounts record; all stress the emotional impact upon those present. To begin with, listeners were startled to hear the recitative (which Garrick in 1760 had called 'the most tedious part of the musical entertainment') *spoken*, against a stringed accompaniment. The speaker was the supreme actor of the age, using all his rhetorical and dramatic skills to persuade his auditors to share in the emotions that he himself was demonstrating, as he implored their 'sympathetic hearts' (line 5) to prepare to adore '"The god of our idolatry!"' (line 14).

On the page, the Ode is seen to conform to the Pindaric model, with varied, irregular patterns of metre and line-length. There are eight

Figure 5 Stratford-on-Avon, 7 September 1769; Garrick and the Drury Lane choir and orchestra perform the Ode, in front of the statue of Shakespeare that Garrick was presenting to the town. Etching, after unknown artist. National Portrait Gallery, London.

passages of recitative, interspersed with seven airs for the choir that reinforce ideas already stated. Two full choruses, one early in the work, the other forming the grand finale, express the overall themes of the Ode; both repeat words first heard in recitative. The final chorus will suffice to give a flavour of their language:

> We will, – his brows with laurel bind,
> Who charms to virtue human kind:
> Raise the pile, the statue raise,
> Sing immortal *Shakespeare*'s praise!
> The song will cease, the stone decay,
> But his Name,
> And undiminish'd fame,
> Shall never, never pass away. (lines 293–300)

With their well-worn phrases and familiar imagery, the choruses are workaday lyrics, not great poetry. The language of the airs and recitatives is similarly cliché-ridden, and often sentimental. Dreams are 'golden' (line 90), the muse is 'heav'n-born' (line 204), Avon's banks are 'hallow'd ground' (line 280). The following, with its echoes of Milton, is a typical stanza:

> *Sweetest bard that* ever *sung,*
> Nature*'s glory,* Fancy*'s Child*;
> *Never sure did witching tongue*
> *Warble forth such wood-notes wild*! (lines 44–47)

Originality, however, was not Garrick's objective. The second half of the book consists of 'testimonies to the genius and merits of Shakespeare', the authors of which include, as well as poets such as Ben Jonson, Milton, Dryden and Pope, Voltaire, Walpole and all the eighteenth-century editors of Shakespeare. When the testimonies are read in conjunction with the Ode, it seems clear that Garrick's aim was to provide a distillation of what contemporary mainstream literary opinion thought were the reasons for honouring Shakespeare. Thus, besides a couple of conventional references to his 'tuneful numbers' (line 209), little or nothing is said in the Ode of Shakespeare's language, and the appended tributes – apart from one fleeting mention by Theobald of his diction and imagery – are similarly silent. Rather, Shakespeare is celebrated for his 'wonder-teeming mind' and ability to raise 'other worlds, and beings' (lines 66–67). He is Nature's heir, admired for his control of the 'subject passions' (line 81). Shakespeare even has the god-like power to force the 'guilty, lawless tribe' (line 102), like Claudius, to confess concealed sins: 'Out bursts the penitential tear! / The look appall'd, the crime reveals' (lines 108–109). Shakespeare ('first of poets, best of men', line 288), is a moral force for good, whose pen '[t]o virtue fir'd / The charm'd, astonish'd, sons of men' (lines 269–270). The peroration goes so far as to address him as a secular saint whom the faithful may invoke: 'Look down blest SPIRIT, from above' (line 265).

The Ode associates Shakespeare with the nation's increasingly self-confident and patriotic mood: 'Britannia's riches and her force, / Shall more harmonious flow in song' (lines 212–213). It also reflects the growing admiration for Shakespeare's ability to create characters so striking that they appear to acquire a life of their own – a view that would come to dominate critical thinking in the following century. Garrick names only one, Falstaff, who seems to have enjoyed a special status in the eighteenth century, probably inspired by Quin's hugely popular performances in the role.[12] Critics of the period frequently singled out Falstaff for praise.[13] Such was the enthusiasm of Johnson, for example, that in his 1765 edition of the *Plays* he quite uncharacteristically shifted out of the third person into direct address in his commentary upon the second part of *Henry IV*: 'But Falstaff unimitated, unimitable Falstaff, how shall I describe thee?' What Johnson valued most in the character was his 'perpetual gaiety', his 'unfailing power of exciting laughter', and Garrick's Ode likewise celebrates him as 'A comic world in ONE' (line 184), born from Shakespeare's mind after a somewhat bizarre conception and parturition. Surrounded by 'a num'rous frolick band' (line 139), which includes Thalia, the muse of comedy, and the nymph Euphrosyne and her sisters,

> [w]ith kindling cheeks, and sparkling eyes
> [. . .] the Bard in transport dies (lines 159–160)

In this state of orgasm, his imagination is impregnated by Fancy, Wit and Humour, who 'spread / Their wings, and hover round his head' (lines 164–165) until

> . . . out a mountain came,
> A mountain of delight!
> LAUGHTER roar'd out to see the sight,
> And FALSTAFF was his name! (lines 170–173)

Garrick's depiction of Falstaff is wholly uncontextualised: 'With sword and shield he, puffing, strides: / The joyous revel-rout [of classical deities and personified abstractions] / Receive him with a shout' (lines 174–176). Like an unanchored barrage balloon, he floats free, the sunny essence of comedy, wholly unshadowed by the grimmer and sadder aspects of the plays in which he originated.

The Jubilee is often mocked because of the absence from the celebrations of any works by Shakespeare himself.[14] Of course, Stratford-upon-Avon had no theatre in 1769, which ruled out the possibility of performing any of the plays to a fashionable audience in the elaborate style then current. The next best thing, a grand procession through the town of actors representing Shakespeare's characters, was planned, but had to be abandoned because of heavy rain. But in fact the Ode itself, while obviously owing much to other poets, is permeated by Shakespearean echoes and quotations. Not all have been accurately remembered, and only sometimes are they marked off by inverted commas. For reasons of space, only a few illustrations can be given here: '"The god of our idolatry!"'(line 14, altered from *Romeo and Juliet* II.i.156); 'He checks, inflames, or turns their [the passions'] mad career; / With that superior skill, / Which winds the fiery steed at will' (lines 83–85, derived from *1 Henry IV* IV.i.110)[15]; 'The marble-hearted monster feels' (line 110, suggested by 'Ingratitude, thou marble-hearted fiend' in *King Lear* I.iv.237); and finally, '"*We ne'er shall look upon his like again!*"' (line 288, altered from 'I shall not look upon his like again', *Hamlet* I.ii.187). The last example was also printed on the tickets to the Jubilee. Each re-reading seems to yield up more examples, by no means all derived from plays in which Garrick acted. Clearly, the Ode is the production of an author who is both soaked in Shakespeare, and ready to alter him to suit the occasion.

Following the Jubilee, the public interest in it was so great that the Ode very quickly appeared in print, first in the monthly magazines, and soon after in book form.[16] It was immediately subjected to extensive critical analysis, both friendly and hostile. In the advertisement to the published text, Garrick was modest: 'Could some gentleman of approved ability have been prevailed upon to do justice to the subject of the following Ode, the present apology would have been unnecessary.' Although he described himself as 'the person perhaps the least qualified to succeed in the attempt', it is clear that in fact he took some pride in the Ode. In a private performance, given for the king and queen at their request, he 'met with much approbation' and later boasted 'I was 3 hours & a quarter with them'.[17] He despatched copies abroad to his French journalist friend, Suard ('I have Sent You my last Child, begot and brought forth in the heigth *[sic]* of Zeal'), and to Voltaire ('my small poetical tribute to the first Genius in the World').[18] Most telling is his long, detailed and highly defensive response to Macklin, who had evidently sent him a sheaf of queries on the language of the Ode, with proposals for improvement.[19]

And yet, in his heart, he knew that the Ode had no great poetic merit. He endorsed his copy of that correspondence: 'Critique of my Ode by Macklin – Ans. by me – I might have spent my time better than supporting a foolish business against a very foolish Man.' But there was comfort in the good sense of the anonymous review of the Ode that appeared in September 1769 in *The Gentleman's Magazine*: 'To examine such a piece as this by the severe rules of literary criticism, would be at once injurious and absurd: it was written for a particular purpose, and that purpose it has perfectly answered.' This comment could well be extended to apply also to Garrick's alterations of his idol's plays.

A foolish business Garrick may have thought the Jubilee when in low spirits. Ultimately, however, it brought substantial profit to him and others, first through the desire of socially mixed London audiences to participate in events at Stratford that had been restricted to a few hundreds of the elite, second through sales of spin-off publications, and third through staged imitations – some respectful, others parodic. Events in the months following the Stratford junketings admirably demonstrate the spirit of competition that drove London's publishing houses as well as its theatres. In both milieux, art and commerce were inseparably entwined, and success went to the swift.

The speed with which managers, actors and publishers exploited Jubilee-mania before it evaporated is astonishing. Within a fortnight the actor Weston was entertaining the Haymarket audience with a new occasional prologue, 'Scrub's Trip to the Jubilee', in which he impersonated a Stratford rustic not over-impressed by the goings-on in his town. This prologue rapidly appeared in book form, fronting a comedy with the catchpenny title of *The Stratford Jubilee*, which the anonymous author (thought to be Francis Gentleman) claimed in the dedication had been '[c]onceiv'd and born within eight days' (line 10).[20] The play brings together at Stratford a group of fashionable visitors, their hangers-on and various tradespeople. Its only point is to show that none of these people has any interest in Shakespeare; probably it was never performed. Pamphlets, both pro- and anti-Garrick and his Ode, appeared within the month.[21] *The Critical Review* of September 1769 reviewed not only the recently published Ode itself, but also *Shakespeare's Garland* (a collection of the songs performed as light entertainment during the celebrations at Stratford),[22] *Shakespeare's Jubilee, a Masque*, by Carey ('very tolerable'), *The Stratford Jubilee* mentioned above ('very dull') and *Garrick's Vagary*, an anonymous collection of six dramatic scenes mocking everything to do with the event.

As Drury Lane's 1769–1770 season opened, Garrick, well aware of the continuing interest of London theatregoers in the Jubilee, shrewdly mounted several performances of the Ode 'in the Manner it was performed at Stratford', in place of an afterpiece. After the first of these, on 30 September 1769, the prompter (Hopkins) noted in his diary: 'Mr G. speaking in this performance is equal to anything he ever did and met with as much applause as his heart could desire.'[23] Garrick himself, in a letter to William Hunt, called his success 'astonishing', but he was not to enjoy it unchallenged for long. Within a month of the Jubilee, his friend George Colman, manager of Covent Garden, had altered a routine matrimonial comedy of his own to set it in Stratford. Its central theme is the dilemma facing a young lady, each of whose parents favours a different suitor for her hand. She solves the problem as Anne Page does: by marrying a third. As *Man and Wife*, a three-act main piece,[24] the comedy now included plenty of topical Jubilee references and snatches of the songs performed during the celebrations. The playbills promised, as the finale, 'a Representation of the AMPHITHEATRE at Stratford upon Avon with a *Masquerade*'. Most challenging of all, Colman staged between Acts II and III 'the Pageant': his own version of the procession of Shakespearean characters through Stratford, which had been cancelled because of heavy rain. Colman's script even included some of the airs from Garrick's Ode. In the prelude to the play the character who represents Colman himself, Dapperwit, while defending his right to raise '[a]n innocent laugh', is careful to distance himself from any intention of mocking Garrick's serious intention: 'As to the Jubilee itself, or the design and conduct of it, I cannot consider them as objects of satire.' He jokes, however, that the Ode 'had one capital fault, [. . .] I understood every word of it'.

Despite Colman's conciliatory words, Garrick could on no account allow Covent Garden to appropriate the Jubilee. As well as the financial health of Drury Lane, his own standing as Shakespeare's personal representative was at stake. Thus, a new skirmish in the endless struggle between the theatres began. Having had advance notice of Colman's astonishing plan, Garrick rushed to devise a response that would outdo his rival's. '[W]e are preparing to Jubilee it upon y[e] Stage – M[r] Colman Enters y[e] lists wth Us, much to my Surprize –', he wrote on 2 October 1769, five days before *Man and Wife* opened at Covent Garden.[25]

Garrick's counter-attraction was a two-act afterpiece, rich in music, spectacle and the sort of humour (naive locals, comic Irishman, exploited visitors) calculated to appeal to a London audience. The combined effect was to make the audience feel that they were sharing in the excitement and fun at Stratford without the expense and inconvenience of the real thing. Garrick's *The Jubilee* was one of the greatest successes of his career. It opened on 14 October 1769, exactly one week after *Man and Wife*. Colman's main piece had run for six nights, during which takings, excellent at first, had dropped sharply. Once Garrick's afterpiece was in the Drury Lane repertoire (it was given every night for the following three weeks and very frequently thereafter), Covent Garden's offering stood little chance. After five more performances, the last on 21 November 1769, Colman reduced *Man and Wife* to an afterpiece, in which form it was occasionally revived.

Garrick later claimed that he had taken only 'a day & a half' to write 'ye petite piece'.[26] Despite this celerity, one marvels that he was able to produce, rehearse, obtain the censor's approval for and stage such an elaborate spectacle in little more than a fortnight. Two manuscripts of *The Jubilee* exist. A shorter, incomplete version, in Garrick's hand, is held in the Boston Public Library; an expanded version, in another hand, but bearing Garrick's own notes and corrections, is in the Huntington Library at San Marino, where the Larpent Collection of plays is housed. Only the fuller, Huntington, version, which belongs to the Kemble-Devonshire Collection, has been published.[27] Its manuscript is not one of the Larpent plays, and therefore does not necessarily represent the text that would have been submitted to the examiner of plays in October 1769 prior to production. Examination of the shorter Boston manuscript suggests that that version was probably the basis for the text submitted to the censor. The Boston manuscript also throws light on working methods of the eighteenth-century theatre that seem to have changed little since Shakespeare's own day.

Though Langhans surmises that the 'wildly scrawled' Boston copy of *The Jubilee* 'may be an early draft',[28] it is considerably more than that, and actually represents an expanded version of what in the film world now would be called a treatment or a scenario. To use another anachronism, those dozen pages could be regarded as Garrick's 'foul papers' for *The Jubilee*. His original handwritten sheets have been incorporated into a bundle that includes cue scripts for several of the characters in the hands of various copyists. These 'sides', however, are based on the fuller Huntington text. Certainly, the Boston manuscript was written in haste; there are blots and many scratchings-out. But the structure of the play, in terms of scenes and acts, is already in place. Garrick has decided on the settings and characters, and most of the dialogue is at least sketched in. He knows when actors, including singers, will enter and leave the stage, and from which side, PS or OP. He knows what sound effects ('guns firing', 'drums beating', 'rain heard') will be needed, and when. Very importantly, he has chosen which songs will be included and at exactly which points in the action they will be sung. He does not write out the lyrics. Some have already appeared in print in *Shakespeare's Garland* and, in any case, the company performed them in Stratford-upon-Avon. So, he simply writes, for example:

> Irish[man] . . . But pray what is all this same Jubilee about –
> Mus[ician]. O, sir, I'll tell you – / *Song*
> *This is, Sir, a Jubilee*, etc. (p. 5)

Similarly, he does not need to include details of the grand procession of Shakespeare's characters ('The Pageant'), since the plan for this had already been drawn up. Only one scene in the Boston manuscript was later to be significantly expanded: the comic encounters of inn staff and gentlefolk in the yard of the White Lion Inn (Part 1, Scene 3). It is not difficult to guess the reason: the new material very closely resembles the parallel and particularly lively scene that opens *Man and Wife*. (When Garrick, at Hampton in September 1769, received word of Colman's intention and started to write his own *Jubilee*, he had not yet, of course, read or seen his rival's effort.) The spectacular all-singing-and-dancing finale, featuring the entire company, is also missing from the Boston copy. This again was probably based on material developed for performance in the Stratford rotunda. The fuller, Huntington, version ends:

> *Every character, tragic and comic, join[s] in the Chorus and go[es] back, during which the guns fire, bells ring, etc. etc.*
> *And the audience applaud[s].*
> *Bravo Jubilee!*
> *Shakespeare forever!* (II.iii.47–51)

Thus, from the moment when he picked up his pen, Garrick was visualising exactly what the Drury Lane audience would see and hear. His rapidly written sheets were probably rushed up from his riverside villa at Hampton to the theatre. They were sufficient, when supplemented by material already in his hands, to enable Hopkins, the prompter, to set copyists to work on scripts for actors and singers, and on a fair copy for the examiner of plays. They also gave Hopkins the information he needed to brief the orchestra and stage crew, organise scenery and effects, and schedule rehearsals. If in the course of rehearsals Garrick should wish – as in the case of *The Jubilee* he clearly did – to expand some of the dialogue, it was no great matter, since the actors worked from easily re-copied cue scripts, not full texts. Thus, the key to the swift staging of *The Jubilee* was the existence at Drury Lane of a team of trusted and experienced professionals, who worked closely with Garrick to develop and realise the production. Tiffany Stern, in *Making Shakespeare: From Stage to Page*, describes a strikingly similar process for bringing to the stage the plays of the sharer-actor-author with whom Garrick felt such affinity.[29]

Just as the Ode provides a summary of mainstream critical opinion on Shakespeare, so the on-stage processions at Drury Lane and Covent Garden give clues to the popularity of individual plays in 1769. *All's Well that Ends Well*, *The Comedy of Errors*, *King Richard II*, *King Henry VI*, *Love's Labours Lost*, *Measure for Measure*, *Titus Andronicus*, *Timon of Athens* and *Troilus and Cressida* were represented neither in *Man and Wife* nor in *The Jubilee*. Managers tended to avoid plays thought to be obscure, indelicate or morally problematical, especially if the principal characters lacked appeal for star performers, and none of these had been performed at either theatre during the previous two seasons. Oddly, no one from *The Taming of the Shrew* was featured in either procession, though Garrick's alteration, *Catharine and Petruchio*, was often staged. However, there is a relevant note on the Huntington manuscript: 'Cath^{e} & Petruchio, with ye same dismal Horse & all P's miserable Geer, as describ'd by Grumio w^{d} have had a fine Effect. I w^{d} introduce C & P in this Manner.' Possibly such a change was made when *The Jubilee* was revived at Drury Lane in 1775 in a revised version, which added new elements to the procession. Garrick's procession featured three plays not included by Colman: *Much Ado about Nothing* (regarded as the sole property of Drury Lane as long as Garrick played Benedick), *The Two Gentlemen of Verona* (rarely staged) and *King Henry V*. The omission of the last from Colman's pageant is puzzling because at this period *King Henry V* was a reliable earner for Covent Garden, but never performed by the rival company. Conversely, Colman, but not Garrick, brought on characters from *King John* (not in the Drury Lane repertoire at that time), *The Winter's Tale* (Florizel, Perdita and Autolicus) and, remarkably, the very rarely seen *Coriolanus* (represented simply by 'Roman Ladies – dishevelled').

Colman organised his procession on themes, each accompanied by appropriate music. One disadvantage of this method was that characters from a single play might need to be divided between two sections. Thus, Hecate and the witches 'two by two', entered to 'Macbeth's musick' with the 'two Baby Spirits' in the supernatural section, following characters from *The Tempest*. However, Macbeth himself ('with Daggers bloody'), Banquo's Ghost and Lady Macbeth ('with the Candle') followed the Tragic Muse. When confronted also by the Muses and the Three Graces, not to mention the 'Cupids, Satyrs, Bacchanals, &c.' who attended on the car containing the bust of Shakespeare that ended the Covent Garden procession, many members of the audience might have had considerable difficulty in identifying the plays represented.

Garrick made no such error. He used the processional entrance of the statue of Shakespeare, led by Apollo and 'supported by the Passions and surrounded by the Seven Muses with their trophies', to separate his two groups of comedies and tragedies. Like Colman, he specified that characters should carry the props that would help audiences to recognise them: Fluellen had his leek and Peter his fan, while Ophelia was 'mad, with straw, *etc*'. And each play was identified, not only by its title carried on a banner, but by the enaction of what in a note on the Huntington manuscript Garrick called 'some capital part of it in Action'. The whole procession entered 'from the top of the stage' and employed the full technical and human resources of Drury Lane. The impact of the spectacle must have been terrific. *The Tempest* featured not only drunken sailors, Ariel, Prospero and Miranda, but also a 'ship in distress sailing down the stage'. Falstaff, Mrs Ford and Mrs Page were on horseback, and after Macbeth and Lady Macbeth came a burning caldron drawn by four demons, 'Hecate and 3 Witches following'. Oberon and Titania rode in a chariot drawn by butterflies. The Comic and the Tragic Muse each had her own chariot and was appropriately attended: Venus and Cupid, satyrs and loves for the former; furies, with Fame, Grief, Pity, Despair and Madness for the latter. Including dancers and singers, the script specifies entrances for at least 320 individuals, three horses and one dog (Crab). Many quick changes would have been involved, with wardrobe resources stretched to the limit. With Dibdin's music, and the added impact of bells, drums, fifes, trumpets and cannons, the effect must have been as overwhelming upon ears as upon eyes. To ensure the triumph of *The Jubilee*, Garrick had one further ace to play: all his leading actors took part in the procession. He himself walked on as Benedick; by the time he retired in 1776 he had done so no fewer than 153 times.[30] He had established the eighteenth century's record run for any London production and at the same time he had wrested back Drury Lane's status as the premier shrine of Shakespeare.

Covent Garden's final salvo in the battle of Stratford-upon-Avon took the form of comic parody. On 27 January 1770 it staged a new pantomime entitled *Harlequin's Jubilee*, which satirised Garrick's *Jubilee*. That both afterpieces, the Drury Lane *Jubilee* and the Covent Garden pantomime, were often performed on the same night suggests that they were not seen by either manager as being in direct competition. Woodward's script for *Harlequin's Jubilee* has not survived, but the words of the songs were printed.[31] The lyrics stress that the rivalry between the theatres was friendly, and for the benefit of the public. Indeed, the songs would mean little to anyone who was not a frequent attender at both houses. For example, Garrick's prologue to *The Jubilee* had characterised the two theatres as inns, each called the Magpie, engaged in a race to bring 'Jubilee Punch' before the public. Garrick had cheerfully acknowledged that Colman had stolen a march on him – 'Young Mag started first, with old Mag hopping after' (line 14) – and that it was the nature of these magpies to 'crib from each other' (line 22). Woodward's riposte is a song, 'The Magpies', which closely parodies Garrick's ballad 'Ye Warwickshire lads and ye lasses', with its famous refrain 'For the lad of all lads was a Warwickshire lad'.[32] Woodward's 'mag of all mags is the *Pantomime Mag*!' (p. 5). He mocks Garrick ('And he that cribs most is the first that cries *Thief*', p. 6), but concedes that competition is the business of both houses:

> To force a good trade is the plan –
> Each magpie will do all he can;
> *Pro Publico bono* will show his best skill,
> For the will of all wills is the *Public's good will*[.] (p. 7)

Certainly there was serious rivalry between the two playhouses, but it was the sort of rivalry experienced in families: that of intimates, speaking a common language and inhabiting a small shared world, to the rules and conventions of which all members subscribe. The battle of the Jubilee ended when Covent Garden ceded the artistic high ground to its rival, thus further strengthening Drury Lane's claim to be the playhouse 'sacred to Shakespeare'.[33]

CHAPTER 6

'Parental and filial capacities' – King Lear *and* Hamlet

Two opposing views of Garrick in relation to Shakespeare's plays were described in the introductory chapter. At one extreme he has been seen as the great restorer of Shakespeare to the stage; at the other, as the actor-manager who for motives of vanity or greed refused to restore when he had the power to do so. That the reality was much more complex is well demonstrated in the ebbs and flows, the advances and retreats, of his engagement, across his long career, with the two supreme tragic roles, King Lear and Hamlet. The term 'roles' rather than 'plays' is used, since the parts themselves would have been Garrick's starting points. His handling of both plays reveals the tensions inherent in the function of actor-alterer, especially one who claims to idolise the originator.

When Garrick's early performances as Lear gained him, almost immediately, huge critical acclaim, the script he was playing was Tate's alteration of 1681.[1] With its love relationship between Edgar and Cordelia, its portrayal of Edmund as 'a Hobbesian villain',[2] its elimination of the Fool and its strict adherence to the morality of poetic justice ending in a reassuring restoration of the *status quo*, this text was all that most contemporary audience members knew of the play. That Garrick himself had read Shakespeare's *King Lear* by 1745 is certain, since in that year he wrote to the artist Francis Hayman suggesting, to illustrate the storm scene, a grouping of characters that included the Fool.[3] Garrick's position as manager from 1747 gave him the authority to restore Shakespeare's tragedy to the stage, but he seems never to have been able to bring himself to do so fully. Over the years he replaced more and more of Tate's lines with Shakespeare's. Nevertheless, his final appearance as Lear in June 1776 was in a version that continued to omit the Fool, and ended with the lovers about to reign as king and queen, while Lear, Gloster and Kent entered upon a calm and reflective retirement together.[4] Yet the audience went home convinced that the play that had moved them to tears had been Shakespeare's – as indeed, in some sense, it had.

Beginning on 11 March 1742, at the surprisingly young age of 25, Garrick played Lear eighty-five times in his career. He last did so on 8 June 1776, two nights before his retirement; it was his final appearance in a play by Shakespeare. Space constraints preclude even a summary of contemporary accounts of his performance and of the strong emotions it generated in audiences over the years.[5] The huge early success Garrick achieved as Lear gave him a stake in Tate's version, making him reluctant to alter a proven audience-pleaser when he took on the responsibilities of management. On the other hand, his sensitivity to Shakespeare's language, and his self-promoted reputation as Shakespeare's idolater, pushed him in the direction of restoration. This internal conflict he never fully resolved.[6]

How early in his career Garrick began the task of restoration, and how extensive a restorer of *King Lear* he actually was, are matters of debate among scholars, though all agree upon three important points of reference. The first is a note about the performance on 28 October 1756 made by Cross, the Drury Lane prompter: 'With Restorations from Shakespear'.[7] The second is the publication by Bell in 1773 of a partially restored text based on a Drury Lane prompt-book.[8] The third is a version incorporating further restorations printed for Bathurst nine years after Garrick's death, which claimed to be Garrick's own alteration and to derive from Drury Lane.[9]

Scholars also agree that Garrick's starting point was Tate's *History of King Lear*. Tate's famous description of the play as 'a Heap of Jewels, unstrung and unpolisht' is often quoted disparagingly. Yet Tate did at least recognise jewels when he found them. Much of his re-writing, particularly in the fifth act, was needed because of the new sub-plots he had devised, and to accommodate the rewarding of the virtuous characters in his new ending. Some re-arrangements were needed because of the elimination of the Fool. And once – but only once – Tate invented an outburst for Lear, in response to Regan's 'What need one?', that out-Herods Herod:

> Blood, Fire! hear – Leaprosies and bluest Plagues!
> Room, room for Hell to belch her Horrors up
> And drench the *Circes* in a stream of Fire;
> Heark how th'Infernals eccho to my Rage
> Their Whips and Snakes – (Tate II.ii.314–318)

But it is important to recognise that, although Tate re-arranged and slightly re-phrased some of Lear's lines prior to Act V and made a number of cuts that bear upon whatever moral message the play may be thought to have (e.g., 'None does offend, none' at IV.v.164), he invented very few lines for the king except, of course, in the totally new prison scene (Tate V.vi) that now ended the play. (The same applies to Edgar's lines as Mad Tom.) Tate left relatively untouched Lear's great set pieces: his calling down of barrenness upon Goneril (Tate I.ii.82–96), the storm scenes in Acts III and, in Act IV, his encounter with Gloucester in his madness. Thus, when Garrick began the long-drawn-out process of restoring Shakespeare's lines to the play at the expense of Tate's, he had surprisingly few major changes to make to his own part. For example, at the start of the third act, the Bell text of 1773 shows that by this date Garrick had restored all nine lines of Lear's difficult first speech ('Blow, winds, and crack your cheeks! rage, blow!' G.III.i.1–9), which Tate had shortened and simplified. But both versions then continued very similarly. Tate had:

> Rumble thy fill, fight Whirlwind, Rain and Fire:
> Not Fire, Wind, Rain or Thunder are my Daughters:
> I tax not you ye Elements with unkindness;
> I never gave you Kingdoms, call'd you Children,
> You owe me no Obedience . . . (Tate III.i.10–14)

Garrick needed to make very few changes in order to restore the original lines:

> Rumble thy belly full! Spit, fire; spout, rain!
> Nor rain, wind, thunder, fire are my daughters.
> I tax not you, you elements, with unkindness.
> I never gave you kingdoms, called you children;
> You owe me no subscription. (G.III.ii.14–18)

Apart from the pluralisation of 'kingdom', these lines are identical in wording (though not in punctuation) with the equivalent passage in the Oxford *Complete Works.*[10]

Another important piece of evidence is the alteration of *King Lear* made by Colman for performance at Covent Garden in the 1767–1768 season, which he published in 1768.[11] Colman stated in his introduction that he had 'endeavoured to purge the tragedy of Lear of the alloy of Tate, which has so long been suffered to debase it'. Up to a point, this is true. Much to Thomas Davies's disapproval, Colman eliminated the love affair between Edgar and Cordelia,[12] and thus reinstated the King of France. Cordelia's confidante, Arante, also disappeared. But he could not bring himself to restore the Fool who, he goes on to say, 'would not be endured on the modern stage'. As one begins to read Colman's alteration, it seems much closer to Shakespeare than Garrick's Drury Lane text of 1773 (the Bell edition). But later one notices unfamiliar lines inserted to expand Cordelia's part, which turn out to be lifted from Tate and, as the play progresses, Colman's text comes closer and closer to Bell's – and therefore to Tate's.

Colman believed that, had it not been for its happy ending, Tate's *King Lear* 'would probably have quitted the stage long ago', and furthermore, *pace* Addison,[13] he had the authority of Johnson to back up his decision to keep Lear and Cordelia alive. In his introduction Colman quotes Johnson's famous pronouncement, made in his notes to the play: 'In the present case the publick has decided. Cordelia, from the time of Tate, has always retired with victory and felicity.' Colman's ending (V.[iii], pp. 67–71) leaves out the betrothal of the lovers, and he invents a few lines for Albany in order to dispose satisfactorily of Cordelia:

> Thy captive daughter too, the wife of France,
> Unransom'd we enlarge, and shall, with speed,
> Give her safe convoy to her royal husband. (V.[iii], p. 70)

Otherwise, Colman's final scene is based on Tate, with just the occasional interpolation of a few words of Shakespeare. Like Garrick's 1773 text, Colman's alteration is sharply focused on Lear. Most of Tate's final speech for Edgar is retained, but the lines are re-assigned, in order to give the star actor the curtain speech. Further, Colman's introduction takes it for granted that his audience will primarily be interested in 'Lear and Cordelia, in their parental and filial capacities', rather than the politics of the play's conclusion. The omission of the first two lines of Edgar's speech ('Our drooping Country now erects her Head, / Peace spreads her balmy Wings, and Plenty Blooms'), coupled with the fact that no reference is made to how Lear will manage to govern his restored kingdom, are clear indications that by 1768, nearly a century after Tate, the emphasis had shifted from the political to the personal. Evidently, *King Lear* was now thought to be less about kingship than about kinship.

Colman's alteration for Covent Garden, though in no sense a full-scale restoration, was sufficiently Shakespearean to act as either a spur or a warning to Garrick – probably both. Colman made it with a complete Shakespeare text (possibly Johnson's 1765 edition), as well as Tate's version, in front of him.[14] But he also had firmly in his mind how *King Lear* was performed at Drury Lane. If, with Stone and other eminent scholars, one makes the assumption (and it *is* only an assumption) that the Bell edition of 1773 is the text that Garrick's company was playing in 1768, several structural similarities will be noticed. For instance, just as at Drury Lane, Colman ends his second act with a general exeunt on Lear's line 'O gods, I shall go mad !' (II.[iv], p. 33) – a sure-fire claptrap. Tate had followed Lear's exit with a single line for Cornwall (Tate II.ii.330), while in the original there is a scene of twenty lines between Regan, Goneril and the two dukes (II.ii.460–481). And Colman like Garrick, but unlike Tate, reduced the horror by having his Gloucester blinded offstage. Probably because of the absence of love interest, however, Colman's version was not very popular with audiences. It was given three times in 1767–1768 and five times the following season: a year when Drury Lane did not offer *King Lear* at all. It was not played at Covent Garden in 1769–1770, when Drury Lane's star performers, Garrick and Barry, were alternating the title role. Performances dwindled to two a year in the two successive seasons, and Colman's version was given for the last time in 1772–1773.

Critics are divided over the extent to which, if at all, Colman's alteration influenced Garrick. Stone, writing in 1948, never mentions it. He sees Garrick as steadily replacing Tate's lines with Shakespeare's from a very early stage in his managerial career, by a process of 'gradual infiltration'.[15] Thus, for Stone, the Bell text of 1773 essentially represented the 'Restorations from Shakespear' announced in 1756. As Pedicord has shown, Stone was followed in this belief by other twentieth-century scholars, including Odell, Hogan and Burnim.[16] Shattuck, too, believed that in 1756 Garrick 'effected a considerable restoration of the original'.[17] However, in 1971, Harris amassed substantial evidence to suggest that Garrick 'did not in 1756 [. . .] restore any sizable portion of Shakespeare's text'. On the contrary, he believed that 'it was George Colman who pressed Garrick to restore more of the original and, failing to persuade his friend, produced his version at Covent Garden in 1768'.[18] Harris thus cast Garrick as a very late and perhaps reluctant restorer. His surmise was dramatically confirmed in 1979 when a prompt-book came to light, made for Drury Lane on a copy of Tate's alteration printed in 1756. In it, 193 lines of Tate's had been cut, but the 'Restorations from Shakespear' amounted to no more than 10 lines.[19]

It is impossible even to be certain that this prompt-book represents what was performed at Drury Lane in 1756. Langhans thinks that the copy 'seems far too sloppy to have served in performance'. The annotations and cuts are made in several different hands, suggesting a process of gradual change over several years. For example, on p. 58, the lightly written warning 'ready to shout', in the margin of Edmund's soliloquy 'To both these Sisters have I sworn my Love' (Tate V.ii.1–10), clearly relates to the instruction 'shout' in the same hand on the opposite page. But at some stage the entire scene was marked for deletion by a prompter with a different, much bolder handwriting. The majority of cuts are in this second hand. If they were, in fact, made later, they show that in 1756 Gloster's blinding was still taking place on stage, and that Edmund was still lasciviously anticipating the rape of Cordelia in language later considered too strong for a polite audience:

> Where like the vig'rous *Jove* I will enjoy
> This *Semele* in a Storm, 'twill deaf her Cries
> Like Drums in Battle, lest her Groans shou'd pierce
> My pittying Ear, and make the amorous Fight less fierce. (Tate III.ii.122–125)

The final two-and-a-half lines are marked for deletion in the bold hand; they do not appear in the Bell edition of 1773 (although restored in the text published by Bathurst in 1786). The majority of the 'bold cuts' are references to the machinations of the Bastard and Lear's elder daughters. The most significant is the deletion of the entire grotto scene (Tate IV.i.) of amorous dalliance between Edmund and Regan. Other characters' lines are also trimmed and, though the play still begins with the Bastard's soliloquy 'Thou Nature art my Goddess' (Tate I.i.1–21), taken together the 'bold cuts' work to shape a version primarily concerned with the sufferings of Lear and Cordelia.

Of particular interest are modifications to the title role made in the 1756 prompt-book, for it is reasonable to assume that it was at Garrick's behest that, over time, the changes to Tate's text that it contains were made. Apart from a single minor cut in Act IV, all the changes that affect the part of Lear are confined to the second scene of Act II: Lear's confrontation with Regan and Goneril. Garrick apparently saw this scene as critical in achieving the right frame of mind in his audience and ensuring that their sympathies remained firmly with the king. After 'Ha! Ask her Forgiveness?' (Tate II.ii.227), a half-line is written in: 'what woo her thus?' This could be an indication that, though Garrick continued to play Tate's version of the next four lines, where no kneeling is implied:

> No, no, 'twas my mistake thou didst not mean so,
> Dear Daughter, I confess that I am old;
> Age is unnecessary, but thou art good,
> And wilt dispense with my Infirmity. (Tate II.ii.228–231)

he early recognised the shock effect of a father sarcastically kneeling to his daughter, and introduced the move well before he substituted the original lines for Tate's. (Colman in 1768 used more or less the original lines; the Drury Lane text published by Bell in 1773 fully restored them.) Certain additions have also been inserted into this scene in what is almost certainly Garrick's own hand. As Lear comes to realise that he can rely upon neither daughter to accommodate him with his hundred knights, the following is written in the margin of p. 27 after Regan's 'My Sister treats you fair' (Tate II.ii.294):

> Lear. O heavens I gave you all. Reg. And in good time you gave it. Thunder Lear. Made you my Guardians, my repositories; what must I come to you with five & twenty, Regan, said you so. Reg. Even so. (Altered from II.ii.423–429)[20]

The most important restoration to the scene is at the bottom of p. 28, again in Garrick's hand:

> If it be you that stir these daughters' hearts
> Against their father, fool me not so much
> To bear it tamely – touch me with noble anger.
> Oh! let not woman's weapons waterdrops
> Stain my man's cheeks. (*cf.* II.ii.448–452)

It is easy to see the appeal of these lines to an actor who specialised in swift transitions between conflicting emotions, and who excelled in moving audiences to tears. Garrick, like Murphy, recognised that '[i]n every Speech in *Lear*'s Mouth, there is such an artful Mixture of thwarting Passions, that the Heart-strings of an Audience are torn on every Side'.[21] The impact of Garrick's performance in this scene was impossible to describe, declared Gentleman in 1770; he nevertheless made the attempt:

> In the second act, where he parlies between Goneril and Regan, who alternately reject him, rage and tenderness, suppressed fury and affectionate condescension, are mingled happily till the conclusive speech, where his breaks of voice, and variation of features, surpass the finest conception that has not been impressed by him, and leave those who have seen him without words to describe.[22]

Garrick's cuts from Tate in the 1756 prompt-book also throw light on his shaping of Lear's character. He deleted Tate's manic outburst for Lear ('Blood, Fire! [. . .] Whips and Snakes'. Tate II.ii.314–318) and the sisters' sardonic responses: Regan: 'How lewd a thing is Passion!' (line 319), Goneril: 'So old and stomachfull' (line 320). Tate had cut Lear's striking of

Figure 6 Garrick in the second storm scene of his alteration of *King Lear*. Note the absence of the Fool. David Garrick, by Charles Spooner, published by Robert Sayer, after Benjamin Wilson. Mezzotint, published 1761. National Portrait Gallery, London.

Oswald – to show a king striking a servant was totally inappropriate – but had expanded to six lines Lear's brief comment ('This is a slave whose easy-borrowed pride / Dwells in the fickle grace of her a follows').[23] Garrick deleted the entire passage – it was a distraction from the main thrust of the scene, family relationships – but he retained Tate's introductory 'More Torture still?' (Tate II.ii.251). He removed the curse on Goneril that Tate had taken from Shakespeare ('strike her young Bones / Ye taking Ayrs with Lameness', Tate II.ii.237–238, *cf.* II.ii.336–337). Clearly, there could be no question of fully restoring this terrible speech, in which Lear calls upon 'the stored vengeances of heaven' to inflict lameness, blindness and sickness upon the daughter who had dared to abate him of half his train (II.ii.332–341). Neither did Garrick restore, either here or in the 1773 Bell edition, Lear's sickening likening of Goneril to a disease within himself, 'a boil, / A plague-sore or embossèd carbuncle / In my corrupted blood' (II.ii.395–398). Such egregious language was completely alien to his conception of Lear, as he set it out in a letter written late in his career:

> *Lear* is certainly a *Weak* man, it is part of his Character – violent, old & *weakly* fond of his Daughters – Here we agree, but I cannot possibly agree with You & Mr Ranby, that the Effect of his distress is diminish'd by his being an *Old Fool* – his Weakness proceeds from his Age (fourscore & upwards) & such an Old Man full of affection, Generosity, Passion, & what not meeting with what he thought an ungrateful return from his best belov'd Cordelia, & afterwards real ingratitude from his other Daughters, an audience must feel his distresses & Madness which is ye Consequence of them –[24]

The key to Garrick's approach to Lear lies in the words 'an audience must feel his distresses'. He continues:

> nay I think I might go farther, & venture to say that had not ye source of his unhappiness proceeded from good qualities carry'd to excess of folly, but from vices, I really think that ye bad part of him would be forgotten in ye space of an Act, & *his distresses at his Years* would become Objects of Pity to an Audience[.]

Essentially, it seems, Garrick shares, and expects his audience to share, Lear's view of himself as 'a man / More sinned against than sinning' (G.III.i.47–48). It was the pathetic elements of a basically good character that he wished to emphasise, and therefore he chose not to restore lines that detracted from this reading of the part.

What Stone hailed as Garrick's 'extended revision of the acting text' in 1756 is now seen to have been minimal. Indeed, of the ten lines restored from Shakespeare in the 1756 prompt-book, three had been cut again by the time that the Bell text was printed in 1773.[25] Despite his professed idolatry of Shakespeare and the pressures put upon him by others, Garrick seems to have been in no hurry to make further restorations. Harris cites a number of critics who, as early as 1747, were vocal in their scorn for Tate,[26] and later in his article he makes a strong case for Colman's having undertaking his own, much fuller, restoration only after he had given up trying to persuade Garrick to do so. But, seen from Garrick's point of view as leading actor and as manager, his reluctance to make major changes to a familiar and popular version is perfectly logical. Most of Lear's greatest moments were already in the script, and audiences continued to be delighted.

Whatever his hesitations may have been, the existence of the Bell edition confirms that Garrick did make, or agree to have made, not later than 1773 a new version for Drury Lane, significantly closer to Shakespeare. Pedicord and Harris both conclude that he did so during the 1770–1771 season, a year in which he did not play Lear at all.[27] The Bell *King Lear* is a hybrid of Tate and Shakespeare, a fact for which, in his introduction to it, Francis Gentleman specifically commends it. Whereas the original was both 'diffuse' and 'obscure',

> we think the following edition, as performed at the theatre in Drury Lane, by judiciously blending of TATE and SHAKESPEARE, is made more nervous [i.e., vigorous, forceful] than that by the Laureat and much more agreeable than Mr. COLMAN's late alteration.

It was Garrick's retention from Tate of the Edgar/Cordelia love story, which Colman had rejected, that made his revision 'much more agreeable' in the eyes of Gentleman. Thomas Davies says that Garrick 'long considered the advantages and disadvantages which might flow from the exclusion or the retaining the scenes of Tate in question; and, after well-weighed reflection, he thought proper to preserve the greatest part of them.'[28] Also retained from Tate was the final prison scene with its morally reassuring ending (G.V.iv), in which the wicked are punished and the good rewarded. Lear's curtain speech (G.V.iv.155–162), as in Colman's version, pictures a peaceful retirement for Lear, Kent and Gloster, while Edgar and Cordelia reign in prosperity. Garrick was not able to bring himself to reinstate the Fool, because, according to Davies, 'he feared, with Mr. Colman, that the feelings of Lear would derive no advantage from the buffooneries of the parti-coloured jester'. Nevertheless, the whole play has clearly been reviewed in the light of a modern edition. The original opening scene is put back, many of Tate's lines removed, and 255 lines of Shakespeare restored.[29]

The existence of yet another version of *King Lear* credited to Garrick, the Bathurst text of 1786, which cut eighteen more lines of Tate's and added another fifty of Shakespeare's, strengthened Pedicord and Bergmann's view that, after the publication of the Bell edition of 1773, Garrick continued to make restorations. Stone, who of course believed that the Bell text represented what was performed at Drury Lane in 1756, also thought that the Bathurst version was evidence of 'further restorations' made by Garrick.[30] Two questions need to be answered about the Bathurst version. First, does it represent the script that Garrick played for his final performance as Lear? Second, was it Garrick himself who made these further alterations?

It can be confidently stated that, when he made his final appearance as King Lear in 1776, Garrick played the text published by Bell in 1773. In the Harvard Theatre Collection is what Pedicord and Bergmann call 'an incomplete promptbook made on the 1773 Bell edition, [which] adds nothing to our knowledge of Garrick's continuing revisions of the play'.[31] Burnim, seeking a prompt-book from which to derive a scene-by-scene account of how Garrick staged the play, calls it 'a document of relatively little value'.[32] Langhans regrets that it is 'only lightly marked. Long passages are untouched, and the notes end part way through V'.[33] These scholars are correct in finding the Harvard copy inadequate as a prompt-book or guide to textual changes, but none of them mentions certain features that indicate that it was intended for a very different purpose. This little book is a single copy of the Bell 1773 edition of *King Lear*, in a very handsome binding. It has been lightly marked up in a hand that Burnim thinks may be that of William Hopkins, the Drury Lane prompter. These notations put right one or two misprints in Lear's lines (e.g., 'bent down' at G.II.v.72 is corrected to 'but down'). They make a few small cuts in his speeches, such as the confusing ''tween her forks' in G.IV.iii.122, and one of Lear's cues is marked for omission (Cordelia's aside: 'What shall Cordelia do? Love and be silent' at G.I.ii.23). The side of the stage from which Lear should enter or exit (PS or OP) is always shown. The entrances and exits of other characters are also sometimes marked, but only when Lear is on stage. Similarly, there are occasional indications of sound effects (flourishes, thunder, rain), but only in scenes in which Lear appears.

When one considers how very rarely Garrick appeared as Lear in the 1770s, it becomes clear that the copy held at Harvard must be a personal *aide memoire*, intended not for the prompt corner but for the star dressing room. In the later years of his career, Garrick shared the exhausting role with Barry and appeared in it only rarely. When at the age of 59 Garrick gave his three final performances in the role (on 13 May, 21 May and 8 June 1776), it was the first time for two years that he had played it, and that previous appearance had been a single performance for the benefit of the Theatrical Fund. Anxieties about the memory's capacity to recall parts not frequently played are common to actors in middle age. Garrick was certainly experiencing them as early as ten years previously when, on holiday in Bath, he received an unwelcome royal command:

> Mr Ramus has spoken to George from his M[ajesty] that I sh^{d} prepare to play y^{e} *Guardian* at my return – did you ever hear ye like? – I have not acted that dawdle these 100 years – w^{t} can I do? – if I don't perform ye best parts, I am undone – I could not get y^{e} *Guardian* into my head for half a year – not a word of *Kitely* – *Ranger* – Hamlet – *Drugger*, *Lear*, &c? – O Tempora![34]

Though humorous in tone, the underlying note of panic is unmistakable. What is more likely than that the ageing actor kept personal copies of rarely played pieces handy to consult during performance? For *King Lear* the case seems proved by the fact that, inside the front cover of the copy held at Harvard, Garrick's personal bookplate has been affixed.

The Bathurst *King Lear* of 1786 claims on its title page to have been 'altered from Shakspeare by David Garrick, Esq'. In considering whether Garrick was himself responsible for making the further changes that it contains, it is necessary to assess how the Bathurst version differs from Bell's of 1773. Whereas Bell had claimed to offer a text 'as performed at the Theatre-Royal, Drury-Lane', and 'regulated from the prompt-book, with permission of the managers, by Mr. Hopkins, Prompter', the Bathurst title page states that the text is 'marked with the variations in the Manager's book' at Drury Lane. Though it lists the entire cast list for Garrick's last appearance as Lear ten years earlier, it also gives one for Covent Garden, with Henderson in the lead. The title page certainly does not go so far as to claim that this is the play 'as performed' by Garrick, and a note preceding the play text states: 'The Passages omitted in the Representation at the Theatres are marked with inverted Commas.' This note suggests that Bathurst is actually a generic 'acting edition', rather than the script last used by Garrick. The most interesting of the passages marked for omission in performance is the brief early exchange between the lovers, Edgar and Cordelia, which had survived wholly unaltered from

Tate (G.I.i.37–45). However, the Bathurst 1786 text follows the 1773 Bell edition exactly in reverting to Tate in Act V, and ends with the re-united couple about to reign. Clearly, the main source for the Bathurst text is the Bell edition; indeed, in at least one case a printing error has been carried over. Both give 'I would divorce me from my mother's tomb' (G.II.v.77), which editors always correct to 'thy mother's'. (In the Harvard text, this correction has been made in ink.)

Essentially, the Bathurst text of 1786 is an expansion of the Bell edition of 1773, but there are important differences, including a number of additions to the part of Lear. If it is accepted that the version played by Garrick for his final appearances was the 1773 Bell edition, then this reduces, though it does not absolutely rule out, the possibility that he made the further alteration published in 1786. Why continue to tinker around with a rarely played part and, in particular, why insert new lines, if he were not going to incorporate them into his performance? The restorations for Lear are mainly, though not exclusively, in the confrontations between father and daughters. For example, the last vestiges of Tate have been removed from the curse on Goneril (which in both versions provides the climax to Act I). In Bell, this begins:

> Hear, Nature! Hear, dear goddess, hear a father!
> If thou didst intend to make this creature fruitful,
> Suspend thy purpose. (G.I.iv.139–141)

Bell then follows the original for ten lines, but reverts to Tate three lines from the end with 'That she may curse her crime, too late, and feel' (G.I.iv.152). The Bathurst version begins:

> Hear, Nature! hear, dear goddess, hear!
> Suspend thy purpose, if thou didst intend
> To make this creature fruitful! (*cf.* I.iv.254–256)

Bathurst continues to follow the Folio wording exactly for the remainder of the speech (lines 257–269), with the exception of the repeat of 'That she may feel' in line 267. However, it is not certain that the Folio's version of the speech was played at Drury Lane. In a copy of the Bathurst text held in the British Library, the whole speech has been struck through, and Tate's version pasted in.

The majority of restorations in the Bathurst text occur in what had been G.II.v. As shown above, Garrick had earlier paid a great deal of attention to this final encounter in life of Lear and his elder daughters.

While he had not totally eliminated all Lear's rage and resentment, he had not restored the lines that expressed those feelings most offensively, and had ensured that the dominant strain was pathos, not anger. The Bathurst text of this scene is closer to Shakespeare, and Lear's part is considerably fuller. Bathurst restores 'Strike her young bones, / You taking airs, with lameness!' (II.ii.336–337), and the five ingratiating lines to Regan beginning: ' 'Tis not in thee / To grudge my pleasures' (II.ii.346–350). Lear's contemptuous description of Oswald ('This is a slave [. . .] follows', II.ii.358–359) is also put back, as is the angry exchange with Cornwall that begins 'How came my man'i' th' stocks?' (II.ii.371–373). The largest restoration is the fifteen lines of dialogue following G.II.v.184 (Regan's 'And in good time you gave it'), as the father weakly shuffles from daughter to daughter, bargaining over the number of knights that each may be prepared to accept. The exchange ends with Regan's icy 'What need one?' (II.ii.437b), but, following Tate and Bell, Lear's tremendous response, beginning 'O, reason not the need!' (II.ii.438–444) is *not* restored, and Bathurst moves straight to Lear's appeal 'You heavens, give me that patience, patience I need!' (line 445), where Bell had printed 'You Heavens, give me that patience which I need!' (G.II.v.185).

There are several other examples of small interpolations to Lear's lines. For instance, in the king's banishment of Kent, Bathurst restores the line 'Our potency made good, take thy reward' (I.i.171) between G.I.ii.126 and 127. After G.I.iv.39, 'How now? Where's that mungrel?' is inserted. In the second storm scene, at G.III.iii.11, the Folio's 'Thou'dst shun a bear, / But if thy flight lay toward the roaring sea / Thou'dst meet the bear i' th' mouth' (III.iv.9–11) is put back into Lear's first long speech. By the end of his acting career, Garrick would have found it difficult to remember to insert new material of this sort into long familiar speeches.

It is clear from the range of textual variations from the 1773 Bell edition that the Bathurst alteration of 1786 was made after a fresh look at Shakespeare's play. For example, where Bell has 'curtesie' (I.[iii.4]), Bathurst has 'curiosity', and in the storm scene that begins Act III, 'kingdoms' [line 17] become 'kingdom', 'pudder' [line 38] is changed to 'pother' and Kent's line 'Th' affliction, nor the force' [line 36] is altered to 'The affliction, nor the fear'. There are other small differences in the way the play is presented. The locations given for scenes are not always identical: for example, at the opening of Act I Bell has 'Scene, an Antichamber in the Palace', whereas Bathurst gives 'Scene, the King's Palace'. Bell breaks the second scene in Act II into two ('A Court before Gloster's Palace' and 'Gloster's Palace'), but Bathurst runs them straight through.

All the differences from the Bell text noted here are consistent with Johnson's and Steevens's 1773 edition,[35] and also with their 1778 edition, but not with Johnson's earlier text of 1765. A link may also be discernible in the fact that the syndicate of thirty-three publishers responsible for Johnson's and Steevens's edition of 1773 was led by Bathurst.

A reversion to Tate in the Bathurst 1786 text that it is particularly difficult to envisage Garrick approving is Edmund's lip-smacking anticipation of the pleasures of seducing Cordelia in 'amorous Fight' (Tate III.ii.123–125). These lines were cut in the 1756 Drury Lane prompt-book as part of the humanisation of Edmund that Marsden has described.[36] If it is accepted that Garrick was likely to be averse to incorporating new material into the part of Lear at the very end of his career, and that the text played for his final appearance as Lear in June 1776 was the Bell edition of 1773, the balance of probabilities, despite the attribution on the title page, lies with the view that Garrick was not responsible for the Bathurst restorations of 1786. It is of course just conceivable that he continued to make alterations to *King Lear* in the two-and-a-half years left to him between his retirement in June 1776 and his death in January 1779. But, if so, the results were not seen in public. *King Lear* was not revived at Drury Lane until two months after his death, and not given there again until a further eight seasons had elapsed.

To the question 'Did Garrick restore *King Lear* to the London stage?', the answer yielded by the printed evidence seems clear: only up to a point. It is true, of course, that every performance is unique. What John Russell Brown says of the textual history of *King Lear* ('We can never have a single definitive text of this tragedy'[37]) is equally true of Garrick's scripts, as the many changes recorded in the 1756 prompt-book testify. The 'snapshot' provided by the 1773 Bell edition will only take us so far. For example, there is one witness to Garrick's speaking on stage in the early 1750s a line ('O me, my heart! My rising heart – but down,' II.ii.292) that appears neither in Tate nor in the 1756 prompt-book.[38] This could well be evidence of flexibility, showing a willingness to experiment with further restorations in performance. However, if Garrick did make such experiments, the lines he selected would have had to accord with his limited view of the play – or rather, of the part. Rosenberg, in *The Masks of King Lear*, analyses a range of approaches to the role adopted by actors. He identifies Garrick as responsible for setting the pattern for a simplified conception of Lear very popular in the nineteenth century: a grieved old father, 'kind, gentle, good, murdered by filial ingratitude.' 'In this version', he goes on, 'the archetype of ruler, and even of man, was subordinated to that of old good father, much put upon.'[39] The enthusiastic reception afforded to this shaping of Tate's version so early in Garrick's career meant that later, more radical, explorations of the role into potentially less sympathetic directions would be risky. It is hard not to regret the opportunities lost to this great actor by adhering so firmly to his reductive interpretation. Compare, for example, Garrick's view of Lear as an 'Old Man full of affection, Generosity, Passion, & what not [...] good qualities carry'd to excess of folly', with that of a recent interpreter:

> Lear himself is the victim of a mutilated sensibility. In his case, his feelings and any tenderness for others that he might have felt have been stifled by the exercise of total power.[...] He is cruel, vain and violent [...]. And only in and through catastrophe and madness, at great cost to others and himself, does he become human.[40]

As with *Hamlet*, for each age there is an approach to *King Lear* that reflects the concerns of the time. Over the years of Garrick's professional career, audiences were increasingly enjoying novels of sensibility and *comedies larmoyantes*, which explored, in highly emotional terms and often in the context of family dramas, the sufferings of the virtuous. 'It is a common observation, that objects which in the reality would shock, are in tragical, and such like representations, the source of a very high species of pleasure', wrote Burke.[41] A particularly popular character with audiences and readers was the loving and dutiful daughter, and alterations of Shakespeare of the period, as Marsden has shown, often highlighted this sympathetic figure.[42] From Garrick's point of view, it would have been perverse to have alienated audiences by reducing the prominence that Tate had given to Cordelia. Garrick carefully retained Tate's references to Cordelia's filial piety as well as her virtuous love for Edgar. Like Colman, he played down the political aspects of Tate's ending. Rather than rejoice over the restoration of the rightful monarch, audiences could enjoy the touching sight of a father restored to sanity giving his beloved daughter in marriage to her faithful lover. But it is significant that, as played at Drury Lane in 1773, the winding-up of the plot, the reunion of the virtuous survivors and Lear's final anticipation of a retirement 'Cheered with relation of the prosp'rous reign / Of this celestial pair' (G.V.iv.159–160), are dealt with very briskly, almost perfunctorily. And the banality of the lines marks them as Tate's, not Shakespeare's.

Perhaps the 'happy ending', for retaining which Garrick has often been criticised, did not matter so very much to audiences. They came for the emotional satisfactions of vicarious suffering, to sympathise, to experience sadness and pity and, above all, to exhibit their sensibility by weeping. Hannah More's account of the effects upon her of seeing Garrick as Lear in 1774 may seem exaggerated, but it is not untypical: 'I thought I should have been suffocated with Grief: It was not like the superficial Sorrow one feels at a well-acted Play, but the deep, substantial Grief of real Trouble. His Madness was the Madness of Nature, of Shakespear, of Lear, of Garrick.'[43] Clearly, and despite the final scene, she considered that she had been present at a tragedy by Shakespeare. Tate's version had been published as *The History of King Lear*, 'reviv'd with Alterations' and with no mention of Shakespeare on the title page. But Hannah More would certainly have maintained that Garrick's alteration was properly labelled in the Bell edition as *King Lear, A Tragedy, by Shakespeare as Performed at the Theatre-Royal, Drury-Lane.*

Garrick might have succeeded in keeping the Fool out of *King Lear*, but George Steevens, who often played a similar role in his personal life, could not be so easily excluded. Steevens was typical of eighteenth-century editors in being closely involved in theatrical as well as literary circles; his letters show him to have been a frequent attender at the playhouse. As well known for his hoaxes as for his achievements as a scholar and editor of Shakespeare, Steevens knew just how to undermine his victims by attacking them at their points of greatest vulnerability.[44] Johnson, his collaborator, defended his fellow club member from the charge of wickedness, but could not deny his tomfoolery. 'No, Sir; he is not malignant. He is mischievous, if you will. He would do no man an essential injury; he may, indeed, love to make sport of people by vexing their vanity.'[45] Vanity, as with many actors, was certainly Garrick's weak spot, and he was especially proud of his reputation as Shakespeare's supreme interpreter. In August 1769, the month before the Stratford Jubilee, the *Public Advertiser* printed a stream of parodies and satirical squibs, designed to ridicule the Jubilee in all its aspects. As just one example, take the parody of Garrick's famous song for Perdita ('Come, come, my good shepherds, our flocks we must shear') included in a letter signed Insomnis. This purports to represent the intention of the people of Stratford to fleece their visitors, and begins 'Come, Brothers of Stratford, these Flocks let us Shear'.[46] Worse was to follow a fortnight later. 'A Man of Letters' wrote to make public some hitherto unannounced details of the Stratford programme:

> the great Vice-regent of Shakespeare will undertake a minute Examination of the Poet's Versification, and will read several Passages [...] pointing out, but with

great good Nature, the Errors of some modern Performers [. . .] Afterwards he will exhibit a specimen of a projected Edition of the Stratford Swan, which a retreat from the stage may, perhaps, some Time or other (O! may that Time be far distant!) enable him to accomplish.[47]

Clearly, the writer was well acquainted with Garrick's weaknesses and knew exactly how best to play upon them. Thomas Davies does not directly name Steevens, but his description identifies him beyond dispute. He was a 'gentleman, supposed to be an intimate friend of Mr. Garrick, and a professed admirer of Shakespeare'.[48] Praising him as 'second only to Dr. Johnson' as a commentator on Shakespeare and his contemporaries, Davies points up the paradox that, while 'the company at Stratford were indulging themselves in a generous and enthusiastic admiration of the greatest and noblest genius', Steevens was 'employing himself in throwing out abusive strictures, sarcasms, and witticisms'. He concludes that 'the man of wit, from his impatience to show the keenness of it, often wounds with this dangerous weapon his best friends, and not seldom himself'.

Garrick and Steevens had never been 'best friends', but their relationship before the Jubilee had apparently been cordial enough. Just like his despised rival, Capell, Steevens badly needed access to Garrick's great collection of old plays, both for his work in assisting Johnson with editing Shakespeare's plays, and for his own edition of twenty quartos published in 1766.[49] Well aware of the coolness between the two old friends that had arisen from Johnson's implying in his 1765 preface that Garrick had been unwilling to share the treasures of his library, Steevens was careful in the advertisement to his own edition to pay tribute as much to Garrick's benevolence as to his acting ability: 'Mr. Garrick's zeal would not permit him to withhold any thing that might ever so remotely tend to show the perfections of that author who could only have enabled him to display his own.' In the advertisement to the 1773 ('Johnson and Steevens') edition of the *Plays*, he was equally complimentary. Speaking of the need for editors to compare Shakespeare's texts with collections of other rare contemporary books in order to understand the allusions, he added: 'It is almost unnecessary to mention any other than Mr. Garrick's, which, curious and extensive as it is, derives its greatest value from its accessibility.' But between these two grateful acknowledgements of Garrick's co-operation had occurred the estrangement that arose from Steevens's mockery of the Jubilee. When Steevens gleefully confessed his guilt, Garrick resolved thereafter to treat him as 'a pest of society'.[50]

Within two years, a relationship of sorts was in the process of being re-established. Steevens badly needed access to Garrick's library; in return he could offer his services as a literary adviser. By 1771 he had his hands on Capell's catalogue of Garrick's old plays. Now he could assist Garrick and at the same time enjoy himself by pointing out the catalogue's inadequacies and the gaps in the collection. His reply to a very respectful letter from Steevens shows Garrick's view of the relationship at this point:

> Mr. Garrick, with his compliments, desires to have that volume of Voltaire which has the critique upon Shakspeare in it. Mr. Garrick takes this opportunity of thanking Mr. Steevens for his intended expedition and operations in the Temple of Shakspeare: whenever he pleases to think of putting it in execution, Mr. Garrick will take care that the windows are kept open.[51]

Garrick is still wary and uses the formal third person, but contact has been re-opened. Garrick was liberal in lending books, and soon the correspondence between the two Shakespeare enthusiasts became much more friendly and frequent.

A topic important to them both was the 1773 edition of the *Plays*. Steevens, mindful of the fuss caused by Johnson's allegation in 1765 that Garrick was reluctant to share his collection of old plays, took care to check the acceptability of his advertisement prior to publication:

> The legitimacy of an edition of Shakspeare can no more be ascertained to satisfaction, without the testimony of the Poet's High Priest, than that of a prince can be lawfully proved, unless the archbishop attends in person. I am therefore desirous that you should glance your eye over the enclosed papers, which are to announce the birth or (not to speak profanely) the regeneration of Dr. Johnson's Edition to the world.[52]

Given his record, Steevens was taking a risk in using such gross flattery. Was he mischievously trying to test how much the actor could be induced to swallow? Or was he simply adopting the language in which appeals to Garrick to endorse Shakespearean projects were customarily couched? When the edition appeared, Garrick's congratulations to Steevens were warm: 'I have the highest regard for Y^{r} great learning & abilities, & most Sincerely esteem You as one of the first Worthies in the literary World – [. . .] Your Notes & Observations upon Shakespeare have done You infinite honour – I am amaz'd at ye Variety & Extent of y^{r} reading.'[53]

By now, Garrick clearly felt that he could confidently consult Steevens on Shakespearean topics. For example, in a letter probably written in January 1775, he asked him not only to settle a wager about the origin of certain lines in Cibber's *Richard III*, but also to advise on possible additions to the Drury Lane repertoire: 'have You Ever thought of any Play unreviv'd in Shakespeare, that would bring Credit to Us well decorated & carefully got up? – What think you of Rich^{d} 2d – ?'[54] By this late stage, Garrick was thinking more about scenic effects than leading roles for himself, for he added: 'I should be glad to Employ our Painter upon some capital *Creditable* Performance.' Steevens responded discouragingly that *Richard II* was 'surely the most uninteresting and flattest of all the number. A few splendid passages will not maintain a play on the stage'. In a second letter he warned of some undesirable political consequences of staging the play: 'There are *four lines* in Shakspeare's play, which if spoken will be applied to the present reign. Whether they should be continued or omitted you are the best judge.'[55] Garrick then turned to Johnson's and Steevens's 1773 edition and read *Richard II*, perhaps for the first time. Reluctantly the manager, still hankering after spectacular scenic effects, found himself in agreement with the assessment of the editor: 'you are perfectly right – it is one of ye least interesting of his Historical plays – it will not do – I could make a fine Scene of the Barriers & particularly if they had made an attack before Rich^{d} had stop'd them'.[56]

Garrick's and Steevens's discussion of *Richard II* admirably exemplifies the close links between stage and page that still existed in the third quarter of the eighteenth century. But indeed their entire surviving correspondence is testimony to that closeness. In the early 1770s, letters between them are frequent. Garrick is asked to act for Steevens as intermediary with the touchy Capell. Steevens offers to index Garrick's collection of old plays correctly, as Capell had failed to do. When an old actor sends to Garrick, the head of his profession, some suggested corrections to Johnson's edition of *Othello*, made after consulting some early texts, Garrick passes them on to Steevens for comment. Meanwhile, the editor takes it for granted that he needs to study the plays in performance and asks the actor-manager for seats: 'I shall think myself under great obligations to you for seven or eight places when you play Hamlet, or any principal character in Shakspeare's tragedies.'[57]

As will be shown below, Steevens's influence is seen at its greatest in his warm encouragement of Garrick's alteration of *Hamlet*. Even here, Steevens was inconsistent. After the actor's death he harshly criticised Garrick for the changes:

This alteration is made in the true spirit of *Bottom the Weaver*, who wishes to play not only the part assigned to him, but all the rest in the piece. Mr. Garrick, in short, has reduced the consequence of every character but himself; and thus excluding Osric, the Gravediggers, &c. contrived to monopolize the attention of the audience.[58]

One wonders just how sincere Steevens's initial encouragement had really been. Is it possible that he had concealed his real opinion in the gleeful hope that Garrick's innovation would be a failure? Tomarken, however, sees Steevens as in some sense the first of the Romantics, genuinely preferring a consistently melancholy prince and believing that 'the variety of *Hamlet*, particularly the low humor, detracts from a coherent resolution of Hamlet's dilemma'.[59] At all events, Steevens seems never to have been able to pass up an opportunity to mock and disparage Garrick, in life and after his death. However cordial their working and social relationships within The Club appeared to be (Steevens was elected in 1775), Garrick knew well that he could not be trusted: 'What a precious Genius is Master Steevens', he wrote exasperatedly to Colman.[60]

Garrick's alteration of *Hamlet* (1772)[61] is fraught with paradox. It is both radical *and* conservative. Outrageous in its cavalier excisions of popular characters and scenes – the grave-diggers, 'Ostrick' and the fencing match – it nevertheless demonstrates respect for 'the original' by its reinstatement of passages long unheard on the London stage. On the strength of this alteration, his last of a play by Shakespeare,[62] Garrick has been hailed as a restorer and condemned as a butcher. This chapter shows that neither response is really appropriate to a text that represents 'work in progress' rather than a finished product, and seeks to explain Garrick's reasons for the changes that he made.

This *Hamlet*, with its restructured ending, can be seen as marking the beginning of the end of re-writing Shakespeare on a grand scale; Garrick composed fewer than thirty-five new lines for his 1772 version. The increasing availability of successive editions, stimulated in part no doubt by Garrick's own activities as Shakespeare's supreme interpreter and fervent publicist, meant that audiences would be far more familiar with the actual words of the plays than had been the case when Garrick brought out his restoration of *Macbeth* in 1744. Yet, while reservations about the acceptability of wholesale re-writing might have been starting to emerge by 1772, what actually made this *Hamlet* so challenging to audiences, as Garrick himself recognised, was nothing to do with its language; it was the loss of well-loved scenes of comedy and action towards the end of the play. After the first performances he wrote to a French friend:

> I have play'd the Devil this Winter, I have dar'd to alter *Hamlet*, I have thrown away the gravediggers, & all ye 5th Act, & notwithstanding the Galleries were so fond of them, I have met with more applause than I did at five & twenty – this is a great revolution in our theatrical history, & for wch 20 years ago instead of Shouts of approbation, I should have had ye benches thrown at my head –[63]

In effect Garrick was daring his public to choose innovation over tradition. Yet, paradoxically, the changes he forced upon them reflected a scarcely revolutionary, indeed conservative, approach to playmaking still highly valued in France but in England increasingly regarded as out of date and irrelevant – if not, indeed, downright unpatriotic.

Hamlet, whether in the second Quarto or first Folio text, is far too long for the comfort of a theatre audience. Companies have almost always pruned the play, and all the more so in the days when afterpieces were also performed. London audiences of the 1760s were accustomed to a much-abbreviated *Hamlet*. The version played at Drury Lane in 1763, with Garrick in the lead, will be referred to below as the Hawes text.[64] It was anything but prosy: reflective, philosophic and descriptive speeches such as the Queen's account of Ophelia's drowning (IV.vii.138–155) were pruned, and many later famous passages were omitted altogether, including Hamlet's speech over the praying Claudius (III.iii.72–96) and his soliloquy 'How all occasions do inform against me' (IV.iv.23–57).[65] Action and variety were at a premium. Although there was no entrance for Fortinbras in the closing moments of the play, the fifth act included most of the graveyard scene, the dialogue with 'Ostrick' and the fencing match.[66] When Garrick first played the title role in 1742, he inherited from his predecessors in the part, Betterton (died 1710) and Robert Wilks (died 1732), a heavily cut text that emphasised the active and downplayed the introspective aspects of Hamlet's character.[67] In 1718 Wilks and his friend John Hughes had published their version of this streamlined text, which contained restorations from Rowe's 1709 edition. It was frequently reprinted and became in effect the standard performance script. Though Garrick is believed to have continued to tinker with the Hughes–Wilks version over the intervening thirty years, it was to a 1747 printing of that familiar text that he turned when preparing his provocative alteration.[68] Long thought to be lost, the copy from which Garrick worked was discovered by George Winchester Stone, then a Harvard research student, in

Figure 7 Garrick as Hamlet sees his father's ghost. This engraving was made in 1769. Engraving after Benjamin Wilson. Artist unknown. The Art Archive/Garrick Club.

the newly opened (1933) Folger Shakespeare Library, where it remains. Stone published Garrick's Act V in 1934, but the full text did not appear in print until the 1980s. The changes Garrick made in his preparation copy provide valuable insight into the business of alteration, but it would be unwise to take them as proof of what was actually played for the first time on 18 December 1772.

Here a caveat is in order. It is all too easy to fall into the trap of assuming that a preparation copy represents the end, rather than the beginning, of a process. A few examples of the need for caution follow. In the base text upon which Garrick made his alterations, a familiar rubric is printed beneath the 1718 cast list: '*This Play being too long to be acted upon the Stage, such Lines as are left out in the Acting, are marked thus* ".' His editors have naturally proceeded on the assumption that passages crossed out by Garrick were not played at Drury Lane from 1772 to 1779, and that the remaining lines, whether or not marked with inverted commas, were included; indeed without them the play would have been extremely short. In fact, Garrick's cuts from the first three acts (restructured into four in his alteration) are relatively few, and mainly from Hamlet's own speeches. As one would expect, bawdry and sexual imagery are excluded, as are mentions of a king and court given over to drunkenness, 'jingle' is avoided, and references to hell, heaven and damned spirits are minimised. According to Hannah More, Garrick as Hamlet 'never once forgot he was a prince',[69] and less courtly aspects of the character – for example, his wild euphoria after the play, some passages of rant, his rhetorical performance of the 'rugged Pyrrhus' speech and harsh references to his mother – are deleted.

On the other hand, there are long passages in Garrick's preparation copy in which '' is printed against every line, which would appear to indicate that the Drury Lane company included several scenes or speeches new to both actors and audience. These passages include most of the cautions given to Ophelia by the departing Laertes (G.II.i.13–46) and more than half of Polonius's advice to his son (G.II.i.61–75), many unfamiliar lines about Pyrrhus, Priam and Hecuba performed by the First Player, several speeches in *The Mousetrap* and the soliloquy 'How all occasions' in full (G.V.ii.27–61). Also included among these apparent restorations are the despatch of the ambassadors to Norway (G.I.ii.26–41) and Polonius's instructions to Reynaldo (G.III.i.1–79). No actors are listed in 1718 for the parts of Voltimand, Cornelius and Reynaldo, whose names and lines in cast list and text are always marked ''. But neither is any of these characters listed on the bill for any performance of *Hamlet* at Drury Lane under Garrick's management from December 1772 (when his alteration was first staged) until his retirement in June 1776. Admittedly, they are minor roles, but the actor entrusted with the tiny part of Messenger (Garrick's invention) is usually named in the bills. One wonders whether their scenes were ever in fact performed, especially as Thomas Davies wrote in 1784 that the Polonius/Reynaldo scene had not been acted 'for more than a century'.[70] His account in *Dramatic Miscellanies* of Garrick's alteration of the play, though not totally accurate (e.g., he says that Laertes dies at the end), strongly suggests that he did see it performed. Additional uncertainty attaches to the prayer scene. On the evidence of the preparation copy alone, it would seem that Garrick played a full though slightly re-worded version of Hamlet's speech over the apparently praying Claudius (see G.IV.i.577–598). Yet Davies, who thought the lines 'reprehensible', commented that '[t]he first actor, who rejected this horrid soliloquy, was Mr. Garrick'.[71] Johnson had also been shocked by it, commenting: 'This speech, in which Hamlet, represented as a virtuous character, is not content with taking blood for blood, but contrives damnation for the man that he would punish, is too horrible to be read or to be uttered.'[72] Davies's remark seems to be confirmed by the short *Hamlet* published by Hawes 'as performed' in 1763, which lists Garrick in the title role. This text, which leaves out all the lines cut in performance, contains no entrance for Hamlet in the prayer scene. Again, one feels unsure: did Garrick play the 'horrid soliloquy' from 1772 to 1776 or not?

Similar doubts arise about the conclusion of the closet scene, with its problematic double ending. The 1763 Hawes text indicates major cuts. After the exit of the Ghost in this version, Hamlet, sane and self-controlled, briefly exhorts Gertrude to repent and adopt a virtuous life, bids her a dignified goodnight and expresses penitence for the death of Polonius. There is no mention of the King's 'reechy kisses', of Hamlet's banishment to England or of hoisting Rosencrantz and Guildenstern with their own petard. As so many nineteenth- and early twentieth-century productions were later to do, the 1763 version ends the scene within thirty lines of the Ghost's exit with 'I must be cruel, only to be kind; / Thus bad begins, and worse remains behind' (III.iv.162–163). However, Garrick's 1772 revision, as published by Pedicord and Bergmann, continues the scene for (after cuts) a further twenty-two lines (G.IV.i.769–790), thus briefly establishing both Hamlet's projected journey to England and Gertrude's promise not to reveal that Hamlet is only 'mad in craft'.

Usually, Garrick placed 'boxes', full or partial, round passages for deletion, or crossed out individual lines. He did not strike through the final nine lines of the closet scene in his preparation copy, and only partially boxed the preceding seven. It is difficult to follow his intentions in the latter passage. Pedicord's and Bergmann's interpretation seems unconvincing. They print:

> My two schoolfellows delve one yard below their mines,
> And blow them at the moon. O, 'tis most sweet
> When in one line two crafts directly meet. (G.IV.i.781–783)

And they end the scene, as indeed the preparation copy seems to indicate, with Hamlet's harsh speech as he drags out Polonius's corpse (G.IV.i. 784–790). Yet it is impossible to imagine Garrick's gentlemanly Hamlet ever voicing the distressingly low line 'I'll lug the guts into the neighb'ring room'. This conclusion is strengthened by a survey of eighteenth-century printings of *Hamlet* 'as performed'. Printings up to 1763 include 'lug the guts', though sometimes the line is marked '' ' for omission. But acting editions after that date (when Hawes published the text that Garrick was currently playing) always cut the line. Probably Garrick in his haste simply forgot to strike through the final nine lines, though this conclusion raises only further uncertainty as to how the scene in performance actually ended.

Indeed, evidence of haste is everywhere in Garrick's preparation copy. His dashing hand has swiftly noted down the cuts and new lines needed to shape his vision of the play, but puzzling loose ends remain. For example, he inserts no change of scene following 'How all occasions' (G.V.ii.62), so that, if his version is followed literally, Ophelia's mad scenes and the rest of the play take place in 'A wood'. Nor are any scene changes indicated in Garrick's fourth act, which comprises the nunnery, play, prayer and closet scenes. The King never has time to tell Laertes that his vengeance should be directed at Hamlet, yet on Hamlet's reappearance Laertes immediately exclaims 'Then my revenge is come' and draws his sword (G.V.ii.272). Ophelia's fate after her last exit (G.V. ii.259) is never mentioned, yet Hamlet boasts in the past tense of his love for her in lines clipped from the cancelled graveyard scene (G.V.ii.281–289), and at the point of death he asks:

> Exchange forgiveness with me, brave Laertes,
> Thy sister's, father's death, come not on me,
> Nor mine on thee! (G.V.ii.315–317)

Sometimes the preparation copy shows Garrick changing his mind – for example, about how to dispose of the Queen in his new ending. Jeffrey Johnson was, it seems, the first to point out that Garrick originally intended to keep Gertrude, in a swoon, on stage, but later changed his mind and wrote in an exit for her at G.V.ii.301.[73] Here again a change of mind is evident. Gertrude's exit line originally began with an echo of Macduff: 'O horror, horror – ', but later it became: 'O mercy, heaven! – Save me from my son – (*Runs out*).' Clearly, this preparation copy is not, *pace* Stone, 'the text that Garrick planned to print'[74]; nor can there be any certainty that it tells us exactly what was played at Drury Lane in December 1772. It represents the beginning of a project, not its completion.

Garrick's starting point for his *Hamlet* project was not, as Pedicord and Bergmann, following Stone, believed, 'the scholarly apparatus that had been built up by 1772, and Johnson's edition chiefly'.[75] Instead, it was the standard performance script on which his 1763 version had also been based, and the first four acts of his alteration offer no evidence that he consulted any other version. Until his new Act V, Garrick incorporated all the familiar textual changes made by Hughes–Wilks. For example, 'Your bedded hair, like life in excrements, / Start up and stand on end' (III.iv.112–113) was modernised in Hughes–Wilks to 'Your hair starts up and stands on end' (G.IV.i.724). As Hughes–Wilks had done, Garrick omitted the dumb show after III.ii.129. And when he needed to change the order of some scenes in his new Act V, he cut out the passages he needed from a copy of his own 1763 (Hawes) version, and pasted them onto pp. 72–74 of his preparation text.[76]

What led Stone to conclude that Garrick was 'interested in presenting to his audiences a more correct text than had been customary' and had been studying modern editions, was the peppering of his fifth act with numerous tiny textual restorations. To look no further than the opening of G.V.i (originally IV.i) on p. 63 of the preparation copy, the following changes were made:

Reference	Preparation copy (Hughes–Wilks 1747)	Amended by hand to
G.V.i.2	You must expound them;	You must translate; 'tis fit we understand them.
G.V.i.7	Mad as the Sea	Mad as the Seas
G.V.i.10	Whips out his Rapier cries a Rat, a Rat,	He Whips his Rapier out and cries a Rat!
G.V.i.19	Should have restrain'd	Should have kept short, restrain'd, and out of haunt
G.V.i.22	A foul Disease	A dire Disease

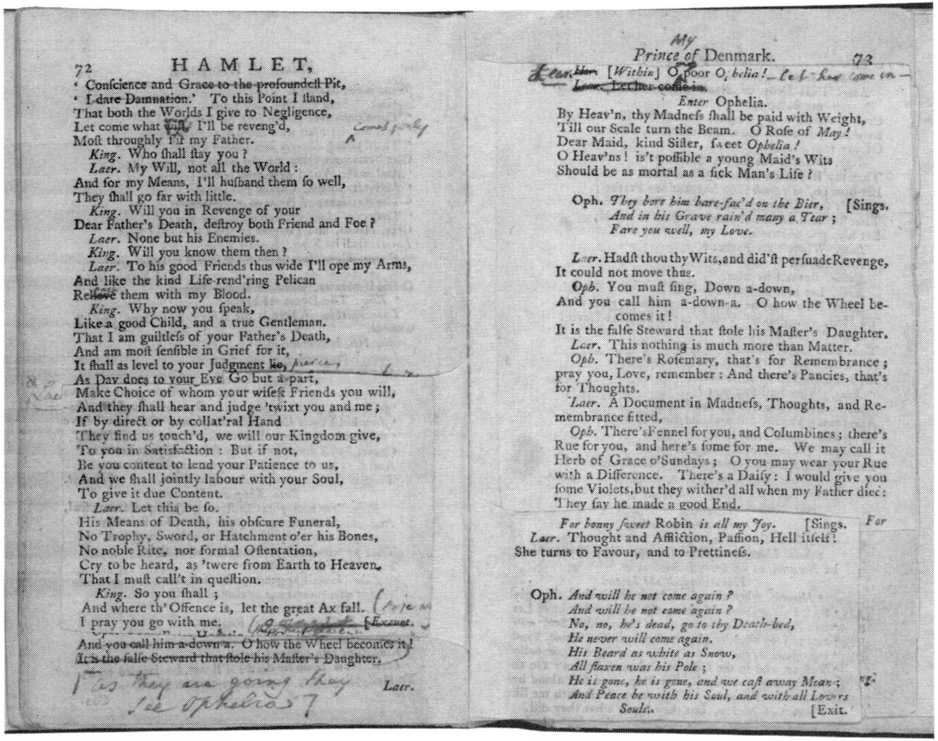

72 HAMLET,

' Conscience and Grace to the profoundest Pit,
' I dare Damnation.' To this Point I stand,
That both the Worlds I give to Negligence,
Let come what will, I'll be reveng'd,
Most throughly for my Father.
King. Who shall stay you?
Laer. My Will, not all the World:
And for my Means, I'll husband them so well,
They shall go far with little.
King. Will you in Revenge of your
Dear Father's Death, destroy both Friend and Foe?
Laer. None but his Enemies.
King. Will you know them then?
Laer. To his good Friends thus wide I'll ope my Arms,
And like the kind Life-rend'ring Pelican
Relieve them with my Blood.
King. Why now you speak,
Like a good Child, and a true Gentleman.
That I am guiltless of your Father's Death,
And am most sensible in Grief for it,
It shall as level to your Judgment lie,
As Day does to your Eye Go but a-part,
Make Choice of whom your wisest Friends you will,
And they shall hear and judge 'twixt you and me;
If by direct or by collat'ral Hand
They find us touch'd, we will our Kingdom give,
To you in Satisfaction: But if not,
Be you content to lend your Patience to us,
And we shall jointly labour with your Soul,
To give it due Content.
Laer. Let this be so.
His Means of Death, his obscure Funeral,
No Trophy, Sword, or Hatchment o'er his Bones,
No noble Rite, nor formal Ostentation,
Cry to be heard, as 'twere from Earth to Heaven,
That I must call't in question.
King. So you shall;
And where th' Offence is, let the great Ax fall.
I pray you go with me. [Exeunt.
And you call him a-down-a. O how the Wheel becomes it!
It is the false Steward that stole his Master's Daughter.
Laer.

Prince of Denmark. 73

[Within] O poor O, belia!
Enter Ophelia.
By Heav'n, thy Madness shall be paid with Weight,
Till our Scale turn the Beam. O Rose of May!
Dear Maid, kind Sister, sweet Ophelia!
O Heav'ns! is't possible a young Maid's Wits
Should be as mortal as a sick Man's Life?
Oph. *They bore him bare-fac'd on the Bier,* [Sings.
And in his Grave rain'd many a Tear;
Fare you well, my Love.
Laer. Hadst thou thy Wits, and did'st persuade Revenge,
It could not move thus.
Oph. You must sing, Down a-down,
And you call him a-down-a. O how the Wheel becomes it!
It is the false Steward that stole his Master's Daughter.
Laer. This nothing is much more than Matter.
Oph. There's Rosemary, that's for Remembrance; pray you, Love, remember: And there's Pancies, that's for Thoughts.
Laer. A Document in Madness, Thoughts, and Remembrance fitted,
Oph. There's Fennel for you, and Columbines; there's Rue for you, and here's some for me. We may call it Herb of Grace o'Sundays; O you may wear your Rue with a Difference. There's a Daisy: I would give you some Violets, but they wither'd all when my Father died: They say he made a good End.
For bonny sweet Robin *is all my Joy.* [Sings.
Laer. Thought and Affliction, Passion, Hell itself!
She turns to Favour, and to Prettiness.
Oph. *And will he not come again?*
And will he not come again?
No, no, he's dead, go to thy Death-bed,
He never will come again.
His Beard as white as Snow,
All flaxen was his Pole;
He is gone, he is gone, and we cast away Moan;
And Peace be with his Soul, and with all Lovers Souls. [Exit.

Figure 8 Garrick's preparation copy for his alteration of *Hamlet* (pp. 72 and 73), showing amendments in two hands. By permission of the Folger Shakespeare Library.

There are many similar amendments on the following nine pages; they cease on p. 72, shortly before Garrick's major re-writing begins. Why this sudden change of approach, from Garrick's customary 'broad-brush' concern with the sweep of the action and its effectiveness on stage, to such meticulous attention to the fine detail of the words on the page? As Stone himself says: 'A man whose interest was only in playing need not have bothered himself with such minute details, for with the rapidity with which words cross the footlights the essential correctness of small phrases passes unnoticed.'[77]

Perhaps because he so much wished to present Garrick as the great restorer of Shakespeare's actual lines, Stone seems not to have observed that most if not all of the textual amendments to Act V of Garrick's *Hamlet* are not in Garrick's hand. The handwriting of these amendments is smaller and more regular than Garrick's, and the ink, though it is badly faded, appears lighter in tone than that used for his own insertions and deletions. At the time that Garrick was preparing his alteration of *Hamlet*, Steevens was working with Johnson on the edition of Shakespeare that they were to bring out in 1773.[78] Comparison of the preparation copy with manuscript letters from Steevens to Garrick of this period leads to the confident conclusion that the annotations are in Steevens's handwriting.[79] There is no doubt that Garrick consulted him about the projected alteration of *Hamlet* in the year prior to its first performance. In a letter dated simply 'Saturday Evening, 1771', which responds to one from Garrick, now lost, Steevens writes that he expects 'great pleasure' from perusal of the alteration. Evidently, Garrick has written outlining his plans for shortening the play by eliminating the comic elements in the last act, and has offered Steevens an advance look at the result. Steevens responds with enthusiasm: 'It is a circumstance in favour of the poet which I have long been wishing for.' He continues:

> In spite of all he [Dr. Johnson] has said on the subject, I shall never be thoroughly reconciled to tragi-comedy; [. . .] I am sure when you personate the Danish Prince, you wish your task concluded with the third act, after which the genius of Shakspeare retires, or only plays bo-peep through the rest of the piece. I confess I am talking a kind of poetical blasphemy; but I am become less afraid of you, since you have avowed your present design.[80]

It seems that Garrick did indeed send his preparation copy of *Hamlet* to Steevens, by whom the small textual amendments to the renumbered Act V were made. Whether these changes were incorporated in the version eventually performed it is now impossible to say. What is clear is that Garrick's alteration does not reveal him to be (as Stone wished) an editor manqué – unless we say that, by amending the standard acting script, he mirrored the practice of those eighteenth-century editors who preferred to 'correct' the editions of their immediate predecessors rather than go back to an original text. Garrick's *Hamlet* is a version designed and shaped for a specific actor at a specific stage in his career. The next section looks briefly at the changes he made, and then seek the reasons for them.

Garrick's alteration of *Hamlet* is intensely focused on Hamlet himself. Garrick re-arranged the traditional act breaks, ending the first on Hamlet's decision to watch for the ghost that night (I.ii.257), the second at the end of the confrontation with his father's spirit (I.v.190), the third at II.ii.606 after Hamlet's soliloquy 'O what a wretch *[sic]* and pleasant *[sic]* slave am I!', and the fourth after the closet scene (III.iv.191). Thus, all four ended with a speech from Hamlet himself. During those four acts, audiences heard a rather fuller text than they were accustomed to, and Garrick inserted only two lines of his own composition, addressed by Polonius to Laertes:

> Though late, very late, the moon is up
> And in full beauty lights you to your vessel. (G.II.i.59–60)

Burnim suggests that the addition was to bridge the time gap 'from the morning court scene to the second ghost scene which follows immediately'. Garrick's handwriting can be difficult to read, and Burnim gives a slightly different wording:

> ... it's very late, ye moon is up
> And in full scanty lights ye go to ye vessell.[81]

The preparation copy confirms that, give or take a comma, Pedicord's and Bergmann's modernised transcription is accurate.

Garrick's major changes and additions begin half way through his fifth act, though even then he adds no more than thirty new lines. The King orders Hamlet to England in G.V.i, following the traditional text, lightly cut. The next scene (based on Q2's expanded version of IV.iv) is set in a wood. Instead of seeing Fortinbras and his army march over the stage, the audience hears 'trumpets and drums at a distance', and Hamlet and Rosencrans enter, meeting Guildenstern. Hamlet asks: 'Well, the news! Have you learnt whence are those powers?' (G.V.ii.1) and, in a rather unlikely exchange, Guildenstern provides the information that in Q2 Hamlet learns from Fortinbras's Captain: for example,

'They go to gain a little patch of ground' (line 13). Rosencrans and Guildenstern are sent to go 'a little before' (line 26) and Hamlet launches into the wholly uncut 'How all occasions' (lines 27–61), a soliloquy that would have been entirely fresh to the ears of most audience members in 1772. Without requiring great physical exertion, it offered opportunities for the swift transitions between 'passions' that were Garrick's speciality. Moving from self-reproach through self-disgust, Hamlet urges himself into action, confirmed in Garrick's alteration by the addition of a final line and a half of (literal) claptrap immediately before his exit:

> O, from this time forth,
> My thoughts be bloody all! the hour is come –
> I'll fly my keepers – sweep to my revenge. (G.V.ii.60–62)

The altered *Hamlet* is now within 300 lines of its ending. No new material is added to Ophelia's first mad scene or to that of Laertes's return, except that the latter is not 'in secret come from France' (IV.v.86) but, in order to compress the time scale of the action, 'tempest-beaten back to Denmark' (G.V.ii.143). Garrick cut very little of IV.v, but slightly reordered the text, pasting into his preparation copy the lines IV.v.201–217 from the Hawes text, so that they preceded Ophelia's second mad scene, and thus ensured that the King, Queen and Laertes remained on stage right through to the brief finale.

Only in the rapid action of the final scene (G.V.ii.260–326) do Shakespeare's inventions give place to Garrick's, or rather to a patchwork of stock phrases, all reminiscent of tragedies familiar to the audience. Hamlet, having flown his keepers, dramatically re-enters – or so we must assume. (Garrick's preparation copy neglects to specify exactly when Hamlet re-enters; he speaks first at G.V.ii.267.) His confrontation with Laertes (G.V.ii.267–291) is based on the graveyard altercation (V.i.250–282). Then the King turns on Hamlet:

> But you have trampled on allegiance,
> And now shall feel my wrath. – Guards! (G.V.ii.295–296)

'First feel mine!', replies Hamlet (line 297), and immediately stabs his uncle. The King (if Thomas Davies's memory can be relied upon)[82] attempts to defend himself before he '[f]alls and dies', and the terrified Queen rushes out. Immediately Laertes, in revenge for 'My father, sister, and my King – ' (line 303), draws his sword, and Hamlet runs upon it. Hamlet prevents Horatio from taking further vengeance: ''Tis the hand of heav'n / Administers by him this precious balm / For all my wounds' (lines 305–307). No Fortinbras or English ambassador appears. Instead, a convenient messenger enters to describe the Queen's collapse:

> Struck with the horror of the scene, she fled.
> But 'ere she reached her chamber door she fell
> Entranced and motionless – unable to sustain the load
> Of agony and sorrow – (lines 308–311)

The last thoughts of Garrick's Hamlet are not concerned with his posthumous reputation or the silence of death, but rather with love, reconciliation and penitence. He dies a model hero. Having urged Horatio to take care of Gertrude when she wakes from her trance (lines 312–314), and then exchanged forgiveness with Laertes (lines 315–318), Garrick's Hamlet completes his earthly business in a short speech calculated to wring tears from his audience:

> O, I die, Horatio! – But one thing more.
> O take this hand from me – unite your virtues – (*Joins* Horatio*'s hand to* Laertes*'*.)
> To calm this troubled land. I am no more;
> Nor have I more to ask but mercy, heav'n! (*Dies*). (lines 319–322)

(Ironically, the two final words are an echo of Richard III's awakening from his nightmare, in which role Garrick had made his debut to huge acclaim back in 1741.) Such a pious death would surely merit 'flights of angels'. The words 'virtues', 'calm', 'mercy' and 'heav'n' would resonate in the audience's ears as Horatio, reverting to Shakespeare, spoke the brief curtain speech cobbled together from V.ii.312–313 and 355–356:

> Now cracks a noble heart. Goodnight, sweet prince,
> And flights of angels sing thee to thy rest.
> Take up the body; such a sight as this
> Becomes the field, but here shows much amiss. (G.V.ii.323–326)

It is not difficult to see why Garrick's ending has been deplored. Boaden called it 'sacrilege'[83], Burnim thought it 'inexcusable',[84] while Holland, despite his sympathy with Garrick's approach to the playing text, acknowledges that '[a]s a piece of brutal cutting it is almost without parallel'.[85] But its very baldness and brevity are an indication that in Garrick's mind the end of the play was not its crown. Throughout his *Hamlet*, just as in his

King Lear, the political takes second place to the personal, and family relationships, as can be seen from the dying Hamlet's concern for his mother at G.V.ii.312–314, are what matter most. Thomas Davies wrote that 'filial piety' was the 'characteristical sign' of Garrick's interpretation[86]. Hannah More, the Garricks' surrogate daughter, said the same in a letter written from the Garricks' house in June 1776, after witnessing one of her host's last appearances as Hamlet:

> Hamlet experiences the conflict of many passions and affections, but filial love ever takes the lead; *that* is the great point from which he sets out, and to which he returns; the others are all contingent and subordinate to it, and are cherished or renounced, as they promote or obstruct the operation of this leading principle.[87]

Garrick's contemporaries never saw his alteration in print but, now that it is available in a modern edition, it can be seen to be structured around two crucial and highly emotional encounters between the Prince and his parents. The climax of the first half takes place on 'the platform before the palace' (G.II.ii). His preparation copy indicates that Garrick intended the famous scene between father and son to be played with a completely full text; he cut not one word of their dialogue (lines 74–170), even leaving in the Ghost's lines 'But virtue [. . .] prey on garbage' (G.II.ii.132–136), strong stuff that had been omitted from the 1763 Hawes version. Davies notes that in this scene Garrick's 'expostulations with the vision, though warm and importunate, were restrained by filial awe'.[88] In the second half of the alteration, Hamlet's confrontation with his mother in the closet scene (G.IV.i.601–790) provides a balancing, and equally dramatic, high point. Again, the text is surprisingly complete. Only eight lines are cut prior to the Ghost's entrance, and none while he is on stage. After Hamlet's final 'Goodnight, mother' (line 790) came the act break, with its music, and a change of scene before the truncated fifth act. The two extended emotional peaks of the tragedy had now been passed, and in this alteration no lightening of the mood could be expected. For an audience that still had to weep at Ophelia's mad scenes, a speedy ending would come as a relief.

What prompted Garrick to make the drastic changes to the ending of *Hamlet* that are the most remarkable – and remarked upon – features of his 1772 alteration? There is evidence of an almost obsessive interest in the playtext in his account of the conversation at a Christmas Eve dinner. Someone had queried the meaning of the word 'mobled' (Garrick's spelling). At first,

Garrick had said that it meant 'clouted' but later, prompted by 'the Demon of Criticism, (slipping down with ye Burgundy)', he had suggested that the word might actually be 'mob-led'. He went home and consulted

> a Memorandum book, where I had collected Every Scrap about Shakespear, I found that I had met with this interpretation of Mobled, in some pamphlet, or Other, and that I had written under it – absurd and ridiculous – and most certainly it is so – Dr Warburton says – Mobled or Mabled signifies, veiled – Johnson – huddled or grosly cover'd – Capel has it – Enobl'd Queen – wch I don't understand –[89]

And if his correspondence following the first performances of his alteration is to be believed, he had long been impatient to revise the play. 'I have ventured to produce Hamlet with alterations it *[sic]* was the most imprudent thing I ever did in all my life but I had sworn I would not leave the Stage till I had rescued that noble play from all the rubbish of the 5th Act', he wrote.[90] Two motivating forces for such imprudence will be suggested below, one cultural, one practical, but both in essence personal to Garrick.

As a very young man, Garrick's views on dramatic theory may well have been influenced by purists who held that comedy and tragedy should be strictly kept apart. Shortly before he and Johnson made their famous journey to London, an anonymous commentator on *Hamlet* had observed:

> The Scene of the Grave-Diggers, (*p.* 344.) I know is much applauded, but in my humble Opinion, is very unbecoming such a Piece as this, and is only pardonable as it gives Rise to Hamlet's fine moral Reflections upon the Infirmity of human Nature.[91]

Further criticism of the same scene appeared in 1752, in an anonymous pamphlet that judged Shakespeare by the standards of the ancients: 'To mix Comedy with Tragedy is breaking through the sacred Laws of Nature, nor can it be defended.'[92] To regard the keeping separate of comedy and tragedy as any concern of 'Nature' now seems bizarre, but had the writer instead referred to the 'sacred laws' of classical drama, he or she would have encountered considerable – though in Britain by that date diminishing – support. There, the correct tragedies of Racine and Corneille were less likely to be held up as models for imitation, as Shakespeare's mingled drama was increasingly seen as a subject for national pride, for which no apologies were necessary.[93] In France, however, tragedies continued to be judged by their adherence to classical principles and conventions.

There is evidence that Garrick was trying to reduce the elements of comedy in *Hamlet* much earlier than 1772, though not without a struggle. That audiences, and especially the upper gallery, valued those elements is well attested. For example, in a Drury Lane playbill for 17 January 1754, apart from Hamlet himself (Garrick) the male character with the best billing is Ostrick. In that role, the popular comedian Woodward enjoys a typeface larger than Davies (King), Berry (Ghost), Havard (Horatio), Taswell (Polonius) or Blakes (Laertes). Again, it was the practice in the eighteenth century to play Polonius, in the words of Thomas Davies, 'to excite laughter and be an object of ridicule'.[94] Davies, then a member of the Drury Lane company, records that he witnessed Garrick persuading Woodward on his benefit night to treat the role more seriously. This must have occurred prior to the opening of the 1758–1759 season, by which date Woodward had left the Drury Lane company. But the experiment was not successful; to the audience, says Davies, Woodward's Polonius seemed 'flat and insipid'.

Garrick, notwithstanding Johnson's approval of *Hamlet*'s scenes 'interchangeably diversified with merriment and solemnity', persisted with his dream of 'regularising' the play, and the resulting alteration is (like Johnson's own *Irene*) undoubtedly a tragedy constructed on classical principles. By eliminating grave-diggers, sailors and Norwegians, it concentrates attention on the principal, and especially the royal, inhabitants of the Danish court. Laertes's trip to France and Hamlet's journey to England never happen, and the entire action takes place either in or near 'Elsinoor'. Thus Garrick's *Hamlet* shows greater respect than Shakespeare's for the unities of place and time. It also reduces the number of bodies on stage at the close: Laertes survives as, apparently, does the Queen. 'Frenchified' was the shorthand term used by Garrick's contemporaries to identify what was different about his alteration of *Hamlet*. Thus, Francis Gentleman, for example, complained that, in omitting the grave-diggers, Garrick had 'too politely frenchified' the play.[95]

It may be relevant that Garrick made his first visit to Paris as a tourist in 1751, enjoying frequent theatre-going, sightseeing and socialising. Yet, fully to appreciate the boldness of his altered *Hamlet*, one must see it in a wider historical context. The victories of British forces during the Seven Years War (1756–1763), and the colonial acquisitions gained under the

Treaty of Paris, had boosted national self-confidence. Britain was now a major player on the world stage, challenging France for supremacy on cultural as well as military battlefields, with notable success. Besterman writes:

> So far as I can discover, only a few hundred English works appeared in a French dress during the three centuries from the invention of printing to 1750, and perhaps fifteen times as many during the second half of the 18th century, a far greater increase than can be accounted for by improved means of communication and the like – and this enormous acceleration took place although England and France were in bitter conflict during much of this period.[96]

As early as 1761, Voltaire, alarmed by his compatriots' increasing tendency 'to praise everything English at the expense of everything French, particularly in literature, and still more precisely on the stage', had published his *Appel à toutes les nations de l'Europe*. This cry to arms against Anglomania contained, says Besterman, 'a minute summary of *Hamlet*' and an analysis of the language of 'To be or not to be' ('a raw diamond full of flaws') in contrasting translations: the first in rhymed alexandrines, the other in blank verse. To Voltaire, there could be

> no better example of the differences which exist in national taste. When the merits of Shakespeare's plays are appreciated there is no point in talking about the 'rules of Aristotle, and the three unities, and decorum [. . .]. It is obvious that an entire nation can be enchanted without so much trouble being taken'.

Voltaire, according to Besterman, saw *Hamlet* as 'a monstrosity, a monstrosity of genius to be sure, but still a monstrosity'. He was obsessed by the fact that 'this ignorant barbarian had succeeded in holding the attention of successive generations against all the rules, and that he was becoming more and more appreciated everywhere, even in Paris, the home of good taste'. Voltaire was now increasingly seen by the English as Shakespeare's enemy. What response would be appropriate from Garrick, Shakespeare's greatest champion?

Probably the *Appel à toutes les nations* of 1761 was 'that volume of Voltaire which has the critique upon Shakspeare in it', about which Garrick had written to Steevens in 1771 when he had begun to work on his alteration of *Hamlet*.[97] By then, Garrick had made his second, much longer, visit to the Continent. In 1763, on his return to Paris he had been lionised as a major celebrity. Perhaps he had begun to think more about his own French roots (his grandfather had come to England as a Huguenot refugee in 1685). Serious ill health later in the tour prevented a planned visit to Voltaire at Ferney. In a letter over which he took considerable trouble – three drafts of it survive – Garrick wrote to explain, and to apologise, adding: '& could I have been the means of bringing our Shakespeare into some favour with Mr Voltaire I should have been happy indeed!'[98] In flattering language that nonetheless made clear that, for the English, adoration of Shakespeare was becoming a quasi-religious duty, he ended his letter: 'No enthusiastic Missionary who had converted the Emperor of China to his religion would have been prouder than I, could I have reconcil'd the first Genius of Europe to our Dramatic faith.' Garrick speaks here as Shakespeare's high priest, *ex cathedrâ*. But a qualifying post-script gives a glimpse of a more private, reflective and analytical Garrick, whose love for Shakespeare, like Jonson's, stopped short this side of idolatry:

PS Tho I have call'd Shakespeare our dramatick faith, yet I must do my countrymen ye Justice to declare, that notwithstanding their deserv'd admiration of his astonishing Powers, they are not bigotted to his errors, as some French Journalists have so confidently affirm'd.

Here Garrick modifies his public stance to align himself more closely with Voltaire's. He acknowledges that 'errors' do exist, and implicitly asserts his right to correct them when he meets them.

Stone and Kahrl record that when Garrick returned to Paris in 1765 a controversy over the respective merits of the French and English dramas was in progress, and Garrick was of course expected to defend Shakespeare.[99] Nevertheless there is no doubt that, in making his 1772 alteration of *Hamlet*, Garrick was hoping to impress his French correspondents. This is clear from the self-congratulatory letters he sent to Pierre-Antoine de Laplace and the Abbé André Morellet following its first performance. The news soon reached Ferney, from whence Garrick eventually received his reward in a gracious reference to his *Hamlet* in Voltaire's letter on Shakespeare, read to the French Academy on 25 August 1776. Intent on cutting England's Bard down to size, Voltaire in this letter gave examples of Shakespeare's indecent and inappropriate language, and his predilection for low characters. Then, after a long and highly critical account of *Hamlet*, and especially of the shocking barbarities of the fifth act, Voltaire quoted Marmontel approvingly:

Nowadays, Shakespeare is always abridged,' he says, 'people refine him; the celebrated Garrick has very recently cut from his theatre the scene of the grave-diggers and almost all the fifth act. Because of this, the play and the author have never received greater acclamation.[100]

Notwithstanding Voltaire's real admiration for Shakespeare and Garrick's genuine respect for Voltaire and private reservations about his idol, both men were now locked into their public roles as, respectively, Shakespeare's fiercest foe and his staunchest defender. Despite the handsome compliment to Garrick in Voltaire's letter to the French Academy, the actor could not be expected to let its denigration of Shakespeare pass without a riposte. Elizabeth Montagu, his friend and fellow crusader, had been in the audience and had sent him a copy. In his reply to her, Garrick mingled religious with military metaphors to deplore Voltaire's article ('this unchristian attack upon Genius'):

> I doubt not, but You have converted Numbers to the faith [a reference to her *Essay on the Writings and Genius of Shakespear* of 1769], not wth Sword as Mahomet did, but by those emanations of Genius, which you have caught from the divinity You have so powerfully, & justly protected & admir'd – this Attack of Voltaire, I hope, is not to pass unnotic'd – If the Champions will not mount with the regulars, the Light horse and hussars must begin a Skirmish –[101]

In her equally flattering response, Mrs Montagu urged Garrick to counter-attack:

> I must say I felt for Shakspeare the anxiety one does for a dead friend, who can no longer speak for himself. When Mr. Garrick was on the stage, I should have defied the utmost malice, as he was then alive, and consequently invincible. Indeed, my dear Sir, you must, from filial piety and paternal duty (for I reckon you both the son and the father of Shakspeare in many respects), defend him against this pert Frenchman.[102]

For by this time, as she acknowledged, Garrick had retired; five months earlier he had played Hamlet for the last time. It was now for others to come to Shakespeare's defence against Voltaire, and in the same month Garrick wrote to Madame Necker that there were 'rods preparing for the Old Gentleman by Several English wits'.[103]

There is no further record of any direct campaigning against Voltaire by Garrick himself in the remaining few years of his life. Meanwhile, Voltaire continued to entertain English visitors by going though his 'anti-Shakespeare' routine. However, to one of these, Richard Neville in 1772, he mentioned his cancelled meeting with Garrick, and continued: 'I am vilified in London as an enemy of Shakespeare; it is true that I am shocked and discouraged by his absurdities, but I am no less struck by his beauties; after my death will be found an edition of his works in which I have marked his fine passages, and in great number.'[104] The long-sought meeting between the two captives of the culture wars never took place; Voltaire died on 30 May 1778, and Garrick outlived him by only eight months.

For reasons of cultural preference, Garrick had certainly frenchified *Hamlet*. More practical considerations also influenced his shaping of the play. In 1772 he was 55 and in poor health. His letters make frequent references to attacks of the stone, gout and headaches; his portraits show a certain stoutness. There were rumours that his powers were in decline. '[W]ill any impartial judicious spectator say that he is the actor he was ten years ago?', enquired the *Town and Country Magazine* in 1773.[105] Also on record is the disappointment of several spectators new to Drury Lane at the signs of age Garrick was displaying as Hamlet by the 1770s. He had given up playing Macbeth in 1768, because of its physical strain. Yet the long role of Hamlet is even more taxing. It demands the greatest bodily exertion from the actor when he is most exhausted. Small wonder, then, that Garrick's alteration omitted both of Hamlet's physical confrontations with Laertes in the final act: the struggle in the grave trap in V.i, and the fencing match in V.ii. In exchange for the loss of these exciting passages, and the popular Ostrick, Garrick's audience heard lines probably not spoken on the London stage since the Restoration.

Jeffrey Johnson considers that Garrick's reinstatements were generally made 'to give characters time to react and to provide proper motivations for their reactions'.[106] More practically, the additions to the roles of Laertes and Polonius in G.II.i and G.III.i, while amusingly pointing up a shared tendency to lecture family members of junior status,[107] provided valuable breathing spaces for the actor cast as Hamlet – particularly following the emotional intensity of his first encounter with the ghost (G.II.ii). This was the taxing scene for which Garrick's performance was most renowned, and of which the descriptions in Lichtenberg's letters and diary (in translation) are probably the most often quoted.[108]

Garrick's alteration of *Hamlet* is a script for performance at a particular theatre at a particular time, under the direction of a particular actor-manager who will either play the leading role himself or occasionally delegate it to a trusted colleague. (Smith played Hamlet at Drury Lane in Garrick's alteration on 4 October 1774 and 23 October 1775.) Garrick was growing tired, and his public knew it. After his return from his Continental sabbatical (1763–1765), the number of his appearances on stage each season sharply declined. Just like tourists such as Lichtenberg, London audiences came, above all, to see him, and he was determined to revise *Hamlet* before he retired. In effect, Garrick was challenging his public to accept *his* version of *Hamlet* while they still had *him*. He had 'destroy'd ye Grave diggers, (those favourites of the people) & almost all of ye 5th Act', and done so specifically in the context of his plans to quit the stage. In the letter from which these words are taken, written in January 1773 to Pierre-Antoine de Laplace, he refers twice to his retirement.

Contemporary critical reactions to Garrick's alteration of *Hamlet* were distinctly mixed. Twelve years later, Thomas Davies wrote: 'To such material changes, in this favourite tragedy, the audience submitted during the life of the alterer; but they did not approve what they barely endured.'[109] Dobson, however, says that most reviewers at the time were highly favourable.[110] Holland quotes praise from the *Westminster Magazine*,[111] while the *London Chronicle* enthused: 'the alterations seem to have been produced by the hand of a master'.[112] (Unfortunately, the latter notice bears signs of having been a puff inserted by Garrick himself.) Garrick's old friend the Reverend John Hoadly wrote to suggest even further changes; he would have preferred an overt love relationship between Hamlet and Ophelia. Against these plaudits can be set the disapproval of, for example, *The Town and Country Magazine*: 'How far the critics will approve these mutations we will not at present determine; but the admirers of Shakespear must certainly be displeased, whenever they find his immortal works thus mutilated.'[113] Garrick was clearly proud of what he had done, and played the title role twelve times before he retired. It is unfair to suggest that audiences 'endured' his alteration simply for the sake of seeing Garrick himself. In the years between his retirement and his death, Garrick's version of *Hamlet* was played frequently at Drury Lane and earned very respectable sums; there were six performances in 1776–1777, seven in 1777–1778 and five in 1778–1779. But the tide which had already turned against French critical principles was also beginning to turn against alteration by re-writing.

Eight months after Garrick's death, the *Morning Chronicle* expressed its astonishment that the Drury Lane managers continued to stage his alteration of *Hamlet*, considering that Shakespeare had been 'materially injured by those [alterations] which Mr. Garrick adopted in complaisance to the French criticks'.[114] Garrick's version had its final performance on 30 October 1779. This was also the first night of Sheridan's *The Critic*, a hilarious burlesque, still funny today, of the conventions and absurdities of blank verse tragedy. The content of this afterpiece may well have contributed to the demise of the main piece. As well as direct quotations from Shakespeare, *The Critic* is full of Shakespearean echoes, such as the heroine's absurdly extended catalogue of the names of flowers and birds, so reminiscent of Perdita.[115] Her later appearance 'stark mad in white satin' (III.i., p. 548, line 3) could not have failed to remind the audience of the Ophelia whom they had just seen. One running gag was Mr Puff's indignation at the amount of 'cutting and slashing' that has been applied to his tragedy, a complaint undoubtedly applicable to the fifth act of Garrick's *Hamlet*. Puff's defence of his ridiculous multiple stabbing scene was all too reminiscent of the final moments of the tragedy just witnessed by the audience:

> Now, gentlemen, this scene goes entirely for what we call SITUATION and STAGE EFFECT, by which the greatest applause may be obtained, without the assistance of language, sentiment, or character: pray mark! (III.i., p. 543, lines 27–30)

When *Hamlet* was next given at Drury Lane (21 April 1780), the grave-diggers and Ostrick were back in the cast.

By this time, prejudice against alteration was gathering strength. Marsden outlines the development from the mid-century of a new critical appreciation of Shakespeare's language, leading inevitably to demands that all alteration should cease.[116] Arthur Murphy's changing attitudes to Garrick's *Hamlet* exemplify this shift. At the time of its first performance he had gaily satirised it in a parodic skit criticising Garrick's reluctance to stage new plays.[117] Twenty-five years later he took a much more serious view of alteration itself:

> The rage for re-touching, and, as it was said, correcting and improving our best authors, was the very error of the times [. . .] and, unhappily, Garrick was infected with the contagion. He lopped, pruned, and cut away, what, he thought, unnecessary branches, and instead of a flourishing tree, left a withered trunk.[118]

(There seems to be a faint unconscious memory here of Mr Puff's complaint: 'The pruning-knife – zounds, the axe! why, here has been such lopping and topping, I shan't have the bare trunk of my play left presently.') Garrick was wrong, says Murphy, because 'the genius of Shakespeare towered above the rules that excluded what he deemed a representation of nature'. Hence the grave-diggers, who are 'an exact imitation of nature', and whose dialogue is 'wonderfully happy', should not have been omitted. Yet Murphy, by then 74 years old, was no

Romantic; he did not regard Shakespeare's text as inviolable, and his surprising conclusion may well have seemed old fashioned to younger readers:

> If Garrick had then used his pruning-knife, and had added from his own invention something of real importance, to bring about a noble catastrophe, he would have shewn his judgement, and might have spared the rest of his labours. It seems, as he never published his alterations, that he saw his error.

Murphy may have been in error himself here. Garrick, of course, published many of his alterations; why his *Hamlet* was not among them is not clear. He was certainly urged to publish it. In 1773 he talked of a plan to bring out his collected works 'in four Vol^{s}', writing to a French friend: 'My alteration of Hamlet is not yet printed, when it is you Shall have it directly, with ye rest, En attendant, till ye whole shall be publish'd togeather.'[119] After Garrick's death, Steevens, in his fierce attack on the altered *Hamlet* that he himself had encouraged the actor to produce, wrote:

> Mr. Garrick had once designed to publish the changes he had made in it, and (as was usual with him in the course of similar transactions) had accepted a compliment from the booksellers, consisting of a set of Olivet's edition of Tully; but, on second thoughts, with a laudable regard to his future credit, he returned the acknowledgment and suppressed the alteration.[120]

Steevens may have had inside knowledge because there is evidence that he at one time assisted Garrick to prepare his alteration for publication. In 1831 Boaden printed a sheaf of notes headed 'Mr. Steevens's Remarks As to the *text* of Shakspeare's play, and Mr. Garrick's alteration of HAMLET', and endorsed by Garrick: 'Mr. Steevens of Hampstead, about "Hamlet," &c'.[121] There is no covering letter to provide a date, and Boaden prints the 'Remarks' as if they were an annex to Steevens's letter of encouragement of 1771. But the notes cannot have been written before December 1772 at the earliest, as in them Steevens refers to Garrick's delivery of certain lines from the newly restored soliloquy 'How all occasions'. Furthermore, Steevens warns: 'In the *Personæ Dramatis* remember to leave out the names of the characters omitted in this alteration of the play', and he gives close attention to the list of editions of *Hamlet* to be cited on that page. The page numbers given by Steevens do not, as Boaden assumed in a footnote, relate to Garrick's preparation copy; in fact they cross-reference almost exactly to Johnson's first edition of 1765. Why this projected printing of the altered *Hamlet* never appeared is unknown; but the mystery provides yet another example of the uneasy relationship between the two men. In fact, Garrick may not have changed his mind as to the merits of his *Hamlet*. When he died it was still being regularly performed, and his original delight at the success of his bold venture may well have remained intact.

In the decade following the performance of Garrick's altered *Hamlet*, signs of the approaching divorce of stage and page begin to be evident. In 1772 Garrick still dominated all matters Shakespearean, straddling the worlds of drama and of literature. While praising and honouring the national bard, enthusiasts, including editors, had not yet reached the point of regarding every line as sacred. They still saw the playhouse, rather than the study, as the proper place to appreciate Shakespeare. But by 1782 a new note could be heard. The article on 'Shakspeare' in *Biographia Dramatica* of that year rejects the 'long and confidently repeated' notion that 'our heroes of the stage' are Shakespeare's '*best commentators*', and calls for 'a line of separation' to be drawn 'between the offices and requisites of the scholar and the mimic'.[122] Garrick had been dead for only three years, but already a gap was opening up between the theatre and the study.

EPILOGUE

Garrick's legacy to Shakespeare studies

With hindsight it can be seen that, had it not been for Garrick, the divorce of page and stage would probably have happened earlier than it did. Logically, the publication by John Bell in 1773–1774 of the scripts performed at the patent houses[1] should have signalled that a rift had opened up, but Garrick's authority held them together. Bell was certainly seen as a threat to more scholarly editions; Johnson's and Steevens's 1773 revision of Johnson's 1765 edition was rushed out early to forestall the appearance of Bell's enterprise, and Steevens's letters to Garrick in late 1773 and early 1774 display his anxiety on the subject. Particularly distressing to Steevens was Garrick's own involvement in Bell's project; he claimed not to believe Bell's assertion that Garrick had offered sanction and assistance. How could Garrick, whose vital help with their own edition had been gratefully acknowledged by Johnson and Steevens in their advertisement, have stooped to give countenance to Bell?

At least part of the answer lay in the fact that Bell's venture honoured Garrick equally with Shakespeare. It was brought forward in the guise of a handsome nine-volume edition, worthy to sit on a gentleman's shelves alongside Warburton and Johnson. Dedicated to Garrick, it came complete with many of the trappings of a scholarly edition: subscribers' list, illustrations, introductions to each play and (very inadequate) 'Notes Critical and Illustrative' by Gentleman. Engraved portraits of Shakespeare and Garrick, of equal size, adorned the first volume. In the dedication, 'The Editors' praised Garrick as 'the best illustrator of, and the best *living comment* [Bell's italics], on Shakespeare, that ever has appeared' and offered him '[t]his compact edition' as thanks for his 'exquisite performance, and judicious remarks'. Bell's advertisement admitted that this was 'not an edition meant for the profoundly learned, nor the deeply studious', but robustly defended the publication of truncated and altered playhouse texts as restoring the plays to 'due proportion and natural lustre, by sweeping off those cobwebs, and that dust of depraved opinion, which Shakespeare was unfortunately forced to throw on them'. The theatres, the advertisement claimed, had been 'generally right in their omissions' of material that a more discriminating age rejected.

During Garrick's acting career, editors of Shakespeare, to a greater or lesser extent, not only saw the playhouse as the primary location for encountering his plays, but accepted that some alteration was necessary to make them fit for modern audiences. Warburton, for example, praised Garrick's alteration of *The Winter's Tale*.[2] The theatre was central to the editors' experience, as it was to the social life of all but the poorest of Londoners. Rowe and Theobald had been playwrights themselves; Johnson too, if only briefly. Capell in his capacity as deputy examiner of plays was closely involved in matters theatrical and had collaborated with Garrick in altering *Antony and Cleopatra* for Drury Lane. Steevens was a frequent playgoer and readily admitted how influential Garrick's performances of Shakespeare had been upon his own interpretations. It was Garrick, he said, who first taught him to admire Shakespeare, and who, in his performances clarified textual difficulties, sometimes by a single look or gesture.[3] As Jacky Bratton has helpfully pointed out, 'British theatre annalists' of the period all shared the assumption 'that Shakespeare is the exemplary dramatist, but that it was on Garrick's stage that his work came to its proper home and finest flower'.[4] Despite Johnson's reservations about Garrick's abilities as a critic and the extent of his old friend's knowledge of the plays,[5] Garrick was regarded by his public as the principal medium through which Shakespeare reached them.

As long as Garrick dominated the stage, editors, consciously or unconsciously, were working in a tradition that aimed to convey to readers, albeit at second hand, an essentially theatrical experience. This is a large claim, but evidence of a shift in editorial focus away from the theatre is discernible when Johnson's and Steevens's first edition (1773)[6] is compared with their second (1778).[7] Often (though not invariably) in the former, scenes are introduced with the formula 'Changes to . . . ' for which, in the latter, a simple statement of location is substituted. Examination of three volumes chosen at random (I, IV and IX) yields the following results:

Number of occurrences of 'Changes to' formula

Vol.	Play	1773	1778
I	*The Merry Wives of Windsor*	10	0
	The Tempest	1	1
	The Two Gentlemen of Verona	2	2
IV	*All's Well that Ends Well*	2	0
	Twelfth Night	5	0
	The Winter's Tale	3	0
	Macbeth	0	0
IX	*Troilus and Cressida*	0	0
	Cymbeline	3	1
	King Lear	7	0

In the case of *Macbeth*, Steevens supplied a note to the 1773 edition, explaining that he had gone back to the First Folio and 'removed such stage-directions as are not supplied by the old copy'. Clearly, Johnson and Steevens were engaged, though far from systematically, in a process of reducing transitory theatrical influences on Shakespeare's enduring works. The retirement of Garrick in June 1776, midway between the dates of their two editions, only accelerated this process. The formulation 'Changes to' reminded playgoers of what they would see in an eighteenth-century theatre; its deletion signalled to readers – or more probably the reader – the need to *imagine* a new location for the scene to follow. When Malone published his definitive edition in 1790, the last vestiges of 'Changes to' were wholly eliminated.[8]

After Garrick's death in 1779 the split between stage and page widened. The publication of alterations of Shakespeare that involved re-writing ended at about the same time. Among the preliminary material to Malone's edition of 1790 is a comprehensive list of alterations with publication details; a few which had not appeared in print, like Garrick's *Hamlet*, are also included. Malone's list effectively ends with the death of Garrick. The entry of most recent date (more than ten years earlier), was Thomas Hull's alteration of *The Comedy of Errors* for Covent Garden. It had been in rehearsal as Garrick lay mortally ill, and opened on 22 January 1779, two nights after his death. The publication of Malone's 1790 edition also marks a further widening of the split between library and theatre. With its sheaves of notes and 746 pages of preliminary matter, it is clearly intended for individual study and not in any sense to evoke the experience of being present during a performance. Hindsight enables us to recognise Malone as the consolidator of the editorial conventions and techniques used to this day in scholarly publishing.[9] But such changes do not happen overnight. While the nineteenth-century editors who were Malone's successors were to pay less and less attention to the performance history and theatrical context of the plays, Malone himself acknowledged two other contributory factors, alongside the scholarly research that was his own speciality, to account for Shakespeare's unquestioned supremacy. He ended his introductory 'Historical Account of the English Stage' at 1741, the year of Garrick's professional debut, with the following tribute:

> Since that time, in consequence of Mr. Garrick's admirable performance of many of his principal characters, the frequent representation of his plays in nearly their original state, and above all, the various researches which have been made for the purpose of explaining and illustrating his works, our poet's reputation has been yearly increasing, and is now fixed upon a basis, which neither the lapse of time nor the fluctuation of opinion will ever be able to shake.[10]

Garrick had been dead for more than a decade when these words were published; Malone had no need to flatter his memory. Yet not only does Malone not downplay the contributions to Shakespeare's abiding status made by Garrick's acting and by frequent performance of (more or less) authentic scripts, he specifically praises Garrick for the 'good taste' that 'led him to study the plays of Shakspeare with more assiduity than any of his predecessors'. Thus Malone retrospectively enrols Garrick into the band of researchers who, like Malone himself, interpret the plays to the public.

Malone might well have revived Pope's term 'stage-editor', though shorn of Pope's contempt, to convey his appreciation of Garrick's contribution to Shakespeare's reputation. But that contribution was already on its way to becoming belittled in the world of literature. Two 'snapshots', taken less than twenty years apart, both prompted by the tombs in Westminster Abbey, illustrate the change. In 1792, W. T. Fitzgerald published in *The Bath Chronicle* a twenty-five-line poem in rhymed couplets, entitled 'Hint for an Inscription to the Memory of Johnson and Garrick'.[11] Equal dollops of praise are lavished upon England's 'sweetest moralist' (line 4) and 'the matchless *Garrick*' (line 11), whose tombs lie side by side beneath 'the shrine of *Shakespeare*' (line 2). Nostalgically, Fitzgerald looks back to an era when the two friends had equally illuminated the Bard:

> Congenial souls! that grac'd a polished age,
> Born to elucidate sweet Avon's page! (lines 18–19)

How different was the reaction of Charles Lamb in 1811. Wandering through the Abbey, he had been 'scandalised' by the 'harlequin figure' adorning Garrick's memorial, and even more so by the 'farrago of false thoughts and nonsense' in his epitaph, which claims equal status for actor and poet.[12] Lamb considered it sacrilege to compare an interpreter – one who simply speaks the words – with the creative genius who originally conceived them. Nor could there be any comparison between the two as human beings. Garrick, he commented scornfully, 'appears to have been as mere a player as ever existed; to have had his mind tainted with the lowest players' vices – envy and jealousy, and miserable cravings after applause', whereas Shakespeare, 'in the plenitude and consciousness of his own powers', exhibited 'noble modesty'. Lamb seems to have believed that his own admiration for Shakespeare gave him insight into Shakespeare's mind. He was unwilling to afford Garrick equal credit, finding himself 'almost disposed to deny to Garrick the merit of being an admirer of Shakspeare'. Certainly, the actor could not have been 'a true lover of his excellencies', or he would not have had any truck with 'such ribald trash as Tate and Cibber'. For Lamb, it seems, the test of a true lover of Shakespeare is adherence to a pure text untainted by the compromises deriving from theatrical conventions, fashion, politics or playhouse economics.

In the thirty years since Garrick's death, a new, individualised approach to appreciating Shakespeare had developed, whose adherents believed that he could be known more profoundly in private study than in a public audience. Marsden locates its origins in critics of the later eighteenth century, for whom

> the subjectivity of the reader and the forces of literary production interlocked at the text, bridging the gap between the reader and the printed page. In this new literary marketplace, the reader was the consumer of printed texts, and dramatic literature was overwhelmingly perceived as text – not performed, but printed. The result was not simply the canonization of Shakespeare but the canonization of his words.[13]

Ironically, Marsden traces the change back to Garrick himself. In 'the schism between Johnson and Garrick, between rational assessment and irrational adoration', it was 'Garrick's Shakespeare that dominated critical discourse'. The critics who reacted against Johnson's 'outmoded theorizing' in his Preface of 1765, proposed 'a variety of new critical standards, focusing especially on the concepts of *character* and *feeling*'. She shows how in the last quarter of the century 'practically every major critic tried his hand at examining Shakespeare's characters in isolation from the plot'. Here Marsden cites as reference Vickers's 'The Emergence of Character Criticism, 1774–1800',[14] an article which contains not a single mention of Garrick. Yet, would it not be extraordinary if powerful performances by popular actors – for example, Quin as Falstaff – had no influence on the development of a species of criticism that was to dominate the following century? Stone was closer to the truth when he spoke of the debt owed to Garrick by eighteenth-century critics, because his

> vital presentation of Shakespeare's characters [was] a proof, acceptable and understandable to the public, of their contention, which grew stronger and clearer the longer Garrick played, that dramatic greatness lay in character delineation and in the whole effect of a play, rather than in selected beauties of speech, in the observance of the rules, or in plot structure.[15]

Clearly, by Lamb's day, a new way of reading Shakespeare had emerged. Whereas Steele in 1722 had written in the preface to his *The Conscious Lovers* that 'the greatest effect of a play in reading is to excite the reader to go see it', Lamb and his contemporaries Coleridge and Hazlitt preferred reading Shakespeare's plays to seeing them. 'It is at this juncture in the history of literary criticism that drama is most firmly commandeered for the practice of private reading', comment Shepherd and Wallis.[16] Not only literary criticism, but also editing and scholarship, came to be affected by a print-based approach that seriously undervalued the theatrical dimension. Thus, Babcock, in *The Genesis of Shakespeare Idolatry 1766–1799,* works in a wholly literary environment.[17] References to the Stratford Jubilee are few and sketchy; Garrick is mentioned only as author of the 'Ode' or as having made some rather regrettable alterations. The contributions to the idolisation of Shakespeare made by Garrick's performances in those alterations, or indeed by the Drury Lane publicity machine, are never mentioned, for Babcock 'reads' his period through the cultural spectacles of nineteenth- and early twentieth-century scholarship.

The aim of this book has been, quite simply, to restore Garrick to a more central position in eighteenth-century Shakespeare studies. Evidence that he sought to present himself as a man of letters can be seen in the frequency with which, in paintings of him in private life, he is shown with a book or pen in his hand. Hogarth depicts him composing the prologue for Samuel Foote's *Taste*. In Batoni's portrait, Garrick holds a Latin and

Italian edition of Terence's comedies. Gainsborough, too, shows him holding a book, while Reynolds has him reading aloud to his wife.[18] The guest list for the first dinner party given by Mrs Garrick in widowhood shows that she continued to set his memory in a literary context. She invited old friends and Club members Johnson, Boswell, Reynolds and Burney, along with Hannah More, Mrs Carter (poet, translator and writer) and Mrs Boscawen, the literary hostess; not a single representative of the theatre was present.[19] The after-dinner conversation recorded by Boswell is all of books and authors.

When Garrick died, he left to the British Museum, along with his collection of early English plays, the statue of Shakespeare made for him by Roubiliac in 1758 to adorn his temple of Shakespeare at Hampton. The figure's resemblance to Garrick himself is striking, and it is believed that Garrick himself posed for it. Today, Garrick-as-Shakespeare is the first image presented to any visitor entering that temple of literature, the British Library. His statue dominates the space it occupies much more powerfully than does the bust of Garrick in the stalls lobby at Drury Lane, and claims a lasting place for Garrick within the world of English letters.

Undoubtedly, Garrick's most enduring contribution to Shakespeare scholarship is his collection of old English plays. By assembling and readily sharing with editors such as Capell and Steevens so many examples of the work of Shakespeare's predecessors and fellow playwrights, he helped to shift the basis for interpreting unfamiliar words from editorial guesswork to systematic comparisons with the usage of other contemporary writers. By leaving the collection to the British Museum, he ensured that this invaluable resource was available to later generations. Lamb might have despised Garrick personally, but as a Shakespeare scholar he was glad enough to make use of what were then called 'the Garrick Plays'.[20] In his introductory letter to the series of extracts he contributed to William Hone's *Table Book*, he called the Garrick Collection 'a treasure rich and exhaustless'.[21] Anderson has shown how vital a resource Garrick's collection has been since 1780 for literary researchers and bibliographers concerned with the sixteenth and seventeenth centuries. For example, the plays were an essential resource for W. W. Greg over the years of preparing his *Bibliography of the English Printed Drama to the Restoration*.[22] As recently as 2004, Lockwood, in tracing the history of a transcript of Marlowe's *Tamburlaine* made by Steevens from a rare volume in Garrick's library, later annotated by Malone and still later owned by the younger Boswell, includes Garrick as one of 'a gathering of scholar collectors' who add value to the provenance of the document.[23]

Now a new generation of researchers is learning to associate the name of Garrick with that of Shakespeare. The British Library web site offers the opportunity to view and compare copies of the twenty-one plays of Shakespeare that were printed in quarto prior to the closing of the theatres in 1642. The provenance of no fewer than forty of the ninety-three quarto texts made available for interrogation – by far the largest single source – is given as 'Garrick'.

As inheritors of the stage/page split that followed Garrick's death, it has taken a long time for editors and scholars of Shakespeare to give due weight to what happens in the playhouse. In seeking to establish a single, fixed, definitive text of each play, the editors of the eighteenth century, and their successors, were pursuing a chimera. Theatre companies, from Shakespeare's day to our own, have always altered scripts by cutting, re-arranging and even at times re-writing them in response to both external and internal factors. These range from the political and cultural climate and changing social attitudes, to the constraints imposed by the size of the company and their individual abilities. The very survival of multiple versions of, for example, *Hamlet*, *King Lear* and *Henry V* is testament to this and provides a direct link between the practices of Shakespeare's theatre and of Garrick's. But later managers were coyer than Garrick about admitting that they dared to alter the Bard. Ironically, Garrick's own enthusiastic bardolatry contributed to the fetishisation of what in his day were already beginning to be perceived as quasi-sacred writings, and so led to the reluctance of later actor-managers like Donald Wolfit (1902–1968) to allow performers to make the slightest deviation from whichever printed text they happened to be using. Even more ironically, those very texts were themselves the products of an editorial process that imposed apparent certainty and finality upon a set of flexible, alterable, performance-driven acting scripts.

Happily, since the Second World War there have been encouraging signs that the rift between stage and page is closing. In academia, the new discipline of Performance Studies has arisen. Leading Shakespeare scholars such as Stanley Wells and Peter Holland, sensitive and open to the power and value of theatrical as well as literary interpretations, have been influential. Meanwhile, the post-war generation of university-educated directors, and their successors, have gained hugely from the study of new critical insights into the plays. Surely the publication in 2007 of a Folio-based *Complete Works*[24] under the auspices of the Royal Shakespeare Company signals a welcome change. On 29 April 2007, during the weekend of Shakespeare's birthday celebrations, Jonathan Bate, co-editor of the *RSC Complete Works*, introduced the new edition to a packed audience in Stratford's new Courtyard Theatre. Working with a group of enthusiastic actors from the company, he demonstrated the significant differences that could result in performance to characterisation and directorial approach from textual changes as minor as the re-assignment of a single speech, the substitution of one word for another or even an adjustment in punctuation. Stage and page, after a long estrangement, are at last developing a warmer and closer relationship based on regained mutual respect. Each recognises that, in Garrick's words, 'each to *Shakespeare*'s genius bows' and that each, as Garrick knew, has much to learn from and to teach the other.

Notes

PROLOGUE GARRICK'S ALTERATIONS OF SHAKESPEARE – A NOTE ON TEXTS

1 *Romeo and Juliet* (first published 1748), *Catharine and Petruchio* (1756), *Florizel and Perdita* (1758), *Cymbeline* (1762), *A Midsummer Night's Dream* (with George Colman, 1763) and *King Lear* (1773). *Macbeth* was published in 1773, 'as performed'. Garrick's truncated version of *Hamlet* (first performed in 1772) was not published in full until 1981.

2 David Garrick, *The Plays of David Garrick: A Complete Collection of the Social Satires, French Adaptations, Pantomimes, Christmas and Musical Plays, Preludes, Interludes, and Burlesques, to Which Are Added the Alterations and Adaptations of the Plays of Shakespeare and Other Dramatists from the Sixteenth to the Eighteenth Centuries*, Harry William Pedicord and Fredrick Louis Bergmann (eds.), 7 vols. (Carbondale, IL: Southern Illinois University Press, 1980–1982). The editors do not explain why volumes 3 and 4 are labelled 'Garrick's adaptations of Shakespeare' and volumes 5–8 'Garrick's alterations of others'.

3 See Pedicord and Bergmann (eds.), *Plays of Garrick*, III and IV. The twelve titles (with dates of first performance as given by Pedicord and Bergmann in parentheses) are *Macbeth* (1744); *Romeo and Juliet* (1748); *The Fairies. An Opera* (1755, from *A Midsummer Night's Dream*); *Catharine and Petruchio* (1756, from *The Taming of the Shrew*); *Florizel and Perdita. A Dramatic Pastoral* (1756, from *The Winter's Tale*); *The Tempest. An Opera* (1756); *King Lear* (1756); *Antony and Cleopatra* (1759); *Cymbeline* (1761); *A Midsummer Night's Dream* (1763); *Hamlet* (1772); *The Tempest* (1773).

4 *William Shakespeare, The Complete Works*, Stanley Wells and Gary Taylor (gen. eds.), (Oxford: Clarendon Press, 1986).

5 Stanley Wells, Intro. to *Shakespeare Complete Works*, Wells and Taylor (gen. eds.), p. xxxvii.

GARRICK AND SHAKESPEARE – BEFORE THE DIVORCE OF STAGE AND PAGE

1 W[illiam] O[land], 'Non-pareil; or, Shakespeare and Garrick', *The Gentleman's Magazine*, 49 (April 1779), p. 208.

2 Thomas Davies, *Memoirs of the Life of David Garrick, Esq.*, 2nd edn, 2 vols. (London: Davies, 1780), facsimile (Hildesheim, New York: Georg Olms Verlag, 1972), vol. 1, p. 43.

3 'He the best Player!' cried Partridge with a contemptuous Sneer, 'why I could act as well as he myself. I am sure if I had seen a Ghost, I should have looked in the very same Manner, and done just as he did'. Henry Fielding, *The History of Tom Jones* (1749), Fredson Bowers (ed.), 2 vols. (Oxford: Clarendon Press, 1974), vol. 2, pp. 856–857. For other fictional accounts of the impact of Garrick's performances upon audiences, see Robert Gale Noyes, *The Thespian Mirror: Shakespeare in the Eighteenth-Century Novel* (Providence, RI: Brown University, 1953).

4 Numbers of performances are taken from George Winchester Stone, Jr., and George M. Kahrl, *David Garrick: A Critical Biography* (Carbondale: Southern Illinois University Press, 1979), appendix B, pp. 656–658.

5 See Michael Dobson, *The Making of the National Poet: Shakespeare, Adaptation and Authorship, 1660–1769* (Oxford: Clarendon Press, 1992). On Garrick, see especially chapters 4 and 5, respectively, 'Embodying the author', pp. 135–184, and 'Nationalizing the corpus', pp. 185–222.

6 'Occasional prologue spoken by Mr. Garrick at the opening of Drury-Lane Theatre, 8 Sept. 1750', in David Garrick, *Poetical Works*, 2 vols. (London: George Kearsley, 1785), vol. 1, pp. 102–103, lines 25–26.

7 See Simon Jarvis, *Scholars and Gentlemen: Shakespearean Textual Criticism and Representations of Scholarly Labour, 1725–1765* (Oxford: Clarendon Press, 1995), pp. 46–47.

8 Marcus Walsh, *Shakespeare, Milton, and Eighteenth-century Literary Editing: The Beginnings of Interpretative Scholarship* (Cambridge: Cambridge University Press, 1997), pp. 117, 125 (n. 40) and 196.

9 See James Boswell, *Life of Johnson*, R. W. Chapman (ed.), J. D. Fleeman (corr.) (London, Oxford and New York: Oxford University Press, 1970), pp. 412–413.

10 See James Boaden (ed.), *The Private Correspondence of David Garrick*, 2 vols. (London: H. Colburn and R. Bentley, 1831–1832), vol. 1, p. 23.

11 Anon., 'To David Garrick Esqr. upon his dedication of a temple to Shakespear', MS poem, lines 7–12, ref. Y.d.184 (26), Folger Shakespeare Library.

12 Alexander Pope (ed.), *The Works of Mr. William Shakespear*, 6 vols. (London: Tonson, 1725), *The Life of Henry the Fifth*, vol. 3, pp. 393–499, n. on p. 422.

13 Arthur Murphy, *The Life of David Garrick, Esq.*, 2 vols. (London: J. Wright, 1801).

14 Davies, *Life of Garrick*, vol. 1, p. 114.

15 Murphy, *Life of Garrick*, vol. 2, p. 137.

16 Anon., 'A description of the monument erected in Westminster Abbey, to the memory of the celebrated David Garrick', *Universal Magazine* (August 1797), p. 73.

17 Percy Fitzgerald, *The Life of David Garrick from Original Family Papers and Numerous Published and Unpublished Sources*, 2nd edn (London: Simkin, Marshall, Hamilton, Kent & Co., 1899).

18 See James Boaden, intro. to Boaden (ed.), *Correspondence*, vol. 1, p. liv: 'If there be any one act of his management which we should wish to blot out from these pages, it is his rash violation of the whole scheme of Shakspeare's *Hamlet*.'

19 Joseph Knight, *David Garrick* (London: Kegan Paul, Trench, Trübrier, 1894).

20 Mrs Clement Parsons, *Garrick and His Circle* (London: Methuen, 1906).

21 Frank A. Hedgcock, *A Cosmopolitan Actor: David Garrick and His French Friends* (London: Stanley Paul, 1912).

22 George C. D. Odell, *Shakespeare from Betterton to Irving*, 2 vols. (London: Constable, 1921), vol. 1, pp. 339–340.

23 W. J. Macqueen Pope, *Theatre Royal Drury Lane* (London: W. H. Allen, 1945), p. 166.

24 See Carola Oman, *David Garrick* (London: Hodder and Stoughton, 1958).

25 George Winchester Stone, Jr., 'Garrick's treatment of Shakespeare's plays and his influence upon the changed attitude of Shakespearean criticism during the eighteenth century', Ph.D. thesis, 2 vols. (Harvard University, 1940).

26 Stone and Kahrl, *David Garrick: A Critical Biography*, p. 247.

27 Robert D. Hume cautions against placing too great reliance on the index of *The London Stage* when trying to assess the popularity of Shakespeare, because plays deriving from Shakespeare but with a change of title (such as Lillo's *Marina* and Otway's *Caius Marius*) are indexed under the name of the alterer. See Hume, 'Before the bard: "Shakespeare" in early eighteenth-century London', *ELH*, 64 (Spring 1997), pp. 41–75, at p. 56.

28 *Ibid*., p. 74, n. 35.

29 Hume, is referring (p. 61) to Arthur H. Scouten, 'The increase in popularity of Shakespeare's plays in the eighteenth century: a caveat for interpreters of stage history', *Shakespeare Quarterly*, 7.2 (Spring 1956), pp. 189–202.

30 George Winchester Stone, Jr., 'David Garrick's significance in the history of Shakespearean criticism: A study of the impact of the actor upon the change of critical focus during the eighteenth century', *Publications of the Modern Language Association of America*, 65 (1950), pp. 183–197, at 186.

31 Brian Vickers, 'Shakespearian adaptations: the tyranny of the audience', in *Returning to Shakespeare* (London and New York: Routledge, 1989), pp. 212–233, at 222.

32 See, e.g., Jean I. Marsden, *The Re-imagined Text: Shakespeare, Adaptation, and Eighteenth-Century Literary Theory* (Lexington: University Press of Kentucky, 1995), and *The Appropriation of Shakespeare: Post-Renaissance Reconstructions of the Works and the Myth*, Jean I. Marsden (ed.) (Hemel Hempstead: Harvester Wheatsheaf, 1991).

33 See Stephen Orgel, 'The authentic Shakespeare', in *The Authentic Shakespeare and Other Problems of the Early Modern Stage* (New York and London: Routledge, 2002), pp. 231–256.

34 Peter Holland, 'The age of Garrick', in Jonathan Bate and Russell Jackson (eds.) *Shakespeare: An Illustrated Stage History* (Oxford: Oxford University Press, 1996), pp. 69–91, at 72.

35 Bernard Shaw, Preface to *Three Plays for Puritans* (1900), in *Prefaces* (London: Constable, 1934), pp. 704–721, at 718.
36 See Stanley Wells, *Shakespeare for All Time* (London: Macmillan, 2002), p. 228.
37 See Hume, 'Before the bard', p. 53.
38 Eliza Haywood, *The Female Spectator*, 4 vols. (London: T. Gardner, 1745), vol. 2. 8, pp. 91–92.

THE CONTEXTS OF GARRICK'S ALTERATIONS OF SHAKESPEARE

1 See *The Private Correspondence of David Garrick*, James Boaden (ed.), 2 vols. (London: H. Colburn and R. Bentley, 1831–1832), vol. I, p. 88, Warburton to Garrick, 12 June 1758.
2 Johnson's defence of Tate is founded on his sense of theatre. He writes of Tate's version: 'I cannot easily be persuaded, that [. . .] the audience will not always rise better pleased from the final triumph of persecuted virtue.' Samuel Johnson, notes to *King Lear*, in *Johnson on Shakespeare*, Arthur Sherbo (ed.), 2 vols. (New Haven and London: Yale University Press, 1968), vol. II, pp. 659–705, at p. 704.
3 For Chetwood's advertisement, see, for example, *The Life and Death of King Lear. By Mr. William Shakespear* (London: J. Tonson, and the Rest of the Proprietors, 1734), p. 92.
4 In only nine other roles did Garrick appear more frequently. They include Benedick, Hamlet, Lear and Richard III. For details, see George Winchester Stone, Jr., and George M. Kahrl, *David Garrick: A Critical Biography* (Carbondale: Southern Illinois University Press, 1979), appendix B, pp. 656–658.
5 See Roy Porter, *Enlightenment: Britain and the Creation of the Modern World* (London: Penguin Books, 2000), p. 37.
6 For the many functions of coffee houses, see John Brewer, *The Pleasures of the Imagination: English Culture in the Eighteenth Century* (London: HarperCollins, 1997), p. 35.
7 Thomas Davies, *Memoirs of the Life of David Garrick, Esq.*, 2nd edn, 2 vols. (London: Davies, 1780), facsimile (Hildesheim, New York: Georg Olms Verlag, 1972), vol. II, p. 17.
8 See Brewer, *Pleasures of the Imagination*, p. 39.
9 See *Annals of the Club, 1764–1914* (London: The Club, 1914), pp. 3–23.
10 Brewer, *Pleasures of the Imagination*, p. 40.
11 James Boswell, *Life of Johnson*, R. W. Chapman (ed.), J. D. Fleeman (corr.) (London, Oxford and New York: Oxford University Press, 1970), pp. 339–340.
12 See Joshua Reynolds, *Johnson and Garrick* (London: Printed by Nichols, Son and Bentley, 1816), p. 2.
13 Horace Walpole, *Correspondence*, W. S. Lewis (ed.), vol. 32 (London and New York: Oxford University Press, Yale University Press, 1965), p. 171, letter to Lady Ossory, 14 December 1773.

14 See Oliver Goldsmith, 'Retaliation', in *Collected Works*, Arthur Friedman (ed.), 5 vols. (Oxford: Clarendon Press, 1966), vol. IV, pp. 341–359.

15 Garrick produced his alteration of Fletcher's *The Chances* at Drury Lane in 1754; *Rule a Wife and Have a Wife* followed in 1756. Both were liked and found a place in the repertoire. His alteration of Jonson's *Every Man in His Humour* (1751) was one of his greatest successes. Hugh Kelly, a former friend of Goldsmith, wrote sentimental comedies. The friends fell out in 1768 when Garrick presented Kelly's *False Delicacy* in opposition to Covent Garden's production of Goldsmith's *The Good Natur'd Man*. Garrick was widely believed to have touched up Kelly's plays. For example, Walpole, writing of Kelly's *School for Wives*, comments: 'Garrick has at least the chief hand in it'; see Walpole, *Correspondence*, vol. XXXII, p. 170.

16 Richard Cumberland, *Memoirs* (London: Lackington, Allen & Co., 1806), p. 463.

17 James Boswell, *The Journal of a Tour to the Hebrides with Samuel Johnson, LL.D* (London: J. M. Dent, 1931), p. 80.

18 For example, *The Revels History of Drama in English*, 8 vols. (London: Methuen, 1975–1983), vol. 5, *1660–1750*, John Loftis *et al.*, and vol. 6, *1750–1880*, Michael R. Booth *et al.*; Allardyce Nicoll, *The Garrick Stage: Theatres and Audience in the Eighteenth Century*, Sybil Rosenfeld (ed.) (Manchester: Manchester University Press, 1980); Harry William Pedicord, *The Theatrical Public in the Time of Garrick* (Carbondale: Southern Illinois University Press, 1954); Cecil Price, *Theatre in the Age of Garrick* (Oxford: Basil Blackwell, 1973); Joseph Donohue (ed.), *The Cambridge History of British Theatre*, vol. 2, *1660–1895*, (Cambridge: Cambridge University Press, 2004); and of course the relevant volumes of *The London Stage 1660–1800, A Calendar of Plays, Entertainments & Afterpieces Together with Casts, Box-receipts and Contemporary Comment Compiled from the Playbills, Newspapers and Theatrical Diaries of the Period*, 5 parts (Carbondale: Southern Illinois University Press, 1960–1968). See also, for a succinct modern summary, Lisa A. Freeman, *Character's Theater: Genre and Identity on the Eighteenth-century English Stage* (Philadelphia: University of Pennsylvania Press, 2002). Freeman's study excludes Shakespearean alterations.

19 See *Letters of Sir Joshua Reynolds*, John Ingamells and John Edgcumbe (eds.) (New Haven, CT: Yale University Press for the Paul Mellon Centre for Studies in British Art, 2000), letters nos. 41, 42 and 43, pp. 52–53.

20 Michael R. Booth, 'Public taste, the playwright and the law', in Michael R. Booth *et al.*, *Revels History of Drama*, vol. VI, pp. 29–57, at p. 30.

21 Pedicord, *Theatrical Public in the Time of Garrick*, appendix C, pp. 198–218, at p. 198.

22 Davies, *Life of Garrick*, vol. I, p. 127.

23 See David Garrick, 'Prologue to 'tis well it's no worse', in *The Poetical Works of David Garrick, Esq.*, 2 vols. (London: George Kearsley, 1785), vol. II, pp. 263–265.

24 Prices and capacities in this section are from Anon., 'A teller's account of a crowded house at *Drury Lane* theatre', *Theatrical Monitor*, 18 (16 April 1768), 2–6.

25 Samuel Johnson, 'Prologue spoken at the opening of the theatre in Drury Lane 1747', in *Poems*, E. L. McAdam, Jr. (ed.) with George Milne (New Haven and London: Yale University Press, 1964), pp. 87–90, at p. 89, line 53. Garrick spoke the prologue on the first night of his management, 15 September 1747, and on 16, 17 and 19 September.

26 See *The Letters of David Garrick*, David M. Little and George M. Kahrl (eds.), 3 vols. (London: Oxford University Press, 1963), no. 178, vol. I, p. 256.

27 Prologue to *The Tempest, An Opera* in Harry William Pedicord and Fredrick Louis Bergmann (eds.), *The Plays of David Garrick*, 7 vols. (Carbondale: Southern Illinois University Press, 1980–1982), vol. III, pp. 267–300.

28 Pedicord and Bergmann (eds.), *Plays of Garrick*, vol. III, pp. 272–273, lines 97–102.

29 David Garrick, *Harlequin's Invasion; or, A Christmas Gambol* (1759) in Pedicord and Bergmann (eds.), *Plays of Garrick*, vol. I, pp. 199–225, I.i.50–53.

30 For more on this topic, see Michael Dobson, *The Making of the National Poet: Shakespeare, Adaptation and Authorship, 1660–1769* (Oxford: Clarendon Press, 1992), pp. 198–207. On *Harlequin's Invasion*, and its predecessor *Harlequin Student* (1741), see also Jonathan Bate, *Shakespearean Constitutions: Politics, Theatre, Criticism 1730–1830* (Oxford: Clarendon Press, 1989), pp. 27–28.

31 Pedicord, *Theatrical Public in the Time of Garrick*, p. 5.

32 Davies, *Life of Garrick*, vol. I, p. 111.

33 'Epilogue spoken by Mrs. Woffington, at the Opening of Drury-Lane Theatre, 1747', in *Poetical Works of Garrick*, vol. I, pp. 96–98, lines 1–6.

34 Mrs Clive was one offender. See Davies, *Life of Garrick*, vol. II. p. 192. Davies himself was said to be guilty of the same fault. See Philip H. Highfill, Kalman A. Burnim and Edward A. Langhans, *A Biographical Dictionary of Actors, Actresses, Musicians, Dancers, Managers and Other Stage Personnel in London, 1660–1800*, 16 vols. (Carbondale: Southern Illinois University Press, 1973–1993), vol. IV, p. 208.

35 Frances Burney, *Evelina* (1778), Kristina Straub (ed.) (Boston: Bedford Books, 1997), p. 126.

36 Burney, *Evelina*, p. 124.

37 For an account of the culture of tears throughout Europe at this period, see Jean Benedetti, *Garrick and the Birth of Modern Theatre* (London: Methuen, 2001), pp. 28–29.

38 *Boswell's London Journal 1762–1763*, Frederick A. Pottle (ed.) (London: Heinemann, 1950), pp. 256–257.

39 Thomas Davies, *Dramatic Miscellanies*, 2nd edn, 3 vols. (London: Davies, 1784), vol. II, pp. 17–18.

40 Boswell, *Journal of a Tour to the Hebrides*, p. 330.

41 William Whitehead, 'To Mr. Garrick' (1747), in *Poems on Several Occasions, with the Roman Father, a Tragedy* (London: Dodsley, 1754), pp. 102–106, at p. 105.

42 Apparently Garrick was not paid for altering old plays. In 1768 he wrote to his brother George: 'You know what sums I have given to y[e] house in altering

Romeo – *Every Man*, &c &c &c without fee or reward – nay have had y[e] most ungratefull return for it –'. See Little and Kahrl (eds.), *Letters of Garrick*, letter no. 512, vol. II, p. 618.

43 For an account of the play's origins in classical comedy, see J. W. Lever, introduction to *Every Man in His Humour: A Parallel-text Edition of the 1601 Quarto and the 1616 Folio*, J. W. Lever (ed.) (London: Edward Arnold, 1972), pp. xiv–xv. All quotations from Jonson's 1601 quarto or 1616 folio are taken from Lever's parallel text edition, and act/scene/line references are preceded by 'Q.' or 'F.', respectively.

44 See R. V. Young, 'Ben Jonson and learning', in Richard Harp and Stanley Stewart (eds.), *The Cambridge Companion to Ben Jonson* (Cambridge: Cambridge University Press, 2000), pp. 43–57, at p. 46. Young also explains (p. 47) that in this play a humour can also mean an affectation.

45 See Boaden (ed.), *Correspondence*, vol. I. p. 64, 4 May 1756, Warbuton to Garrick.

46 See *A Catalogue of the Library, Splendid Books of Prints, Poetical and Historical Tracts of David Garrick, Esq.* (London: 1823).

47 Advertisement to the 1752 edition in Pedicord and Bergmann (eds.), *Plays of Garrick*, vol. VI, p. 53. All quotations from Garrick's alteration of *Every Man in His Humour* are from this edition, and act/scene/line references are preceded by 'G.'

48 *Ibid.* pp. 54–55.

49 Martin Butler, 'Jonson's London and its theatres', in Richard Harp and Stanley Stewart (eds.), *The Cambridge Companion to Ben Jonson* (Cambridge: Cambridge University Press, 2000), pp. 15–29, at p. 22.

50 By 1751, Garrick was already well established in his self-assigned public role of Shakespeare's greatest fan, and a note printed on the verso of the title page of *Every Man in His Humour* in the 1640 folio could not have failed to catch his attention. Heading the list of 'principal Comedians' when the play was 'First Acted in the yeare 1598' is 'Will. Shakespeare'. This information from Ben Jonson, *Works*, C. H. Herford, Percy and Evelyn Simpson (eds.), 11 vols. (Oxford: Clarendon Press, 1925–1952), vol. III, p. 403. In the first folio of 1616, details of the play's first performance, including the list of actors, appear at the *end* of the play.

51 Lever, parallel-text edition, pp. xxiv–xxvi. *Cf. Othello* III.iii.187–188 and 287–288.

52 On 11 March 1759 Garrick wrote to the earl of Bute about *Every Man in His Humour* : 'the Language & Characters of Ben Jonson (and particularly of the Comedy in question) are much more difficult than those of any other Writer, & I was three years before I durst venture to trust the Comedians with their Characters, when it was first reviv'd –'. See Little and Kahrl *Letters of Garrick*, no. 227, vol. I, pp. 303–304.

53 Davies, *Life of Garrick* vol. I, p. 50.

54 Douglas Grant, in his notes to Churchill's *Rosciad*, says that 'Mrs. Davies as an actress received little respect, but her beauty was generally praised'. See

Charles Churchill, *Poetical Works*, Douglas Grant (ed.) (Oxford: Clarendon Press, 1956), n. 320, p. 462. He quotes the anonymous *Theatrical Examiner: An Enquiry into the Merits and Demerits of the Present English Performers in General* (London: J. Doughty, 1757), p. 53: 'Mrs D ... s is a showy *figure*, and her *figure* plays her parts.'

55 Ian McIntyre, *Garrick* (London: Allen Lane, The Penguin Press, 1999), p. 195.

56 Pedicord and Bergmann (eds.), *Plays of Garrick*, vol. VI, p. 53. They note that some later editions slightly amended the advertisement so that it ended: 'the distance of 150 years had rendered some of the humour too obsolete to be hazarded in the representation at present'.

57 Davies, *Life of Garrick*, vol. II, p. 296.

58 *Ibid.*, vol. I, p. 112. Here, and in *Dramatic Miscellanies*, Davies writes in such detail about rehearsals for *Every Man in His Humour* that it is surprising to note that he, unlike his wife, never played in it at Drury Lane.

'TO GIVE THE ACTOR MORE ECLAT' – GARRICK'S EARLIEST ALTERATIONS OF SHAKESPEARE

1 See, for example, *Shakspeare's Romeo and Juliet: A Tragedy, Adapted to the Stage by David Garrick; Revised by J. P. Kemble: As Acted at the Theatre Royal Drury Lane* (London: T. Rodwell, 1818). The Folger Shakespeare Library holds Kemble's promptbook of 1811, which includes Garrick's final scene for the lovers.

2 Robert D. Hume, 'Before the Bard: "Shakespeare" in early eighteenth-century London', *ELH*, 64 (1997), 41–75, at p. 47.

3 *Macbeth*, 'as performed at the Theatre Royal, Drury-Lane', was the first play to be printed in Bell's edition of *Shakespeare's Plays. As They Are Now Performed at the Theatres Royal in London ; Regulated from the Prompt Books of Each House, by Permission*, 9 vols. (London: John Bell and C. Etherington, 1773–1774), vol. I, pp. 1–71. The title page of each volume is dated 1774, although the early volumes appeared late in 1773. Each play has its own separate title page; *Macbeth* 's is dated 1773.

4 William Davenant, *Macbeth, a Tragedy* (1674), in Christopher Spencer (ed.), *Five Restoration Adaptations of Shakespeare* (Urbana: University of Illinois Press, 1965), pp. 33–107. All quotations from Davenant's *Macbeth* are from this edition, and act/scene/line references are prefixed by 'D'. For a summary of this version's playing history, and of the changes to Shakespeare made by Davenant, see Christopher Spencer's introduction to *Five Restoration Adaptations of Shakespeare*, pp. 14–16.

5 Samuel Johnson, *Miscellaneous Observations on the Tragedy of Macbeth* (1745), in Arthur Sherbo (ed.), *Johnson on Shakespeare*, 2 vols. (New Haven and London: Yale University Press, 1968), vol. I, pp. 3–45. All quotations from *Miscellaneous Observations* are from this edition.

6 W. Jackson Bate, *Samuel Johnson* (New York and London: Harcourt Brace Jovanovich, 1977), p. 227.

7 See George Winchester Stone, Jr., 'Garrick's handling of *Macbeth*', *Studies in Philology*, 38 (1941), 609–28, at pp. 614–615. Stone is supported by a comment in an anonymous pamphlet (probably by Garrick), *An Essay on Acting: In which Will Be Consider'd the Mimical Behaviour of a Certain Fashionable Faulty Actor, and the Laudableness of such Unmannerly, as well as Inhumane Proceedings. to which Will Be Added a Short Criticism on His Acting Macbeth* (London: W. Bickerton, 1744). The writer (p. 2) expresses shock that the public should flock to see '*Macbeth Burlesqu'd*, or *Be . . g . .k* 'd [. . .] when they might read *Mr. Theobald's Edition of him*, without throwing away their Money'. See Lewis Theobald (ed.), *The Tragedy of Macbeth*, in *The Works of Shakespeare*, 2nd edn, 8 vols. (London: H. Lintott, C. Hitch, J. and R. Tonson, C. Corbet, R. and B. Wellington, J. Brindley and E. New (1740), vol. VI, pp. 267–345.

8 Samuel Johnson, *Proposals for Printing, by Subscription, the Dramatick Works of William Shakespeare* (1756), in Arthur Sherbo (ed.), *Johnson on Shakespeare*, vol. I, pp. 51–58, at p. 51.

9 Act/scene/line references preceded by 'G' are to *Macbeth, A Tragedy* (1744), in Harry William Pedicord and Fredrick Louis Bergmann (eds.), *The Plays of David Garrick*, 7 vols. (Carbondale: Southern Illinois University Press, 1980–1982), vol. III, pp. 6–74.

10 Scrope went on to ask permission to publish the emendation which, 'not having met with it in print', he regarded as Garrick's private property. Dr Scrope clearly had not read Johnson's *Miscellaneous Observations*, and admitted that he had not read Johnson's first edition (1765) of the *Plays*. Garrick's reply has not survived. For the full text of Dr Scrope's letter, see *The Private Correspondence of David Garrick*, James Boaden (ed.), 2 vols. (London: H. Colburn and R. Bentley, 1831–1832), vol. I, pp. 342–343.

11 Samuel Johnson, *The Rambler*, W. J. Bate and A. B. Strauss (eds.), 3 vols. (New Haven and London: Yale University Press, 1969), no. 168 (1751), vol. III, pp. 125–129, at p. 127. Act/scene/line references not preceded by 'D' or 'G' are to *The Tragedy of Macbeth*, in *William Shakespeare: The Complete Works*, Stanley Wells and Gary Taylor (gen. eds.) (Oxford: Clarendon Press, 1986), pp. 1099–1126.

12 Johnson, *Miscellaneous Observations*, p. 23. Davenant had deleted the line in its entirety.

13 Stone, 'Garrick's handling of *Macbeth*', p. 615.

14 See John Nichols, *Literary Anecdotes of the Eighteenth Century*, Colin Clair (ed.) (Fontwell: Centaur Press, 1967), p. 393; also Stone, 'Garrick's handling of *Macbeth*', p. 614.

15 Warburton's 'crotchety edition' (Franklin's description) of *The Works of Shakespear* did not appear until 1747; see Colin Franklin, *Shakespeare Domesticated* (Aldershot: Scolar Press, 1991), pp. 24–25. Bate speaks of Johnson's gratitude for the praise, albeit anonymous, that Warburton in his edition gave to *Miscellaneous Observations* ; see W. Jackson Bate, *Samuel Johnson*, p. 228.

16 Boaden (ed.), *Correspondence*, head-note to vol. I, p. 63.

17 *Ibid.*, pp. 74–75, Warburton to Garrick, 19 December 1756.
18 See David M. Little and George M. Kahrl (eds.), *The Letters of David Garrick*, 3 vols. (Cambridge, MA: Harvard University Press, 1963), vol. II, p. 726, letter no. 622, 6 February 1771, to Peter Fountain.
19 Boaden (ed.), *Correspondence*, vol. I, pp. 412–413, 18 February 1771. Warburton strongly disapproves of the '[e]ditions on editions of our immortal favourite [that] are daily springing up', brought out by 'all these idiots'. His greatest contempt is heaped upon 'one Capell': 'While others have procured for themselves the advantage of being embalmed alive in the liquid amber of the poet, this man seems to have been only able to gibbet himself above ground over his grave.'
20 The original portrait was destroyed in a fire in 1946; we know it now only through copies and engravings. For more details of the commission, see Rosie Broadley *et al.*, exhibition catalogue *Every Look Speaks: Portraits of David Garrick* (Bath: Holburne Museum of Art, 2003), pp. 65–67.
21 Arthur Murphy, *The Life of David Garrick, Esq.*, 2 vols. (London: J. Wright, 1801), vol. I, p. 71.
22 Garrick's 1773 text shows that he rose to the challenge and restored the entire speech except for the notoriously difficult 'th'assassination [. . .] success' (lines 2–4). See G.I.vii.1–8.
23 *The Diary of Samuel Pepys*, Robert Latham and William Matthews (eds.), vol. 8 (London: G. Bell and Sons, 1974), p. 171.
24 The flying witches became so essential a feature that Rowe, in his 1709 edition, inserted a stage direction at the end of the first scene: 'They rise from the stage, and fly away.' Theobald retained the direction, as did Johnson.
25 Joseph Addison, *The Spectator*, no. 45 (21 April 1711), Donald F. Bond (ed.), 5 vols. (Oxford: Clarendon Press, 1965), vol. I, pp. 191–195, at p. 194. Addison was complaining of the lady's noisiness, a bad habit that she had picked up in France.
26 Scouten (ed.), *The London Stage Part 3*, vol. II, p. 673.
27 Thomas Davies, *Dramatic Miscellanies*, 2 vols. (London: Davies, 1784), vol. II, p. 116.
28 Stone, 'Garrick's Handling of *Macbeth*', p. 618.
29 See Kalman A. Burnim, *David Garrick, Director* (Pittsburgh: University of Pittsburgh Press, 1961), p. 109. Working from a prompt-book based on the 1773 Bell edition, now in the Folger Library, Burnim gives a fascinating scene-by-scene account of how *Macbeth* would have been staged at Drury Lane during, or shortly after, Garrick's reign.
30 Davies, *Dramatic Miscellanies*, vol. II, p. 118.
31 Paul Prescott, 'Doing all that becomes a man: The reception and afterlife of the Macbeth actor, 1744–1889', *Shakespeare Survey*, 57 (2004), 81–95.
32 Dennis Bartholomeusz, for example, in *Macbeth and the Players* (Cambridge: Cambridge University Press, 1969), in his chapter 'Garrick and Mrs Pritchard' (pp. 38–81), attempts to discover how Garrick played the role by studying Garrick's correspondence, press reports and contemporaries' accounts, and by

drawing conclusions from textual alterations. For a brief account of Garrick's approach to the role, and of some contemporaries' views thereon, see also Simon Williams, 'Taking Macbeth out of himself: Davenant, Garrick, Schiller and Verdi', *Shakespeare Survey*, 57 (2004), 54–68. See also, Burnim, *David Garrick, Director*, pp. 108–125. More recently, James P. Lusardi and June Schlueter, in '"I have done the deed": *Macbeth* 2.2', in Frank Occhiogrosso (ed.), *Shakespeare in Performance* (Newark and London: University of Delaware Press and Associated University Presses, 2003), pp. 71–83, have included Garrick's and Mrs Pritchard's interpretations in their historical survey of performers' approaches to the play.

33 Anon., *An Essay on Acting*.

34 George Winchester Stone, Jr., and George M. Kahrl, *David Garrick: A Critical Biography* (Carbondale: Southern Illinois University Press, 1979), call the pamphlet (p. 550) 'a mocking attack upon himself'. Ian McIntyre in *Garrick* (London: Allen Lane, The Penguin Press, 1999), p. 85, concurs.

35 Stephen Orgel, 'The authentic Shakespeare', in *The Authentic Shakespeare and Other Problems of the Early Modern Stage* (New York and London: Routledge, 2002), pp. 231–256, at p. 246.

36 McIntyre, *Garrick*, p. 84.

37 Brian Vickers, *Shakespeare: The Critical Heritage*, 6 vols. (London and Boston: Routledge & Kegan Paul, 1974–1981), vol. III, p. 130.

38 See Harry William Pedicord, '*Ragandjaw* : Garrick's Shakespearian parody for a private theatre', *Philological Quarterly*, 60.2 (1981), 197–204, which includes the full text (186 lines) of Garrick's extremely vulgar parody of the tent scene in *Julius Caesar*, including the quarrel between Brutus [Brutarse] and Cassius [Cassiarse], written for private theatricals in 1746.

39 Francis Gentleman, in his note to the Bell edition of 1773, vol. I, p. 51, commented: 'Here *Shakespeare* [. . .] has given us a most trifling superfluous dialogue, between Lady *Macduff*, *Rosse*, and her son, merely that another murder may be committed, on the stage too. We heartily concur in, and approve of, striking out the greatest part of it.'

40 See Marvin Rosenberg, 'Macbeth and Lady Macbeth in the eighteenth and nineteenth centuries', in John Russell Brown (ed.), *Focus on Macbeth* (London, Boston and Henley: Routledge & Kegan Paul, 1982), pp. 73–86, esp. p. 73.

41 Davies, *Dramatic Miscellanies*, vol. II, p. 152.

42 For an interesting discussion of these pictures, see Stephen Leo Carr and Peggy A. Knapp, 'Seeing through *Macbeth*', *Publications of the Modern Language Association of America*, 96.5 (October 1981), 837–847.

43 James Boswell, *Life of Johnson*, R.W. Chapman (ed.), J. D. Fleeman (corr.) (Oxford: Oxford University Press, 1970), p. 616.

44 Sherbo (ed.), *Johnson on Shakespeare*, vol. II, p. 795.

45 Anon., 'Remarks on the Tragedy of the Orphan', *Gentleman's Magazine*, 18 (November 1748), 502–506, at p. 503.

46 Sherbo (ed.), *Johnson on Shakespeare*, vol. II, p. 795.

47 Peter Holland, 'The age of Garrick', in Jonathan Bate and Russell Jackson (eds.), *The Oxford Illustrated History of Shakespeare on Stage* (Oxford: Oxford University Press, 2001), pp. 69–91, at p. 87.
48 Francis Gentleman, *The Dramatic Censor; or, Critical Companion*, 2 vols. (London: J. Bell and C. Etherington, 1770), vol. I, p. 104.
49 Bartholomeusz, *Macbeth and the Players*, p. 78.
50 Stanley Wells, *Shakespeare for All Time* (London: Macmillan, 2002), p. 217.
51 Burnim, *David Garrick, Director*, p. 125.
52 McIntyre, *Garrick*, p. 83.
53 Stone, 'Garrick's handling of *Macbeth* ', p. 619.
54 Jean Georges Noverre, *Letters on Dancing and Ballets,* Cyril W. Beaumont (trans.) (London: Beaumont, 1930), p. 82.
55 *Ibid.*, p. 84.
56 Colley Cibber, *The Tragical History of King Richard III* (1700), in *Five Restoration Adaptations of Shakespeare*, Christopher Spencer (ed.) (Urbana: University of Illinois Press, 1965), pp. 273–344, V.v.60–68. Cibber's preface (p. 279) explains the typography. Italicized lines are 'intirely *Shakespear's* '; those preceded by a single inverted comma 'are generally his thoughts, in the best dress I could afford 'em'; the rest are wholly Cibber's.
57 Desmond Shawe-Taylor, ' "The Beautiful Strokes of a Great Actor": Garrick and his painters', in Broadley *et al.*, *Every Look Speaks*, pp. 11–30, at p. 14.
58 Davies, *Dramatic Miscellanies,* vol. II, p. 118.
59 *Shakespeare's Plays. As They Are Now Performed,* vol. I, p. 69.
60 Wells, *Shakespeare for All Time*, p. 217.
61 For the contents of Garrick's collection, see George M. Kahrl, in collaboration with Dorothy Anderson, *The Garrick Collection of Old English Plays: A Catalogue with an Historical Introduction* (London: The British Library, 1982); for the *Faustus* editions, see items 699–702 of the catalogue.
62 Russ McDonald, *Shakespeare and the Arts of Language* (Oxford: Oxford University Press, 2001), pp. 158–159.
63 Little and Kahrl (eds.), *Letters of Garrick*, vol. II, p. 670, letter no. 565, [?] October 1769, to Charles Macklin.
64 *The Historical Tragedy of Macbeth (Written Originally by Shakespear) Newly Adapted to the Stage, with Alterations, as Performed at the Theatre in Edinburgh* (Edinburgh: W. Cheyne, 1753). No author is cited. On the title page is printed this forlorn warning: 'NB. Whoever shall presume to print or publish this Play, shall be prosecuted to the Extent of the Law, and no Copies are authentick but such as are signed by Edward Salmon.' The signature of Edward Salmon, prompter, appears on the copies held in the New York Public Library and British Library.
65 *The Historical Tragedy of Macbeth, (Written Originally by Shakespeare:) With the Songs, Alterations and Additions* (Dublin: W. Whitestone, 1761). The Dublin text is single spaced whereas the Edinburgh version is double spaced. The Dublin text omits the list of *errata* appended (p. 88) to the earlier version, and there are very occasional slight differences in spelling,

capitalisation and bracketing conventions. Otherwise the two appear to be identical.

66 For a full account of John Lee's career, see Philip H. Highfill, Jr., Kalman A. Burnim and Edward A. Langhans, *A Biographical Dictionary of Actors, Actresses, Musicians, Dancers, Managers & Other Stage Personnel in London, 1660–1800*, 16 vols. (Carbondale: Southern Illinois University Press, 1973–1993), vol. IX, pp. 201–209.

67 Lee is said to have made an alteration of *Romeo and Juliet* for Edinburgh, but there is no record of its being published. See James C. Dibdin, *The Annals of the Edinburgh Stage* (Edinburgh: Richard Cameron, 1888), p. 73. Dibdin speculates (p. 74) that an alteration of *Much Ado about Nothing* published in Edinburgh in 1754 was also made by Lee.

68 See, for example, the advertisement appearing in the *Bath and Bristol Chronicle*, 19 January 1769, p. 4, for a performance 'with the Original Music, Dance, and New Decorations'. Lee and Mrs Lee are billed as playing Macbeth and Lady Macbeth, for the latter's benefit. Also noteworthy is that two of the three speaking witches were to be played by women.

69 See Little and Kahrl (eds.), *Letters of Garrick*, vol. II, pp. 837–838, letter no. 726, 17 December [1772?], to Grey Cooper.

70 For Macklin's 'old Caledonian' *Macbeth*, see Rebecca Rogers, 'How Scottish was "the Scottish play?" *Macbeth*'s national identity in the eighteenth century', in Willy Maley and Andrew Murphy (eds.), *Shakespeare and Scotland* (Manchester: Manchester University Press, 2004), pp. 104–123, at pp. 108–111.

71 Pedicord and Bergmann (eds.), *Plays of Garrick*, vol. III, p. 398.

72 Jonathan Bate, 'The romantic stage', in Jonathan Bate and Russell Jackson (eds.), *The Oxford Illustrated History of Shakespeare on Stage* (Oxford: Oxford University Press, 2001), pp. 92–111.

73 For publishing details of these editions and reprintings, see Pedicord and Bergmann (eds.), *Plays of Garrick*, vol. III, p. 413. Each volume of Bell's *Shakespeare's Plays. As They Are Now Performed* is preceded by a title page dated 1774, though the earliest volumes came out in time for the Christmas trade in 1773. The individual plays are dated either 1773 (vols. 1–5) or 1774 (vols. 6–8). *Romeo and Juliet* is in the second volume.

74 See 'To the reader' (1748), 'Advertisement' (1750), 'Advertisement' (1753), in Pedicord and Bergmann (eds.), *Plays of Garrick*, vol. III, pp. 77–79. All quotations from Garrick's alteration of *Romeo and Juliet* are from this edition (vol. III, pp. 75–149) and are preceded by 'G.'

75 Thomas Otway, *The History and Fall of Caius Marius* (1680), in J. C. Ghosh (ed.), *The Works of Thomas Otway*, 2 vols. (Oxford: Clarendon Press, 1932), vol. I, pp. 433–519, 'Prologue', p. 437, lines 30–33.

76 'Mr. Cibber opened with a full house, and Romeo and Juliet, or rather Caius Marius.' See Little and Kahrl (eds.), *Letters of Garrick*, vol. I, pp. 43–45, letter no. 28, 16 September 1744, to Somerset Draper, p. 43.

77 The passages from *Caius Marius* are I.318–359, II.89–209 and IV.34–85. See Theophilus Cibber, *Romeo and Juliet, A Tragedy* (London: C. Corbett and

G. Woodfall, 1748), facsimile (London: Cornmarket Press, 1969), pp. 7–8, 11–13 and 42–43, respectively.

78 Otway, *Caius Marius*, V.361–410; *cf.* Cibber, *Romeo and Juliet*, pp. 62–63.

79 See *The Prompter*, 10 (11 November 1789), 58. The article is anonymous, but Vickers identifies the author as James Fennell, For an account of Otway's and Cibber's alterations, see George C. Branam, 'The Genesis of David Garrick's *Romeo and Juliet*', *Shakespeare Quarterly*, 35.2 (Summer 1984), 170–179. Branam shows (pp. 172–173) that Sheridan made his alteration for the 1746–1747 Dublin season. 'Mr. Marsh' is presumably Charles Marsh.

80 Nancy Copeland, 'The source of Garrick's *Romeo and Juliet* text', *English Language Notes*, 24.4 (June 1987), 27–33.

81 Sherbo (ed.), *Johnson on Shakespeare*, vol. II, pp. 939–957.

82 'To the reader', in *Romeo and Juliet* (1748), Pedicord and Bergmann, *Plays of Garrick*, vol. III, p. 77. The original title page described the play as 'By Shakespear. With some ALTERATIONS, and an additional SCENE : As it is Performed at the *Theatre-Royal*, in *Drury-Lane*'.

83 Johnson, 'Preface to Shakespeare' (1765), in Sherbo (ed.), *Johnson on Shakespeare*, vol. I, pp. 59–113, at p. 74.

84 See Vickers, Introduction to *Shakespeare: The Critical Heritage*, vol. VI, p. 36. But Vickers mentions some, including Capell, who, exceptionally, took a contrary view.

85 For a scene-by-scene account of cuts made in film and stage productions, and of the interpretations of actors and directors during and since the eighteenth century, see James N. Loehlin (ed.), *Shakespeare in Production: Romeo and Juliet* (Cambridge: Cambridge University Press, 2002), pp. 89–251.

86 George Winchester Stone, Jr., '*Romeo and Juliet* : The source of its modern stage career', *Shakespeare Quarterly*, 15.2 (Spring 1964), 191–206, at p. 192. Stone's article contains a detailed act-by-act account of Garrick's cuts and scene transpositions.

87 Loehlin, *Shakespeare in Production: Romeo and Juliet*, p. 242, n. 2.

88 Nancy Copeland, 'The sentimentality of Garrick's *Romeo and Juliet*', *Restoration and Eighteenth-century Theatre Research*, 4.2 (Winter 1989), 1–13, at pp. 7–8.

89 MacNamara Morgan, *A Letter to Miss Nossiter Occasioned by Her First Appearance on the Stage: In which Is Contained Remarks Upon Her Manner of Playing the Character of Juliet* (London, 1753), p. 49.

90 Jay L. Halio, '*Romeo and Juliet* in performance', in Frank Occhiogrosso (ed.), *Shakespeare in Performance: A Collection of Essays* (Newark and London: University of Delaware Press and Associated University Presses, 2003), pp. 58–70, at p. 61. The 'acting edition' from which Halio worked (London: Tonson, 1763) continues for a further fifty lines after Juliet's suicide.

91 For details, see Branam, 'The genesis of David Garrick's *Romeo and Juliet*', p. 176.

92 Little and Kahrl (eds.), *Letters of Garrick*, vol. I, p. 153, letter no. 93, 27 July 1750. Miss Bellamy was not new to the role. She had played Juliet opposite Lee at Covent Garden in the previous season (1749–1750).

93 David Garrick, 'An occasional epilogue, spoken by Mrs. Clive, at Drury-Lane Theatre, October, 1750', in *The Poetical Works of David Garrick, Esq.*, 2 vols. (London: George Kearsley, 1785), vol. I, pp. 104–106, lines 9–10.

94 Little and Kahrl (eds.), *Letters of Garrick*, vol. I, pp. 156–157, letter no. 96, 13 October 1750, to the countess of Burlington.

95 Sherbo (ed.), 'Notes on *King Lear*' (1765), in *Johnson on Shakespeare*, vol. II. pp. 659–705, at p. 704.

96 Nevertheless, Gentleman's comment in the Bell 1773–1774 edition, II. 98, has some force: 'This masquerade scene, is well designed to give *Romeo* an opportunity of unfolding himself: but we rather think the lady's catching fire, so very suddenly, shows her to be composed of tinder-like materials.'

97 See Arthur Murphy (writing as 'Theatricus'), 'Free remarks on the tragedy of *Romeo and Juliet*', *The Student*, 2, 58–64, at p. 62. The essay is dated 20 October 1750.

98 Fennell, *The Prompter*, pp. 10, 58–59. *Cf.* Johnson's comment: 'Juliet plays most of her pranks under the appearance of religion; perhaps Shakespeare meant to punish her hypocrisy.' See Sherbo (ed.), *Johnson on Shakespeare*, vol. II, p. 953.

99 Murphy, 'Free remarks on *Romeo and Juliet*', p. 63. For a fuller account of contemporary critical reactions to the funeral processions, both favourable and otherwise, see Burnim, *David Garrick, Director*, pp. 136–137.

100 See Count Frederick Kielmansegge, *Diary of a Journey to England in the Years 1761–1762*, Countess Kielmansegg (trans.) (London: Longmans, Green & Co., 1902), pp. 221–222.

101 Loehlin, *Shakespeare in Production: Romeo and Juliet*, p. 19.

102 These details are taken from Brian Gibbons's introduction to *Romeo and Juliet*, Brian Gibbons (ed.) (London: Arden, 1980), p. 36.

103 Charlotte Lennox, *Shakespear Illustrated: or the Novels and Histories, On which the Plays of Shakespear Are Founded, Collected and Translated from the Original Authors. With Critical Remarks*, 3 vols. (London: A. Millar, 1753–1754), published anonymously, as 'By the Author of the Female Quixote'. For an account of what he calls '[t]his labour of learning and originality', see Franklin, *Shakespeare Domesticated*, pp. 224–225 and 228–233. For the dedication written by Johnson to *Shakespear Illustrated*, see Sherbo (ed.), *Johnson on Shakespeare*, vol. I, pp. 47–50.

104 Rintz shows that Garrick cut from his 1753 edition three lines for Juliet that were particularly closely based on Otway (G.V.iv.196–198). See Don Rintz, 'Garrick's "protective reaction" to a charge of plagiarism', *Restoration and Eighteenth-century Theatre Research*, 14.1 (1975), 31–35. However, Pedicord and Bergmann (eds.), in *Plays of Garrick*, vol. III, p. 143, seventh footnote, indicate that the lines were included in 1753, but cut from editions of 1754 onwards.

105 Copeland, 'The sentimentality of Garrick's *Romeo and Juliet*', p. 8.

106 Jean I. Marsden, *The Re-imagined Text: Shakespeare, Adaptation, and Eighteenth-century Literary Theory* (Lexington: University Press of Kentucky, 1995), p. 90.

'RE-BOTTLING' SHAKESPEARE – GARRICK IN MID-CAREER (1753–1768)

1 For the creation of Shakespeare as national Bard, see Michael Dobson, *The Making of the National Poet: Shakespeare, Adaptation and Authorship, 1660–1769* (Oxford: Clarendon Press, 1992), especially chapter 5, 'Nationalizing the corpus', pp. 185–222.

2 Samuel Johnson, 'Proposals for printing, by subscription, the dramatick works of William Shakespeare' (1756), in Arthur Sherbo (ed.), *Johnson on Shakespeare*, 2 vols. (New Haven and London: Yale University Press, 1968), vol. I, pp. 51–58, at p. 56. In naming his predecessors, Johnson conspicuously did *not* mention Hanmer.

3 For details of these contributors, see Arthur Sherbo, *The Birth of Shakespeare Studies: Commentators from Rowe (1709) to Boswell-Malone (1821)* (East Lansing, MI: Colleagues Press, 1986), pp. 15–26. Warburton was unique in not acknowledging the help given by other commentators in preparing his edition.

4 The note supplied by Garrick (to *Hamlet* I.v.156) refers to the custom of swearing on one's sword. It cites the historian Pierre de Bourdeille, and thus demonstrates the actor's ability to read, in the original, the French of a contemporary of Shakespeare. For details, see James Gray, '"Swear by my sword": A note in Johnson's *Shakespeare*', *Shakespeare Quarterly*, 27.2 (Spring 1976), 205–208. This is the only note in the whole of Johnson's *Shakespeare* to refer to Garrick by name.

5 For modern editions of these libretti, see Harry William Pedicord and Fredrick Louis Bergmann (eds.), *The Plays of David Garrick*, 7 vols. (Carbondale: Southern Illinois University Press, 1980–1982), vol. III, pp. 151–186 (*The Fairies*) and vol. III, pp. 267–300 (*The Tempest*). In the prologue to *The Fairies* (pp. 155–156) Garrick jokes:

> I dare not say WHO wrote it – I could tell ye,
> To soften matters – Signor Shakespearelli. (lines 31–32)

The prologue to the operatic version of *The Tempest* is discussed in Chapter 2, this volume. For more about the challenge posed by opera in Italian, see Ian Woodfield, *Opera and Drama in Eighteenth-century London: The King's Theatre, Garrick and the Business of Performance* (Cambridge: Cambridge University Press, 2001).

6 Although Garrick did not appear in it, this alteration was very popular and became a staple item in the Drury Lane repertoire until his retirement. For further details, and an account of Garrick's various stagings of *The Tempest* between 1747 and 1776 (including the Dryden/Davenant version), see George Winchester Stone, Jr., 'Shakespeare's *Tempest* at Drury Lane during Garrick's management', *Shakespeare Quarterly*, 7.1 (Winter 1956), 1–7. For a broader discussion of changing cultural attitudes to the play, and of the increasing identification of Prospero with Shakespeare himself, see also Michael Dobson, '"Remember/first to possess his books": The appropriation of *The Tempest*, 1700–1800', *Shakespeare Survey*, 43 (1990), 99–107.

7 *Cymbeline. A Tragedy. By Shakespear. With Alterations.* (London: J. and R. Tonson, 1762). Published anonymously, this was the most popular, and the most frequently reprinted, of the several alterations of the play made between the Restoration and Garrick's death. The other alterers were D'Urfey, 1682; Marsh, 1755; Hawkins, 1759 and Brooke, 1778. For details, see George C. Branam, *Eighteenth-century Adaptations of Shakespearean Tragedy* (Berkeley and Los Angeles: University of California Press, 1956), p. 182. For a modern edition, see Pedicord and Bergmann (eds.), *Plays of Garrick*, vol. IV, pp. 95–169.

8 Quoted in George Winchester Stone, Jr. (ed.), *The London Stage Part 4, 1747–1776*, 3 vols. (Carbondale: Southern Illinois University Press, 1962), vol. II, p. 1021.

9 For a full account of the successive modifications of *A Midsummer Night's Dream* by Garrick and Colman, see George Winchester Stone, Jr., '*A Midsummer Night's Dream* in the hands of Garrick and Colman', *Publications of the Modern Language Association of America*, 54 (1939), 467–482. As ever, Stone's object was to defend Garrick from blame for the play's failure in November 1763. Stone consulted the copy of the text printed by Tonson in 1734 (held in the Folger Shakespeare Library) in which Garrick had made his amendments, as well as Colman's autograph list of further changes, together with the version published in Garrick's absence. For a sympathetic account of Garrick's approach to *A Midsummer Night's Dream*, see Peter Holland, 'The age of Garrick' in Jonathan Bate and Russell Jackson (eds.), *The Oxford Illustrated History of Shakespeare on Stage* (Oxford: Oxford University Press, 2001), pp. 69–91, at pp. 79–82.

10 Ann Thompson, intro. and ed., *The Taming of the Shrew* (Cambridge: Cambridge University Press, 2003), p. 20. For a modern edition of *Catharine and Petruchio*, see Pedicord and Bergmann (eds.), *Plays of Garrick*, vol. III, pp. 187–220.

11 Though billed on first performance as *The Winter's Tale*, the alteration was first published (London: Tonson, 1758) as *Florizel and Perdita, a Dramatic Pastoral, in Three Acts. Alter'd from The Winter's Tale of Shakespear. By David Garrick*. Quotations from the text are from Pedicord and Bergmann (eds.), *Plays of Garrick*, vol. III, pp. 221–266, and are preceded by 'G'. The prologue is at pp. 223–225.

12 Brian Vickers, *Returning to Shakespeare* (London and New York: Routledge, 1989), pp. 224–225.

13 Theophilus Cibber, *Dissertations on Theatrical Subjects* (London: Griffiths, 1756), p. 36. Cibber's jealous diatribe envisages '*Shakespear*'s ghost' rising to condemn 'this pilfering pedlar in poetry [. . .] who thus shamefully mangles, mutilates, and emasculates his plays'.

14 Gary Taylor, *Reinventing Shakespeare* (London: The Hogarth Press, 1990), p. 120. Taylor could have gone on to point out that *The Winter's Tale* had scarcely been 'forsaken' until Garrick turned his attention to it: it had been revived in London as recently as the early 1740s.

15 Horace Howard Furness, preface to New Variorum edition of *The Winter's Tale*, H. H. Furness (ed.), 5th edn (Philadelphia: J. B. Lippincott Co., 1898), p. xiii.

16 George Winchester Stone, Jr., 'Garrick's treatment of Shakespeare's plays and his influence upon the changed attitude of Shakespearean criticism during the eighteenth century', Unpublished Ph.D. Thesis, 2 vols. (Harvard University, 1940), vol. I, p. 257.
17 See Branam, *Eighteenth-century Adaptations*, pp. 5–7.
18 Samuel Johnson, notes to *The Winter's Tale* (1765) in Sherbo (ed.), *Johnson on Shakespeare*, vol. I, p. 310.
19 The term 'the rules' has been avoided since, as Jean Marsden has shown, by the mid-century most critics demonstrated a 'strong antirule sentiment'. See Jean I. Marsden, *The Re-imagined Text: Shakespeare, Adaptation, and Eighteenth-century Literary Theory* (Lexington: University Press of Kentucky, 1995), pp. 108–109. Even the conservative Johnson, Garrick's early mentor, concluded in his famous preface that 'the unities of time and place are not essential to a just drama'. See Samuel Johnson, 'Preface to Shakespeare' (1765), in Sherbo (ed.), *Johnson on Shakespeare*, vol. I, pp. 59–113, at p. 80. In his only play, however, he was careful to observe those unities. See Samuel Johnson, *Irene* (London: R. Dodsley, 1749), facsimile (Ilkley: The Scolar Press, 1973).
20 Thomas Davies, *Memoirs of the Life of David Garrick, Esq.*, 2nd edn, 2 vols. (London: Davies, 1780), facsimile (Hildesheim and New York: Georg Olms Verlag, 1972), vol. I, p. 277. Davies played Camillo in Garrick's alteration.
21 'Shakespeare had here introduced a bear – a most fit actor for pantomimes or puppet shows; but blushing criticism has excluded the rough gentleman', wrote Francis Gentleman in his notes to *The Winter's Tale*, vol. III, p. iii. See *Shakespeare's Plays. As They Are Now Performed at the Theatres Royal in London; Regulated from the Prompt Books of Each House by Permission*, 9 vols. (London: John Bell and C. Etherington, 1773–1774), vol. V, pp. 149–225, at p. 185.
22 Gentleman, intro. to *The Winter's Tale*, in Bell's *Shakespeare's Plays. As They Are Now Performed*, vol. V, p. 151. He is commenting upon an alteration made by '[t]he ingenious Mr. Hull, of Covent-Garden'. The title page classifies the play as 'A tragedy' – a perfectly logical attribution, since it deals with the misfortunes of persons of royal birth.
23 See Janet Todd, *Sensibility: An Introduction* (London: Methuen, 1986). See also Markman Ellis, *The Politics of Sensibility: Race, Gender and Commerce* (Cambridge: Cambridge University Press, 1996), esp. pp. 5–48.
24 For details, see Marvin Spevack, *A Complete and Systematic Concordance to the Works of Shakespeare*, 9 vols. (Hildesheim: Georg Olms Verlag, 1968–1980), vol. I, pp. 1252–1260.
25 Garrick's re-written and condensed version of the scene conflates Second and Third Gentleman in the person of Camillo. It can be assumed that the serious and dignified Thomas Davies would have played these lines absolutely straight, and this is confirmed by Garrick's cutting the affectation of 'caught the water, though not the fish'.
26 'I could wish that You would think of giving a Comedy of Character to y[e] Stage – One calculated more to make an Audience Laugh, than cry – the

Comedie Larmoyante is getting too Much ground upon Us, & if those who can write the better Species of y[e] Comic drama don't make a Stand for y[e] Genuine Comedy & vis comic the Stage in a few Years, will be (as Hamlet says) like Niobe all tears – ', he wrote to the Revd Charles Jenner. See Little and Kahrl (eds.), *Letters of Garrick*, vol. II, pp. 689–690, letter no. 583, 30 April 1770.

27 Compare, for example, Harriet Byron: 'O the blessing of a benevolent heart!' in Samuel Richardson, *The History of Sir Charles Grandison* (1753–1754), Jocelyn Harris (ed.), 3 parts (London: Oxford University Press, 1972), vol. II, p. 134. Richardson and Garrick were on good if not intimate terms. A very flattering reference to Garrick appeared in the third volume of *Clarissa*. For Garrick's letter of thanks, see Little and Kahrl (eds.), *Letters of Garrick*, vol. I, p. 95, letter no. 56, 12 December 1748. In September 1753, Richardson sent an advance copy of *Sir Charles Grandison* to the Garricks. For their enthusiastic reception of this favour, see letter no. 133, 4 September 1753, vol. I, pp. 201–202.

28 See *The Private Correspondence of David Garrick*, James Boaden (ed.), 2 vols. (London: H. Colburn and R. Bentley, 1831–1832), vol. II, p. 122, Steevens to Garrick, 'Tuesday night', [?] January 1775.

29 Marsden, *The Re-imagined Text*, p. 86. Garrick's Polixenes is also presented as a family man. His line 'Kings are no less unhappy, their issue not being gracious' (IV.ii.26–27) is altered to 'Fathers are no less unhappy . . . ' (G.I.i.84).

30 A concomitant reason for expanding Hermione's part in the statue scene could have been that the role was taken by Mrs Pritchard, one of the Drury Lane company's three leading actresses in the 1755–1756 season. The second, Mrs Cibber, played Perdita; the third, Mrs Clive, played Catharine in the afterpiece, *Catharine and Petruchio*.

31 Irene G. Dash, 'A penchant for Perdita on the eighteenth-century English stage', in *The Woman's Part: Feminist Criticism of Shakespeare*, Carolyn Ruth Swift Lenz, Gayle Greene and Carol Thomas Neely (eds.) (Urbana: University of Illinois Press, 1980), pp. 271–284, at p. 274.

32 See Macnamara Morgan, *The Sheep-shearing, or, Florizel and Perdita. A Pastoral Comedy Taken from Shakespear* (London: J. Truman, 1762). The English Short Title Catalogue (ESTC) warns that 'the imprint may be fictitious'. Although *The Sheep-shearing* was new to London, it had previously been performed in Dublin.

33 A slightly longer version is given in a later edition; see *The Sheep-shearing: or, Florizel and Perdita. A Pastoral Comedy. Taken from Shakespear. As It Is Acted at the Theatre-Royal in Dublin. The Songs Set by Mr. Arne* (Dublin: Peter Wilson, 1767), p. 27.

34 *Florizel and Perdita. A Dramatic Pastoral, in Three Acts, Alter'd from The Winter's Tale of Shakespear. by David Garrick. As It Is Performed at the Theatre Royal in Drury-Lane* (London: J. and R. Tonson, 1758). By contrast, Morgan's two-act *The Sheep-shearing, or, Florizel and Perdita,*when published in London in 1762, was shown on the title page as 'a pastoral comedy'.

35 See Gerald Maclean, Donna Landry and Joseph P. Ward, introduction to *The Country and the City Revisited: England and the Politics of Culture, 1550–1850,*

Gerald Maclean, Donna Landry and Joseph P. Ward (eds.) (Cambridge: Cambridge University Press, 1999), pp. 1–23.

36 The full list of mainpiece comedies given at Drury Lane between 13 September 1755 and 17 January 1756, with author and numbers of performances in brackets following the title, is as follows: *As You Like It* (Shakespeare, 2); *Every Man in His Humour* (Jonson, altered by Garrick, 2); *Love for Love* (Congreve, 1); *Love Makes a Man* (Colley Cibber, 1); *Much Ado about Nothing* (Shakespeare, 2); *The [Beaux'] Stratagem* (Farquhar, 2); *The Alchemist* (Jonson, altered by Garrick, 5); *The Careless Husband* (Colley Cibber, 2); *The Chances* (Fletcher, altered by Buckingham and later by Garrick, 2); *The Conscious Lovers* (Steele, 2); *The Drummer* (Addison, 1); *The Fair Quaker of Deal* (Charles Shadwell, 9); *The Inconstant* (Farquhar, 1); *The Man of Mode* (Etheredge, 1); *The Provok'd Wife* (Vanbrugh, altered by Garrick, 3); *The Recruiting Officer* (Farquhar, 1); *The Rehearsal* (Buckingham, heavily cut by Garrick, 5); *The Relapse* (Vanbrugh, 1); *The Suspicious Husband* (Hoadly, 3).

37 Davies, *Life of Garrick*, vol. I, p. 278.

38 For details, see Mary E. Knapp, *A Checklist of Verse by David Garrick* (Charlottesville: University of Virginia Press, 1955), p. 58.

39 A slip-song, *The Sheep-sheering Song. A New Song Sung by Mr. Beard at the Theatre Royal in Covent-Garden* ('Come, come, my good shepherds, our flocks we must sheer'), is held in the British Library. It was not unusual to hand out song-sheets.

40 See James Boswell, *Life of Johnson*, R. W. Chapman (ed.), J. D. Fleeman (corr.) (London, Oxford and New York: Oxford University Press, 1970), p. 408.

41 In a prompt-book made on a copy of the first edition (1758) of Garrick's alteration, now held in the Folger Shakespeare Library, two new songs for Florizel and other notes relating to Drury Lane have been inserted in a hand that is either Garrick's or Colman's. There are also significant cuts, notably the first and last scenes. For detailed discussion, see Irene Dash, 'Garrick or Colman?' *Notes and Queries*, 216 (April 1971), 152–155; also Harry William Pedicord, 'George Colman's adaptation of Garrick's promptbook for *Florizel and Perdita*', *Theatre Survey*, 22.2 (1981), 185–190. If Pedicord is correct in assigning the inserted songs to Garrick, then they date from the Drury Lane revival in the 1761–1762 season. In that case, the prompt-book must have been used later by Colman to make further cuts some time prior to his production of *The Sheep-shearing* at the Haymarket on 18 July 1777.

42 Davies, *Life of Garrick*, vol. I, p. 279.

43 The confusion is evident in the index of *The London Stage Part 4*, for example, and even, in at least one instance, in the catalogue of the British Library. For an account of the difficulties that scholars have faced in trying to attribute performances to authors correctly, see Dash, 'Garrick or Colman?' This chapter's conclusions are based on *The London Stage Part 4*, but not on its index. For the randomness of this index in relation to alterations of *The Winter's Tale*, see Judith Milhous and Robert D. Hume, 'The Drury Lane Theater Library in 1768', *Yale University Library Gazette*, 68.3–4 (April 1994), 116–134, at p. 132.

44 Charles Marsh, *The Winter's Tale, a Play, Alter'd from Shakespear* (London: Charles Marsh [Sen.], 1756). The biographical information about Marsh contained in this chapter is drawn from Valerie Edden's introduction to the facsimile published by the Cornmarket Press (London: Cornmarket Press, 1970).

45 Edden, intro. to Marsh's *Winter's Tale*, p. iii.

46 Thomas Hull, 1728–1808, actor, singer, manager, playwright, novelist. His career at Covent Garden lasted 48 years, and included a period (1775–1776 to 1781–1782) as acting manager. He made two alterations of *The Comedy of Errors* (1762 and 1779), and one of *Timon of Athens* (1786). For a full account of his career, see Philip H. Highfill, Jr., Kalman A. Burnim and Edward A. Langhans, *A Biographical Dictionary of Actors, Actresses, Musicians, Dancers, Managers and Other Stage Personnel in London, 1660–1800*, 16 vols. (Carbondale: Southern Illinois University Press, 1973–1993), vol. VIII, pp. 32–40.

47 Marsh, *The Winter's Tale*, V.iii, p. 78.

48 *The Winter's Tale*, V.ii, in Bell's *Shakespeare's Plays. As They Are Now Performed*, vol. V, p. 225.

49 See *The Sheep-shearing: A Dramatic Pastoral. In Three Acts. Taken from Shakespeare. As It Is Performed at the Theatre Royal in the Hay-Market* (London: G. Kearsly, 1777). The British Library catalogue lists George Colman the elder as author, but erroneously attributes the facsimile published by Cornmarket (London: Cornmarket Press, 1969) to Macnamara Morgan.

50 Dash states that 'Hermione was not always retained in stage productions of *Florizel and Perdita*', citing as evidence the omission of 'the entire last section, the statue scene' from the text included in *Dramatic Works of David Garrick, Esq.*, 3 vols. (London: A. Millar, 1798), vol. I, pp. 242–275; see Dash, 'A penchant for Perdita', p. 279, and p. 284, n. 18. Unfortunately, this edition is faulty; it is identified in Cardiff University's catalogue as a false imprint. All other texts in this volume mark their endings either in words (usually 'Finis') or with a pictorial colophon, often with both. *Florizel and Perdita* has neither and ends abruptly at G.III.iii.47, before the conclusion of the penultimate scene. But Mrs Pritchard as Hermione is listed among the *dramatis personae*, and Paulina's invitation to the reunited royal families to view her statue (G.III.ii.96–106) is included. This looks more like a printer's error than evidence of a change of mind on Garrick's part.

51 See Stone, 'Garrick's treatment of Shakespeare's plays', vol. I, pp. 255–263. See also Pedicord and Bergmann (eds.), *Plays of Garrick*, vol. III, pp. 434–435.

52 For information about the Lord Chamberlain's department and the system of pre-censorship of plays in the eighteenth-century theatre, this chapter has drawn largely upon L. W. Conolly, *The Censorship of English Drama 1737–1824* (San Marino: The Huntington Library, 1976).

53 For details of the system of fees charged ('quite illegal', says Conolly), see Conolly, *Censorship*, pp. 16–17.

54 See Little and Kahrl (eds.), *Letters of Garrick*, vol. I, p. 332, letter no. 260, 3 December 1760, to Capell.

55 Conolly, *Censorship*, p. 31.

56 *Ibid.*, p. 73. The examples Conolly gives of the changes on political grounds that Capell occasionally required from Garrick are very trivial; see pp. 75–76.

57 See Conolly, *Censorship*, pp. 137–139. Conolly records (pp. 144–146) only one wholesale rejection by Capell ('not fit to be acted') of an entire piece. This was a farce by Joseph Reed, *The Universal Register Office*, submitted by Garrick and his partner Lacy in March 1761. Capell objected to the frequent *double entendres* arising from the linking of sexual and religious language. See also G. J. Barker-Benfield, *The Culture of Sensibility: Sex and Society in Eighteenth-century Britain* (Chicago and London: University of Chicago Press, 1992), pp. 297–299.

58 George M. Kahrl in collaboration with Dorothy Anderson, *The Garrick Collection of Old English Plays: A Catalogue with an Historical Introduction* (London: The British Library, 1982), pp. 7–15.

59 For details, see George Winchester Stone, Jr., and George M. Kahrl, *David Garrick: A Critical Biography* (Carbondale: Southern Illinois University Press, 1979), p. 187. Their chapter 'The literary world of scholarship', pp. 165–199, explores very fully Garrick's contributions to that world, his interaction with scholars and his interest in early plays.

60 Boaden (ed.), *Correspondence*, vol. I, p. 355, Warton to Garrick, 23 June 1769.

61 See Kahrl with Anderson, *Garrick Collection*, pp. 34–39.

62 Johnson, 'Proposals for printing the works', in Sherbo (ed.), *Johnson on Shakespeare*, vol. I, p. 55.

63 Johnson, 'Preface to Shakespeare', in Sherbo (ed.), *Johnson on Shakespeare*, vol. I, p. 105.

64 See Boswell, *Life of Johnson*, p. 493.

65 See Boaden (ed.), *Correspondence*, vol. I, p. 183, Johnson to Garrick, 18 May 1765: 'Dear Sir, I know that great regard will be had to your opinion of an edition of Shakspeare. I desire therefore to secure an honest prejudice in my favour by securing your suffrage; and that this prejudice may really be honest, I wish you would name such plays as you would see, and they shall be sent you by, Sir, Your most humble servant, Sam. Johnson.'

66 Boswell, *Life of Johnson*, p. 411. Boswell's other guests in his Old Bond Street lodgings that night included two prominent members of The Club, Reynolds and Goldsmith, as well as Garrick's two earliest biographers, Thomas Davies and Arthur Murphy.

67 *Mr William Shakespeare His Comedies, Histories, and Tragedies, Set Out by Himself in Quarto, or by the Players His Fellows in Folio, and Now Faithfully Republish'd from Those Editions in Ten Volumes Octavo; with an Introduction*, 10 vols. (London: J. and R. Tonson, 1767–1768). Garrick had a set in his personal library. For a full appraisal of Capell's edition, see Alice Walker, 'Edward Capell and his edition of *Shakespeare*', in *Proceedings of the British Academy*, 46 (1960), 131–145.

68 See Boaden (ed.), *Correspondence*, vol. II, pp. 238–239, Capell to Garrick, 18 July 1777. Capell, writing from his Hastings retreat, was convinced that a

conspiracy existed to prevent him from completing the publication of his *Notes and Various Readings of Shakespeare*. For a Victorian attempt to polish up Capell's tarnished reputation, see J. O. Halliwell [Halliwell-Phillipps], *A Few Words in Defence of the Memory of Edward Capell* (London: Privately printed, 1861).

69 *Antony and Cleopatra, an Historical Play, Written by William Shakespeare: Fitted for the Stage by Abridging only; and Now Acted, at the Theatre-Royal in Drury-Lane, by His Majesty's Servants* (London: J. and R. Tonson, 1758). Capell presented a copy to the British Museum nine days after the first performance. For a modern edition, see Pedicord and Bergmann (eds.), *Plays of Garrick*, vol. IV, pp. 1–93.

70 George Winchester Stone, Jr., 'Garrick's presentation of *Antony and Cleopatra*', *Review of English Studies*, 13 (January 1937), 20–38, at p. 25.

71 See Pedicord and Bergmann (eds.), *Plays of Garrick*, vol. IV, p. 398, n. 14.

72 See Stone, 'Garrick's presentation of *Antony and Cleopatra*', p. 28.

73 *Cf.* G.I.ii.1–56. This episode was marked for deletion in the version (not Garrick's alteration) in Bell's *Shakespeare's Plays. As They Are Now Performed*, vol. VI, pp. 259–366. Gentleman commented: 'The whole of this scene might well be spared in representation: it has a blameable relish of indecency' (p. 265).

74 Richard Madelaine, intro. to Richard Madelaine (ed.), *Shakespeare in Production: Antony and Cleopatra* (Cambridge: Cambridge University Press, 1998), p. 33.

75 Little and Kahrl (eds.), *Letters of Garrick*, vol. III, p. 982, letter no. 885, 10 [?] January [?] 1775.

76 Edward Capell (ed.), *Prolusions, or Select Pieces of Antient Poetry* (London: Tonson, 1760), pp. v–vi. The selection included *Edward the Third* ('a Play, thought to be writ by Shakespeare'), a 1599 edition of which was one of the rarities in Garrick's collection of old plays.

77 Edward Capell (ed.), *Mr. William Shakespeare, His Comedies, Histories, and Tragedies*, 10 vols. (London: J. and R. Tonson, 1767–1768). *Antony and Cleopatra* is found in vol. 8. Capell employed his system of marks in that edition, though occasionally one was replaced by a newly composed stage direction. For example, the fourth scene of Act I in Garrick and Capell's 1758 alteration begins: 'You may see, ± Lepidus, and henceforth know', whereas Capell's edition ten years later has: 'You may see, *Lepidus*, and henceforth know [*giving him a letter to read*]'. Only one of the 'conjectural readings' appended to the 1758 alteration (see Pedicord and Bergmann (eds.), *Plays of Garrick*, vol. IV, p. 93) was adopted in Capell's 1768 edition of the play.

78 Samuel Pegge, 'Memoirs of Edward Capell, Esq.', in John Nichols, *Illustrations of the Literary History of the Eighteenth Century*, 8 vols. (London: Nichols, 1817–1858), vol. I, pp. 465–476, at p. 471.

79 For a detailed discussion of Garrick's alteration of *Cymbeline*, see George Winchester Stone, Jr., 'A century of *Cymbeline*; or Garrick's magic touch', *Philological Quarterly*, 54 (1975), 310–322.

80 Pedicord and Bergmann (eds.), *Plays of Garrick*, vol. IV, p. 97, lines 1–9.

81 For an account of Steevens's advertisement 'To the public' of 1 February 1766, see Sherbo, *Birth of Shakespeare Studies*, pp. 27–28.

82 Richard Warner, *A Letter to David Garrick, Esq., Concerning a Glossary to the Plays of Shakespeare, On a More Extensive Plan than Has Hitherto Appeared. To Which Is Annexed, a Specimen* (London: Printed for the author, 1768), p. 92. Sherbo comments that Warner's notes show that he 'quite evidently regarded Shakespeare's plays as just that, plays put on before an audience and with that audience constantly in the playwright's mind'. See Sherbo, *Birth of Shakespeare Studies*, pp. 46–49.

83 Letter from Francis Wheler to William Hunt, 28 November 1767, held in the Shakespeare Birthplace Trust Records Office, ref. no. ER1/38.

84 See Boaden, *Correspondence*, vol. I, pp. 322–323, Wheler to Garrick, December 1768.

85 David Scott Kastan, *Shakespeare and the Book* (Cambridge: Cambridge University Press, 2001), p. 96.

86 See Marsden, *The Re-imagined Text*, chapter 3, 'Adaptation in decline', pp. 75–102, esp. pp. 77–78.

(ENTR'ACTE): CELEBRATING SHAKESPEARE ON PAGE AND STAGE IN 1769

1 D. G., *An Ode upon Dedicating a Building, and Erecting a Statue, to Shakespeare, at Stratford upon Avon* (London: T. Becket and P. A. de Hondt, 1769).

2 David Garrick, *The Jubilee*, in Harry William Pedicord and Fredrick Louis Bergmann (eds.), *The Plays of David Garrick*, 7 vols. (Carbondale: Southern Illinois University Press, 1980–1982), vol. II, pp. 97–126.

3 See, for example, Anon., '[E]xtract of a letter to a gentleman in London', *The Gentleman's Magazine*, 39 (September 1769), 421–423.The best-known record by an eye-witness is Boswell's journal. See Frank Brady and Frederick A. Pottle (eds.), *Boswell in Search of a Wife, 1766–1769* (London: Heinemann, 1957), pp. 295–303, and appendix A, pp. 373–374. For the fullest contemporary account, upon which later writers have heavily relied, see Benjamin Victor, *The History of the Theatres of London and Dublin from the Year 1730 to the Present Time*, 3 vols. (London: T. Davies etc., 1761–1771), vol. III, pp. 200–232. For a lively satirical account in verse, see Edward Thompson, *Trinculo's Trip to the Jubilee* (London: C. Moran, W. Flexney and R. Riddley, 1769).

4 Thomas Davies, *Memoirs of the Life of David Garrick, Esq.*, 2nd edn, 2 vols. (London: Davies, 1780), facsimile (Hildesheim, New York: Georg Olms Verlag, 1972), vol. II, pp. 213–228.

5 Peter Holland, 'The age of Garrick', in Jonathan Bate and Russell Jackson (eds.), *The Oxford Illustrated History of Shakespeare on Stage* (Oxford: Oxford University Press, 2001), pp. 69–91, at pp. 72–75.

6 Ian McIntyre, *Garrick* (London: Allen Lane, The Penguin Press, 1999), pp. 412–432.

7 Jonathan Bate, *Shakespearean Constitutions: Politics, Theatre, Criticism, 1730–1830* (Oxford: Clarendon Press, 1989), pp. 30–31.

8 Susan Green, 'A cultural reading of Charlotte Lennox's *Shakespear Illustrated*', in J. Douglas Canfield and Deborah C. Payne (eds.), *Cultural Readings of Restoration and Eighteenth-century English Theater* (Athens, GA: University of Georgia Press, 1995), pp. 228–257, at p. 241.

9 Péter Dávidházi, ' "He drew the liturgy, and framed the rites": The changing role of religious disposition in Shakespeare's reception', *Shakespeare Survey*, 54 (2001), 46–56.

10 Gillian Russell, 'Theatrical culture', in Thomas Keymer and Jon Mee (eds.), *The Cambridge Companion to English Literature 1740–1830* (Cambridge: Cambridge University Press, 2004), pp. 100–118.

11 Maria Rosaria Cocco, 'Under the mulberry tree: The Garrick/Shakespeare Jubilee of 1769', in Mariacristina Cavecchi and Mariangela Tempera (eds.), *EuroShakespeares: Exploring Cultural Practice in an International Context* (Bologna: University of Bologna, 2002), pp. 7–33.

12 James Quin (1693–1766) first played Falstaff, the role with which he was most identified, at Drury Lane in the 1740–1741 season. His final appearance in the part had been in 1753, after his retirement had officially begun.

13 For an accessible selection of eighteenth-century criticism relating to Falstaff, see Brian Vickers (ed.), *Shakespeare: The Critical Heritage*, 6 vols. (London: Routledge & Kegan Paul, 1974–1981), vol. II, pp. 195, 237–238, vol. III, pp. 122–129, vol. VI, pp. 64–80, 440–446, 469–479 and 490–499.

14 See, for example, Michael D. Bristol, *Big-time Shakespeare* (London and New York: Routledge, 1996), p. 70, and Richard Dutton, *William Shakespeare: A Literary Life* (Basingstoke: Macmillan, 1989), pp. 2–3.

15 Garrick confirmed in a letter to Charles Macklin that in composing these lines he had had in mind 'y[e] Skill of Harry Monmouth To turn & wind a fiery Pegasus [/] And witch y[e] world wth Noble Horsemanship!' See David M. Little and George M. Kahrl (eds.), *The Letters of David Garrick*, 3 vols. (Cambridge, MA: Harvard University Press, 1963), vol. II, pp. 670–674, letter no. 565, undated, probably October 1769.

16 According to Knapp, within the month of September, the Ode was reproduced in *The London Chronicle*, *St. James's Chronicle*, *Lloyd's Evening Post*, *Bath Chronicle*, *Warwickshire Journal*, *Weekly Magazine or Edinburgh Amusement*, *London Magazine*, *Scots Magazine*, *Town and Country Magazine* and *Universal Magazine*. See Mary E. Knapp, *A Checklist of Verse by David Garrick* (Charlottesville: University of Virginia Press, 1955), p. 26.

17 See Little and Kahrl (eds.), *Letters of Garrick*, vol. II, pp. 661–662, letter no. 554, 27 August 1769, to William Hunt.

18 Little and Kahrl (eds.), *Letters of Garrick*, vol. II, p. 668, letter no. 562, 15 October 1769 and vol. II, p. 669, no. 564, September or October 1769.

19 See Little and Kahrl (eds.), *Letters of Garrick*, vol. II, pp. 670–674, letter no. 565, undated.

20 Anon., *The Stratford Jubilee, a New Comedy of Two Acts, as It Has Been Lately Exhibited at Stratford upon Avon, with Great Applause, to Which Is Prefixed Scrub's Trip to the Jubilee* (London: T. Lowndes and J. Bell, 1769). Each act has obviously been set by a different printer: confirmation that the play was rushed out to cash in on public interest in the Jubilee. The play was offered first to Foote for the Haymarket, and then to Colman for Covent Garden. Neither manager accepted it.

21 See, for example, Anon., *Anti-Midas : A Jubilee Preservative from Unclassical, Ignorant, False, and Invidious Criticism* (London: 1769). This defence of the Ode, published anonymously, may have been written by Garrick himself, or at any rate at his behest. It appends (pp. 23–35) a series of very offensive anti-Ode articles signed Longinus, reprinted from the *Public Ledger*. Their author may well have been Thomas Sheridan.

22 *Shakespeare's Garland. Being a Collection of New Songs, Ballads, Roundelays, Catches, Glees, Comic-serenatas, &c. Performed at the Jubilee at Stratford upon Avon. The Musick by Dr. Arne, Mr. Barthelimon, Mr. Ailwood, and Mr. Dibdin* (London: T. Becket and P. A. de Hondt, 1769). Most, but not all, of the items are marked 'By Mr. G.'

23 Quoted in George Winchester Stone, Jr. (ed.), *The London Stage Part 4, 1747–1776*, 3 vols. (Carbondale: Southern Illinois University Press, 1962), vol. III, p. 1425.

24 George Colman, *Man and Wife, or, The Shakespeare Jubilee, a Comedy, of Three Acts, as It Is Performed at the Theatre Royal in Covent Garden*, 2nd edn (London: T. Becket & Co. and R. Baldwin, 1770).

25 See Little and Kahrl (eds.), *Letters of Garrick*, vol. II, pp. 665–666, letter no. 560, 2 October 1769, to Joseph Cradock.

26 Little and Kahrl (eds.), *Letters of Garrick*, vol. II, pp. 675–676, letter no. 567, 4 December 1769, to the Revd Evan Lloyd. Garrick says that *The Jubilee* 'has now had more success than any thing I Ever remember'.

27 First by Elizabeth P. Stein in *Three Plays by David Garrick* (New York: William Edwin Rudge, 1926), and later by Pedicord and Bergmann (eds.), *Plays of Garrick*, vol. II, pp. 97–126. While *The Jubilee* was not published in full until the twentieth century, the words of the songs, as was common practice, were printed immediately, in a sixpenny booklet. See *Songs, Chorusses, &c. Which Are Introduced in the New Entertainment of the Jubilee. At the Theatre Royal. In Drury-Lane.* (London: T. Becket and P. A. de Hondt, 1769). There was, of course, considerable overlap between these and the songs in *Shakespeare's Garland.*

28 Edward A. Langhans, *Eighteenth Century British and Irish Promptbooks: A Descriptive Bibliography* (New York and London: Greenwood Press, 1987), p. 77.

29 See Tiffany Stern, *Making Shakespeare: From Stage to Page* (London: Routledge, 2004).

30 See George Winchester Stone, Jr., and George M. Kahrl, *David Garrick: A Critical Biography* (Carbondale: Southern Illinois University Press, 1979), appendix B, p. 656.

31 [Henry Woodward], *Songs, Chorusses, &c. As They Are Performed in the New Entertainment of Harlequin's Jubilee, at the Theatre Royal in Covent-Garden* (London: W. Griffin, 1770).

32 See Garrick, *The Jubilee*, I.ii.89, in Pedicord and Bergmann (eds.), *Plays of Garrick*, vol. II, pp. 108–109. In successive stanzas the Warwickshire lad becomes 'the Bard of all bards' (line 96), 'the Will of all Wills' (line 103), 'the wag of all wags' (line 110) and 'the thief of all thieves' (line 117) – this last because 'Of all she was worth he robbed nature' (line 115).

33 See 'Occasional prologue spoken by Mr. Garrick at the opening of Drury-Lane Theatre, 8 Sept. 1750', in David Garrick, *Poetical Works*, 2 vols. (London: George Kearsley, 1785), vol. I, pp. 102–103, line 25.

'PARENTAL AND FILIAL CAPACITIES' – *KING LEAR* AND *HAMLET*

1 See Nahum Tate, *The History of King Lear* (1681), in Christopher Spencer (ed.), *Five Restoration Adaptations of Shakespeare* (Urbana: University of Illinois Press, 1965), pp. 201–274. All quotations from Tate's *Lear* are from this edition.

2 See Nancy Klein Maguire, 'Nahum Tate's *King Lear* : "The king's blest restoration" ', in Jean I. Marsden (ed.), *The Appropriation of Shakespeare: Post-Renaissance Reconstructions of the Works and the Myth* (Hemel Hempstead: Harvester Wheatsheaf, 1991), pp. 29–42, at p. 36. Maguire sets Tate's alteration in the context of the politics of the exclusion crisis of 1678–1683.

3 'Suppose Lear Mad upon the Ground with Edgar by him; His Attitude Should be leaning upon one hand & pointing Wildly towards the Heavens with his Other, Kent & Fool attend him & Glocester *[sic]* comes to him with a Torch; the real Madness of Lear, the Frantick Affectation of Edgar, and the different looks of Concern in the three other Characters will have a fine Effect.' See David M. Little and George M. Kahrl (eds.), *The Letters of David Garrick*, 3 vols. (Cambridge, MA: Harvard University Press, 1963), vol. I, pp. 52–55, letter no. 33, *post* 10 October 1745, to Francis Hayman.

4 *King Lear, a Tragedy*, in Harry William Pedicord and Fredrick Louis Bergmann (eds.), *The Plays of David Garrick*, 7 vols. (Carbondale: Southern Illinois University Press, 1980–1982), vol. III, pp. 301–390. Quotations from this edition, which is based on the Bell edition of 1773, are preceded by 'G'.

5 For a useful collation of detailed accounts of, and reactions to, Garrick as Lear, see Jane Freeman, 'Beyond Bombast: David Garrick's performances of Benedick and King Lear', *Restoration and Eighteenth-century Theatre Research*, 14.2 (1999), 1–21. Jean Benedetti, in *David Garrick and the Birth of Modern Theatre* (London: Methuen, 2001), pp. 100–110, gives a vivid picture of the actor's delivery of the part. See also Leigh Woods, 'Crowns of straw on little men: Garrick's new heroes', *Shakespeare Quarterly*, 32.1 (Spring 1981), 69–79, and 'Garrick's King Lear and the English malady', *Theatre Survey*, 27.1–2 (1986), 17–35. The latter article relates Garrick's performance to contemporary theories of madness.

6 For example, on Garrick's change of mind about restoring the Fool, see Peter Holland, 'The age of Garrick', in Jonathan Bate and Russell Jackson (eds.), *The Oxford Illustrated History of Shakespeare on Stage* (Oxford: Oxford University Press, 2001), pp. 69–91, at p. 83, and Thomas Davies, *Dramatic Miscellanies*, 3 vols. (London: Davies, 1784), vol. II, pp. 266–267.

7 See George Winchester Stone, Jr. (ed.), *The London Stage Part 4, 1747–1776*, 3 vols. (Carbondale: Southern Illinois University Press, 1962), vol. II, p. 561.

8 See *King Lear. A Tragedy*, in *Shakespeare's Plays. As They Are Now Performed at the Theatres Royal in London*; *Regulated from the Prompt Books of Each House, by Permission*, 9 vols. (London: John Bell and C. Etherington, 1773–1774), vol. II, pp. 1–80. This text is the basis of Pedicord's and Bergmann's modern edition.

9 *King Lear, a Tragedy: Altered from Shakspeare by David Garrick, Esq., Marked with the Variations in the Manager's Book at the Theatre-Royal in Drury-Lane* (London: C. Bathurst and 29 ors, 1786).

10 See *William Shakespeare: The Complete Works*, Stanley Wells and Gary Taylor (gen. eds.) (Oxford: Clarendon Press, 1986), *The Tragedy of King Lear*, pp. 1063–1098, III.ii.14–18. Quotations from Shakespeare's *Lear* not otherwise assigned are from this Folio-based edition.

11 George Colman, *The History of King Lear. As It Is Performed at the Theatre Royal in Covent Garden* (London: R. Baldwin and T. Becket and Co., 1768), facsimile (London: Cornmarket Press, 1969).

12 See Davies, *Dramatic Miscellanies*, vol. II, pp. 261–264. Mrs Davies had played Cordelia at Drury Lane to 'no inconsiderable share of approbation'. See *Dramatic Miscellanies*, vol. II, p. 321.

13 In his introduction (p. iii), Colman acknowledges that 'in the catastrophe he [Tate] has incurred the censure of Addison'. The latter had written that, as 'reformed according to the chymerical Notion of Poetical Justice', *King Lear* had 'lost half its Beauty'. See *The Spectator*, Donald F. Bond (ed.), 5 vols. (Oxford: Clarendon Press, 1965), no. 40, 16 April 1711, vol. I, pp. 168–173, at p. 170.

14 Because of the quotations from Johnson in Colman's preface, Tomarken is certain that Johnson's 1765 edition of *Lear* did influence Colman. See Edward Tomarken, *Samuel Johnson on Shakespeare: The Discipline of Criticism* (Athens, GA: The University of Georgia Press, 1991), p. 94. However, as well as similarities, there are textual differences between Johnson's 1765 edition and Colman's 1768 version; the latter is sometimes closer to Bell (1773). This suggests that Colman had access to the Drury Lane prompt-book.

15 George Winchester Stone, Jr., 'Garrick's production of *King Lear* : A study in the temper of the eighteenth-century mind', *Studies in Philology*, 45 (1948), 89–103, at p. 94.

16 Harry William Pedicord, 'Shakespeare, Tate, and Garrick: New light on alterations of *King Lear*', *Theatre Notebook*, 36.1 (1982), 14–21, at p. 16. This article contains (pp. 17–19) a complete account of the cuts in Garrick's hand in the 1756 prompt-book.

17 Charles H. Shattuck, 'Drama as promptbook', in George Winchester Stone, Jr. (ed.), *The Stage and the Page: London's 'Whole Show' in the Eighteenth-century Theatre* (Berkeley: University of California Press, 1981), pp. 163–191, at p. 180.
18 Arthur John Harris, 'Garrick, Colman and *King Lear* : A reconsideration', *Shakespeare Quarterly*, 22.1 (Winter 1971), 57–66, at p. 66.
19 The 1756 prompt-book can be consulted in the British Library (shelfmark c 119 dd 22). That it was connected with Drury Lane is confirmed by the fact that some of the additions are in Garrick's hand. Langhans tentatively identifies also the hands of two Drury Lane prompters, Cross (1756) and Harwood (1780s). See Edward A. Langhans, *Eighteenth Century British and Irish Promptbooks: A Descriptive Bibliography* (New York and London: Greenwood Press, 1987), pp. 164–165.
20 Apart from the direction for 'thunder', all that survives of this restoration in the Bell 1773 text is the first two-line exchange, with 'O heavens' changed to the equally unShakespearean 'O gods! ' See G.II.v.183.
21 Arthur Murphy, 'On the Tragedy of King *Lear*' (12 January 1754), in *The Gray's Inn Journal*, 2 vols. (London: P. Vaillant, 1756), vol. II, pp. 73–80, at p. 75.
22 Francis Gentleman, *The Dramatic Censor; or, Critical Companion*, 2 vols. (London: J. Bell and C. Etherington, 1770), vol. I, p. 370.
23 *William Shakespeare: The Complete Works*, Stanley Wells and Gary Taylor (gen. eds.) (Oxford: Clarendon Press, 1986), *The History of King Lear*, pp. 1025–1061, Scene 7.343–344.
24 Little and Kahrl (eds.), *Letters of Garrick*, vol. II, pp. 682–683, letter no. 574, 23 February [1770?], to Edward Tighe.
25 '*Lear*. Made you my Guardians, my repositories. / What must I come to you with five and twenty, Regan, said you so? / *Regan*. Even so' (altered from II.ii. 425–429).
26 Harris, 'Garrick, Colman and *King Lear*', pp. 59–61.
27 See Pedicord, 'Shakespeare, Tate, and Garrick', p. 20, and Harris, 'Garrick, Colman and *King Lear*', pp. 65–66. It is therefore slightly surprising that Pedicord and Bergmann assign the date of 1756 to the Bell text of 1773 that they include in their edition. See Pedicord and Bergmann (eds.), *Plays of Garrick*, vol. III, p. 301.
28 Davies, *Dramatic Miscellanies*, vol. II, pp. 263–264.
29 See Pedicord and Bergmann (eds.), *Plays of Garrick*, vol. III, p. 448.
30 See Stone, 'Garrick's production of *King Lear*', p. 100.
31 Pedicord and Bergmann (eds.), *Plays of Garrick*, vol. III, p. 448, n. 14.
32 Kalman A. Burnim, *David Garrick, Director* (Pittsburgh: University of Pittsburgh Press, 1961), p. 146.
33 Langhans, *Eighteenth Century Promptbooks*, pp. 166–167.
34 Little and Kahrl (eds.), *Letters of Garrick*, vol. II, pp. 498–499, letter no. 393, 19 March 1766, to Richard Berenger. See also his panicky letter to his brother written the following year: 'I have forgot it all [the part of Oakly in *The Jealous Wife*] & am very uneasy indeed': vol. II, pp. 556–557, letter no. 445, 8 February 1767, to George Garrick.

35 Samuel Johnson and George Steevens (eds.), *The Life and Death of King Lear*, in *The Plays of William Shakespeare*, 10 vols. (London: C. Bathurst, and 32 ors, 1773), vol. IX, pp. 309–495.

36 See Jean I Marsden, *The Re-imagined Text: Shakespeare, Adaptation, and Eighteenth-century Literary Theory* (Lexington: University Press of Kentucky, 1995), p. 92.

37 John Russell Brown, *Shakespeare: The Tragedies* (Basingstoke: Palgrave, 2001), p. 229.

38 Joseph Warton, *The Adventurer*, no. 113 (4 December 1753), 253–258, at p. 255. Colman (1768), Bell (1773) and Bathurst (1786) all restored this line.

39 Marvin Rosenberg, *The Masks of King Lear* (Berkeley, Los Angeles and London: University of California Press, 1972), p. 27.

40 Corin Redgrave, 'The king and I', *The Guardian*, 17 January 2005, pp. 14–15.

41 Edmund Burke, *A Philosophical Enquiry into the Origin of Our Ideas of the Sublime and Beautiful*, 2nd edn (London: Dodsley, 1759), facsimile (Menston: Scholar Press, 1970), p. 71.

42 Jean I. Marsden, 'Daddy's girls: Shakespearian daughters and eighteenth-century ideology', *Shakespeare Survey*, 51 (1998), 17–26.

43 See Little and Kahrl (eds.), *Letters of Garrick*, vol. III, pp. 1355–1358, appendix D, p. 1358.

44 For a full account of Steevens's life and work, see Arthur Sherbo, *The Achievement of George Steevens* (New York, Bern, Frankfurt am Main and Paris: Peter Lang, 1990), and also Arthur Sherbo, 'Steevens, George (1736–1800)', in *Oxford Dictionary of National Biography*, online edn (Oxford University Press, 2004), May 2006.

45 13 April 1778, James Boswell, *Life of Johnson*, R. W. Chapman (ed.), J. D. Fleeman (corr.) (London, Oxford and New York: Oxford University Press, 1970), p. 939.

46 'Insomnis', letter to *The Public Advertiser*, 15 August 1769, pp. 1–2.

47 A man of letters', letter to *The Public Advertiser*, 29 August 1769, p. 2. A very similar 'Letter to Mr. Urban', unsigned, appeared in *The Gentleman's Magazine*, 39 (August 1769), 375.

48 Davies, *Life of Garrick*, vol. II, pp. 220–222.

49 Samuel Johnson (ed.), *The Plays of William Shakespeare*, 8 vols. (London: Tonson, 1765), and George Steevens (ed.), *Twenty of the Plays of Shakespeare, Being the Whole Number Printed in Quarto During His Life-time*, 4 vols. (London: Tonson, 1766).

50 See Little and Kahrl (eds.), *Letters of Garrick*, vol. II, pp. 678–679, letter no. 570, conjectured date shortly after the Jubilee in September 1769, recipient unknown.

51 For Steevens's letter, see James Boaden (ed.), *The Private Correspondence of David Garrick*, 2 vols. (London: Henry Colburn and Richard Bentley, 1831–1832), vol. I, pp. 449–450, dated 1771. For Garrick's reply, see vol. I, p. 450; also Little and Kahrl (eds.), *Letters of Garrick*, vol. II, pp. 780–781, letter no. 669, Tuesday, 1771, day and month not given.

52 Boaden (ed.), *Correspondence*, vol. I, pp. 500–501, 3 December 1772, Steevens to Garrick. He goes on to acknowledge that the public would consider the 1773 edition to be over-burdened with notes ('the child is wrapped up in too many swaddling clothes'), and to blame Johnson's obstinacy for this.

53 Little and Kahrl (eds.), *Letters of Garrick*, vol. II, pp. 907–908, letter no. 808, 6 December [1773], to George Steevens. The letter is subscribed 'Y^{r} sincere friend & hum^{le} Ser D Garrick'.

54 Little and Kahrl (eds.), *Letters of Garrick*, vol. III, p. 982, letter no. 885, [conjectured date 10 January 1775].

55 Boaden (ed.), *Correspondence*, vol. II, pp. 112–113, 12 [January] 1775. Boaden identifies the lines as Salisbury's:

> I see thy glory, like a shooting star,
> Fall to the base earth from the firmament.
> Thy sun sets weeping in the lowly west,
> Witnessing storms to come, woe, and unrest. (II.iv.19–22)

He speculates that they would have been taken as applicable to the troubles in the American colonies.

56 Little and Kahrl (eds.), *Letters of Garrick*, vol. III, p. 985, letter no. 888, 13 [January 1775].

57 Boaden (ed.), *Correspondence*, vol. I, p. 501, 3 December 1772.

58 David Erskine Baker, Isaac Reed (ed.), *Biographia Dramatica or a Companion to the Playhouse*, 2 vols. (London: Rivington, and 7 ors, 1782), vol. II, pp. 143–144. For evidence that the satirical passages in the 1782 *Biographia Dramatica* were written for Reed by his friend Steevens, see Sherbo, *Achievement of George Steevens*, p. 139. See also Sherbo, 'Steevens, George', *ODNB*, online edn, May 2006.

59 Tomarken, *Samuel Johnson on Shakespeare*, pp. 133 and 144.

60 Little and Kahrl (eds.), *Letters of Garrick*, vol. III, p. 1041, letter no. 948, [*ante* 28 October 1775], to George Colman.

61 *Hamlet, Prince of Denmark, a Tragedy*, in Pedicord and Bergmann (eds.), *Plays of Garrick*, vol. IV, pp. 241–323. Quotations from this edition are preceded by 'G'.

62 Pedicord and Bergmann include *The Tempest*, published by Bell in 1773, among Garrick's adaptations of Shakespeare (*Plays of Garrick*, vol. IV, pp. 325–387), but in their notes they point out (vol. IV, p. 444) that it was first staged in 1757. In any case it is not an alteration.

63 Little and Kahrl (eds.), *Letters*, vol. II, pp. 841–843, letter no. 730, 4 January 1773, to the Abbé André Morellet.

64 *Hamlet, Prince of Denmark: A Tragedy. As It Is Now Acted at the Theatres Royal, in Drury-Lane, and Covent-Garden. Written by William Shakespear* (London: Hawes and Co., B. Dodd, J. Rivington, S. Crowder, T. Longman, B. Law, T. Caslon, T. Lownds and C. Corbett, 1763).

65 Quotations from 'the original' are from *The Tragedy of Hamlet, Prince of Denmark* in Wells and Taylor (gen. eds.), *Shakespeare: Complete Works*,

pp. 735–777. Because Wells and Taylor base their edition on the Folio text, 'How all occasions . . . ' is printed at the end of the play (pp. 776–777) among the 'additional passages' found in Q2.

66 For a list of the main omissions, for which Charles Beecher Hogan is credited, see Pedicord and Bergmann (eds.), *Plays of Garrick*, vol. IV, pp. 432–433. Those cited here have been checked against the Hawes version.

67 See Anthony B. Dawson, *Shakespeare in Performance: Hamlet* (Manchester and New York: Manchester University Press, 1995), pp. 39–40. For details of the Davenant version played by Betterton, and of the restorations made by Wilks, see George Winchester Stone, Jr., 'Garrick's long lost alteration of *Hamlet*', *Publications of the Modern Language Association of America*, 49 (1934), 890–921, at pp. 895–896.

68 See Pedicord and Bergmann (eds.), *Plays of Garrick*, vol. IV, pp. 432–433. They cite two published texts which they consider may be associated with Garrick: *Hamlet, Prince of Denmark: A Tragedy. As It Is Now Acted by His Majesty's Servants. Written by William Shakespear* (London: J. and P. Knapton, T. Longman, C. Hitch, and the Rest of the Proprietors, 1751), and *Hamlet, Prince of Denmark* (London: Hawes and Co., B. Dodd, J. Rivington, S. Crowder, T. Longman, B. Law, T. Caslon, T. Lownds and C. Corbett, 1763). The former seems to be no more than yet another reprinting of Hughes–Wilks. For the Hughes–Wilks text used by Garrick as the basis of his 1772 alteration, see *Hamlet, Prince of Denmark: A Tragedy. As It Is Now Acted by His Majesty's Servants. Written by William Shakespear* (London: J. and P. Knapton, T. Longman, C. Hitch and the Rest of the Proprietors, 1747).

69 R. Brimley Johnson (ed.), *The Letters of Hannah More* (London: John Lane the Bodley Head Ltd, 1925), p. 46.

70 Davies, *Dramatic Miscellanies*, vol. III, p. 36.

71 III.iii.73–96, *cf.* G.IV.i.577–598, and see Davies, *Dramatic Miscellanies*, vol. III, p. 101.

72 See Johnson, notes to *Hamlet*, in *Johnson on Shakespeare*, Sherbo (ed.), vol. II, pp. 958–1011, at p. 990.

73 See Jeffrey Lawson Laurence Johnson, 'Sweeping up Shakespeare's "rubbish": Garrick's condensation of Acts IV & V of *Hamlet* ', *Eighteenth Century Life*, 8.3 (1983), 14–25, at pp. 22–23.

74 Stone, 'Garrick's long lost alteration', p. 900.

75 See *ibid* ., and Pedicord and Bergmann (eds.), *Plays of Garrick*, vol. IV, p. 434.

76 For details, see Stone, 'Garrick's long lost alteration', pp. 916, 917 and 919. Stone says that Garrick cut out these passages from pp. 54–55 and p. 66 of a printing by H. Woodfall and others (London: 1767) of the 1763 Hawes version.

77 Stone, 'Garrick's long lost alteration', p. 900.

78 Samuel Johnson and George Steevens (eds.), *The Plays of William Shakespeare*, 10 vols. (London: C. Bathurst, and 32 ors, 1773). *Hamlet* is in vol. X.

79 See the Forster Collection in the National Art Library, vol. 38, pressmark Forster 48.F.42.

80 Boaden (ed.), *Correspondence*, vol. I, pp. 451–452.
81 Burnim, *David Garrick, Director*, p. 159.
82 Davies, *Dramatic Miscellanies*, vol. III, p. 146. When a member of the Drury Lane company, Davies had played Claudius. Steevens had earlier advised Garrick to take care that the King reacted appropriately: 'An Englishman loves a spirited, but abhors a phlegmatic exit.' See Boaden (ed.), *Correspondence*, vol. I, p. 452, 'Saturday Evening' 1771, Steevens to Garrick.
83 James Boaden, 'Biographical memoir', preface to Boaden (ed.), *Correspondence*, vol. I, pp. iii–lxiv, at p. liv. Boaden mistakenly gives 8 February 1774 and not 18 December 1772 as the date of the first performance of Garrick's 'rash violation of the whole scheme of Shakspeare's *Hamlet* '.
84 Burnim, *David Garrick, Director*, p. 154.
85 Holland, 'Age of Garrick', p. 72.
86 Thomas Davies, *Memoirs of the Life of David Garrick, Esq.*, 2nd edn, 2 vols. (London: Davies, 1780), facsimile (Hildesheim and New York: Georg Olms Verlag, 1972), vol. I, p. 57.
87 See R. B. Johnson (ed.), *Letters of Hannah More*, p. 47.
88 Davies, *Life of Garrick*, vol. I, p. 56.
89 Little and Kahrl (eds.), *Letters of Garrick*, vol. II, pp. 631–632, letter no. 525, 25 December 1768, to the Hon. Charles Yorke.
90 Little and Kahrl (eds.), *Letters of Garrick*, vol. II, pp. 845–846, letter no. 733, 10 January 1773, to Sir William Young.
91 Anon., *Some Remarks on the Tragedy of Hamlet Prince of Denmark, Written by Mr. William Shakespeare* (London: Wilkins, 1736), p. 46.
92 Anon., *Miscellaneous Observations on the Tragedy of Hamlet, Prince of Denmark* (London: W. Clarke, 1752), p. 47.
93 See, for example, Horace Walpole, preface to *The Castle of Otranto: A Gothic Story*, 2nd edn (London: William Bathoe and Thomas Lownds, 1765). Walpole's comments are aimed at Voltaire; he specifically defends (p. ix) 'the humour of the grave-diggers, [and] the fooleries of Polonius'.
94 Thomas Davies, *Dramatic Miscellanies*, vol. III, pp. 41–42.
95 See Gentleman's note to V.i. of *Hamlet* in *Bell's Edition*, vol. III, p. 71.
96 Theodore Besterman, introduction to *Voltaire on Shakespeare* (1967), in Theodore Besterman (ed.), *Studies on Voltaire and the Eighteenth Century*, 71 vols. (Geneva: Institut et Musée Voltaire, 1955–1973), vol. LIV, p. 15.
97 Little and Kahrl (eds.), *Letters of Garrick*, vol. II, pp. 780–781, letter no. 669, Tuesday, 1771, day and month not given, to Steevens.
98 Little and Kahrl (eds.), *Letters of Garrick*, vol. II, p. 428, letter no. 340, [*ante* 10 November 1764]. Garrick wrote in English, a language which Voltaire understood well.
99 Stone and Kahrl, *David Garrick: A Critical Biography*, p. 422.
100 Besterman, *Voltaire on Shakespeare*, p. 192 (my translation).
101 Little and Kahrl (eds.), *Letters of Garrick*, vol. III, p. 1135, letter no. 1055, 26 October 1776, to Elizabeth Montagu.
102 See Boaden (ed.), *Correspondence*, vol. II, pp. 188–189, 3 November 1776, p. 189.

103 Little and Kahrl (eds.), *Letters of Garrick*, vol. III, p. 1141, letter no. 1061, 10 November 1776, to Suzanne Necker.

104 See Lord Braybrooke, 'An evening with Voltaire', *Gentleman's Magazine*, n.s. 34 (November 1850), 571–573, where Voltaire's words are given in French. The translation is by Besterman, who also comments that Voltaire's library contained 'no trace' of such an edition. See Besterman, *Voltaire on Shakespeare*, p. 171.

105 'Dramaticus', 'Present state of the stage, with strictures upon the most celebrated performers', *Town and Country Magazine and Universal Repository*, 5 (March 1773), 127–128.

106 Jeffrey Johnson, 'Sweeping up Shakespeare's "rubbish" ', p. 16.

107 Doubts were expressed above as to the reliability of the preparation copy as a guide to identifying which of the apparent restorations were actually played. However, a notice following the first night specifically mentions the reinstatement, among 'many other fine passages, which have been hitherto overlooked', of Polonius's advice to his son ('a fine lesson for young travellers'). See *The London Chronicle*, 17–19 December 1772, p. 592.

108 See, for example, Burnim, *David Garrick, Director*, pp. 159–162, and R. B. Sutton, 'Further evidence of David Garrick's portrayal of Hamlet from the diary of Georg Christoph Lichtenberg', *Theatre Notebook*, 50.1 (1996), 8–14. Lichtenberg attended the performances of *Hamlet* given at Drury Lane on 2 and 12 December 1774.

109 Davies, *Dramatic Miscellanies*, vol. III, p. 146.

110 Michael Dobson, *The Making of the National Poet: Shakespeare, Adaptation and Authorship, 1660–1769* (Oxford: Clarendon Press, 1992), p. 172.

111 Holland, 'Age of Garrick', p. 72.

112 *The London Chronicle*, 17–19 December 1772, p. 592.

113 Anon., 'The theatre, *Numb.* XVI', *Town and Country Magazine*, 5 (December 1772), 655–658, at p. 658.

114 Anon., 'Theatrical intelligence', *The Morning Chronicle*, 20 September 1779, p. 2.

115 See Richard Brinsley Sheridan, *The Critic*, in Cecil Price (ed.), *Dramatic Works*, 2 vols. (Oxford: Clarendon Press, 1973), vol. II, pp. 463–550 (II.ii. pp. 529–530). Price does not number lines sequentially, but starts each page afresh at line 1.

116 Marsden, *The Re-imagined Text*, p. 152.

117 For an account of Murphy's critique of Garrick's *Hamlet*, see Richard W. Schoch, ' "A supplement to public laws": Arthur Murphy, David Garrick, and Hamlet, with alterations', *Theatre Journal*, 57.1 (March 2005), 21–32. See also Dobson, *Making of the National Poet*, p. 172. Murphy's skit can be found, as 'Hamlet, with alterations; a tragedy, in three acts', in Jesse Foot, *The Life of Arthur Murphy, Esq.* (London: J. Faulder, 1811), pp. 256–274.

118 Arthur Murphy, *The Life of David Garrick, Esq.*, 2 vols. (London: J. Wright, 1801), vol. II, pp. 82–83.

119 Little and Kahrl (eds.), *Letters of Garrick*, vol. II, p. 861, letter no. 753, 7 March 1773, to Pierre-Antoine de Laplace.

120 Baker, Reed (ed.), *Biographia Dramatica*, vol. II, p. 144.
121 Boaden (ed.), *Correspondence*, vol. I, pp. 453–454.
122 Baker, Reed (ed.), *Biographia Dramatica*, vol. I, p. 404.

EPILOGUE GARRICK'S LEGACY TO SHAKESPEARE STUDIES

1 *Shakespeare's Plays. As They Are Now Performed at the Theatres Royal in London; Regulated from the Prompt Books of Each House by Permission*, 9 vols. (London: John Bell and C. Etherington, 1773–1774).
2 See James Boaden (ed.), *The Private Correspondence of David Garrick*, 2 vols. (London: H. Colburn and R. Bentley, 1831–1832), vol. I, p. 88, Warburton to Garrick, 12 June 1758.
3 See Boaden (ed.), *Correspondence*, vol. I, pp. 216–217, Steevens to Garrick, 27 December 1765.
4 Jacky Bratton, *New Readings in Theatre History* (Cambridge and New York: Cambridge University Press, 2003), pp. 20–21.
5 Boswell, writing after Garrick's death, recounts an anecdote dating from the actor's retirement in 1776: ' "Now I have quitted the theatre," cried Garrick, "I will sit down and read Shakespeare." – " 'Tis time you should," exclaimed Johnson, "for I much doubt if you ever examined one of his plays from the first scene to the last." ' See James Boswell, *The Journal of a Tour to the Hebrides with Samuel Johnson LLD* (1785), (London: J.M. Dent, 1931), p. 199, n. 1.
6 Samuel Johnson and George Steevens (eds.), *The Plays of William Shakespeare*, 10 vols. (London: C. Bathurst, and 32 ors, 1773).
7 Samuel Johnson and George Steevens (eds.), *The Plays of William Shakspeare*, 2nd edn, 10 vols. (London: C. Bathurst and 33 ors, 1778).
8 Edmond Malone (ed.), *The Plays and Poems of William Shakspeare, in Ten Volumes* (London: J. Rivington and Sons and 31 ors, 1790).
9 Bratton claims, further, that Malone's principles 'established the dogmas of scholarly theatre history'. See Bratton, *New Readings*, p. 87.
10 Malone (ed.), *Plays and Poems of Shakspeare*, vol. I. ii, pp. 283–284.
11 William Thomas Fitzgerald, 'Hint for an inscription to the memory of Johnson and Garrick, who are both buried at the base of Shakespeare's statue, in Westminster-Abbey', *The Bath Chronicle*, 19 April 1792, p. 4. The poem was subsequently published in William Thomas Fitzgerald, *Miscellaneous Poems* (London: Bulmer & Co., 1801), pp. 127–128. Fitzgerald notes there that he had sent a copy to Boswell, 'at his very earnest request, on the 24th of May, 1793', with a view to including the lines in a future edition of his *Life of Johnson*.
12 Charles Lamb, 'On the tragedies of Shakspeare, considered with reference to their fitness for stage representation' (1811), in E. V. Lucas (ed.), *Miscellaneous Prose by Charles and Mary Lamb* (London: Methuen, 1912), pp. 112–130, at p. 113.
13 Jean I. Marsden, 'The individual reader and the canonized text: Shakespeare criticism after Johnson', *Eighteenth Century Life*, 17.1 (1993), 62–80, at p. 63.

14 Brian Vickers, 'The emergence of character criticism, 1774–1800', *Shakespeare Survey*, 34 (1981), 11–21.

15 George Winchester Stone, Jr., 'David Garrick's significance in the history of Shakespearean criticism: A study of the impact of the actor upon the change of critical focus during the eighteenth century', *Publications of the Modern Language Association of America*, 65.2 (March 1950), 183–197, at p. 196.

16 Simon Shepherd and Mick Wallis, *Drama/Theatre/Performance* (London and New York: Routledge, 2004), p. 24. For a study of Shakespeare's influence on the English Romantic poets, see Jonathan Bate, *Shakespeare and the English Romantic Imagination* (Oxford: Clarendon Press, 1989).

17 Robert Witbeck Babcock, *The Genesis of Shakespeare Idolatry 1766–1799: A Study in English Criticism of the Late Eighteenth Century* (Chapel Hill: University of North Carolina Press, 1931).

18 Reproductions of these examples can be seen in Rosie Broadley *et al.*, exhibition catalogue *Every Look Speaks: Portraits of David Garrick* (Bath: Holburne Museum of Art, 2003), pp. 15, 57–58, 70–71 and 75.

19 For details, see James Boswell, *Life of Johnson*, R. W. Chapman (ed.), J. D. Fleeman (corr.) (London, Oxford and New York: Oxford University Press, 1970), pp. 1139–1142. Dr Burney, though still composing and teaching, was by this stage in his career chiefly known as a writer.

20 Charles Lamb, *Specimens of English Dramatic Poets Who Lived about the Time of Shakspeare* (London: Longman, Hurst, Reeves, and Orme, 1808).

21 See Charles Lamb, letter to the editor, 27 January 1827, in William Hone (ed.), *The Table Book of Daily Recreation and Information* (1827), vol. III of Hone's *Works* (London: William Tagg and Co., 1878), p. 56. Lamb eventually contributed forty-six extracts.

22 Dorothy Anderson, 'Reflections on librarianship: Observations arising from examination of the Garrick collection of old plays in the British Library', *British Library Journal*, 6 (1980), 1–6, at p. 2.

23 Tom Lockwood, 'Edmond Malone and early modern textual culture', *Yale University Library Gazette*, 79 (October 2004), 53–69, at p. 68.

24 Jonathan Bate and Eric Rasmussen (eds.), *The RSC Shakespeare: The Complete Works* (Basingstoke: Macmillan, 2007).

Bibliography

PRIMARY TEXTS

Alterations of Shakespeare and Jonson by Garrick

The Alchymist. A Comedy, in Harry William Pedicord and Fredrick Louis Bergmann (eds.), *The Plays of David Garrick*, 7 vols. (Carbondale: Southern Illinois University Press, 1980–1982), vol. V, pp. 55–156.

Antony and Cleopatra; an Historical Play, Written by William Shakespeare: Fitted for the Stage by Abridging Only [by Edward Capell and David Garrick]; *and Now Acted, at the Theatre-Royal in Drury-Lane, by His Majesty's Servants* (London: J. and R. Tonson, 1758).

Antony and Cleopatra: An Historical Play, in Harry William Pedicord and Fredrick Louis Bergmann (eds.), *The Plays of David Garrick*, 7 vols. (Carbondale: Southern Illinois University Press, 1980–1982), vol. IV, pp. 1–93.)

Catharine and Petruchio. A Comedy [from *The Taming of the Shrew*], in Harry William Pedicord and Frederick Louis Bergmann (eds.), *The Plays of David Garrick*, 7 vols. (Carbondale: Southern Illinois University Press, 1980–1982), vol. III, pp. 187–220.

Cymbeline. A Tragedy. by Shakespear. With Alterations (London: J. and R. Tonson, 1762).

Cymbeline, A Tragedy, in Harry William Pedicord and Fredrick Louis Bergmann (eds.), *The Plays of David Garrick*, 7 vols. (Carbondale: Southern Illinois University Press, 1980–1982), vol. IV, pp. 95–169.

Every Man in His Humour. A Comedy. Written by Ben Jonson. With Alterations and Additions. As It Is Perform'd at the Theatre-Royal in Drury-Lane (London: J and R. Tonson and S. Draper, 1752).

Every Man in His Humour, as altered by David Garrick, Esq. (London: John Bell, 1791).

Every Man in His Humour. A Comedy, in Harry William Pedicord and Fredrick Louis Bergmann (eds.), *The Plays of David Garrick*, 7 vols. (Carbondale: Southern Illinois University Press, 1980–1982), vol. VI, pp. 51–133.

The Fairies. An Opera [from *A Midsummer Night's Dream*], in Harry William Pedicord and Fredrick Louis Bergmann (eds.), *The Plays of David Garrick*, 7 vols. (Carbondale: Southern Illinois University Press, 1980–1982), vol. III, pp. 151–186.

Florizel and Perdita. A Dramatic Pastoral, in Three Acts. Alter'd from The Winter's Tale of Shakespear. By David Garrick. As It Is Performed at the Theatre Royal in Drury-Lane (London: J. and R. Tonson, 1758).

Florizel and Perdita. A Dramatic Pastoral [from *The Winter's Tale*], in Harry William Pedicord and Fredrick Louis Bergmann (eds.), *The Plays of David Garrick*, 7 vols. (Carbondale: Southern Illinois University Press, 1980–1982), vol. III, pp. 221–266.

Hamlet, Prince of Denmark: A Tragedy, in Harry William Pedicord and Fredrick Louis Bergmann (eds.), *The Plays of David Garrick*, 7 vols. (Carbondale: Southern Illinois University Press, 1980–1982), vol. IV, pp. 241–323.

King Lear. A Tragedy, in *Shakespeare's Plays. As They Are Now Performed at the Theatres Royal in London; Regulated from the Prompt Books of Each House by Permission*, 9 vols. (London: John Bell and C. Etherington, 1773–1774), vol. II, pp. 1–80.

King Lear, a Tragedy: Altered from Shakspeare by David Garrick, Esq., Marked with the Variations in the Manager's Book at the Theatre-Royal in Drury-Lane (London: C. Bathurst and 29 ors, 1786).

King Lear. A Tragedy, in Harry William Pedicord and Fredrick Louis Bergmann (eds.), *The Plays of David Garrick*, 7 vols. (Carbondale: Southern Illinois University Press, 1980–1982), vol. III, pp. 301–390.

Macbeth, in *Shakespeare's Plays. As They Are Now Performed at the Theatres Royal in London*; *Regulated from the Prompt Books of Each House by Permission*, 9 vols. (London: John Bell and C. Etherington, 1773–1774), vol. I, pp. 1–71.

Macbeth, a Tragedy, in Harry William Pedicord and Fredrick Louis Bergmann (eds.), *The Plays of David Garrick*, 7 vols. (Carbondale: Southern Illinois University Press, 1980–1982), vol. III, pp. 6–74.

A Midsummer Night's Dream, in Harry William Pedicord and Fredrick Louis Bergmann (eds.), *The Plays of David Garrick*, 7 vols. (Carbondale: Southern Illinois University Press, 1980–1982), vol. III, pp. 171–240.

Romeo and Juliet. By Shakespear. With Alterations, and an Additional Scene; by D. Garrick. As It Is Performed at the Theatre-Royal in Drury-Lane (London: J. and R. Tonson and S. Draper, 1753).

Romeo and Juliet. By Shakespear, With Alterations, and an Additional Scene; by D. Garrick. As It Is Performed at the Theatre-Royal in Drury-Lane (London: Tonson, 1763).

Romeo and Juliet, in Harry William Pedicord and Fredrick Louis Bergmann (eds.), *The Plays of David Garrick*, 7 vols. (Carbondale: Southern Illinois University Press, 1980–1982), vol. III, pp. 75–149.

Shakspeare's Romeo and Juliet: A tragedy, Adapted to the Stage by David Garrick; Revised by J. P. Kemble: As Acted at the Theatre Royal Drury Lane (London: T. Rodwell, 1818).

The Sheep-shearing: A Dramatic Pastoral. In Three Acts. Taken from Shakespeare. As It Is Performed at the Theatre Royal in the Hay-Market [Garrick's alteration of *The Winter's Tale*, further altered by George Colman the elder], (London: G. Kearsly, 1777).

The Tempest. A Comedy, in Harry William Pedicord and Fredrick Louis Bergmann (eds.), *The Plays of David Garrick*, 7 vols. (Carbondale: Southern Illinois University Press, 1980–1982), vol. IV, pp. 325–387.

The Tempest, an Opera, in Harry William Pedicord and Fredrick Louis Bergmann (eds.), *The Plays of David Garrick*, 7 vols. (Carbondale: Southern Illinois University Press, 1980–1982), vol. III, pp. 267–300.

Other Works by Garrick

Anon., [probably David Garrick], *Anti-Midas: A Jubilee Preservative from Unclassical, Ignorant, False and Invidious Criticism* (London: 1769).

Dramatic Works of David Garrick, Esq., 3 vols. (London: A. Millar, 1798).

An Essay on Acting, In Which Will Be Consider'd the Mimical Behaviour of a Certain Fashionable Faulty Actor (London: W. Bickerton, 1744).

Harlequin's Invasion; or, A Christmas Gambol (1759), in *The Plays of David Garrick*, Harry William Pedicord and Fredrick Louis Bergmann (eds.), 7 vols. (Carbondale: Southern Illinois University Press, 1980–1982), vol. I, pp. 199–225.

The Journal of David Garrick: Describing His Visit to France and Italy in 1763, George Winchester Stone Jr. (ed. and intro.) (New York: The Modern Language Association of America, 1939).

The Jubilee (1769), in *The Plays of David Garrick*, Harry William Pedicord and Fredrick Louis Bergmann (eds.), 7 vols. (Carbondale: Southern Illinois University Press, 1980–1982), vol. II, pp. 97–126.

Letters of David Garrick and Georgiana Countess Spencer 1759–1779, The Earl Spencer and Christopher Dobson (eds.) (Cambridge: For Presentation to Members of the Roxburghe Club, 1960).

The Letters of David Garrick, David M. Little and George M. Kahrl (eds.), 3 vols. (London: Oxford University Press, 1963).

'The new sheep-shearing song in the *Winter's Tale*', *The Gentleman's and London Magazine*, 25 (February 1756), 84.

'The new sheep-shearing song in the *Winter's Tale*', *The Universal Magazine*, 18 (March 1756), 126.

An Ode upon Dedicating a Building, and Erecting a Statue, to Shakespeare, at Stratford upon Avon (London: T. Becket and P.A. de Hondt, 1769).

The Plays of David Garrick, Harry William Pedicord and Fredrick Louis Bergmann (eds.), 7 vols. (Carbondale: Southern Illinois University Press, 1980–1982):

- Vol. 1, *Garrick's Own Plays, 1740–1766*, 1980.
- Vol. 2, *Garrick's Own Plays, 1767–1775*, 1980.
- Vol. 3, *Garrick's Adaptations of Shakespeare, 1744–1756*, 1981.
- Vol. 4, *Garrick's Adaptations of Shakespeare, 1759–1773*, 1981.
- Vol. 5, *Garrick's Alterations of Others, 1742–1750*, 1982.
- Vol. 6, *Garrick's Alterations of Others, 1751–1756*, 1982.
- Vol. 7, *Garrick's Alterations of Others, 1757–1773*, 1982.

The Poetical Works of David Garrick, Esq., 2 vols. (London: George Kearsley, 1785).

The Private Correspondence of David Garrick, James Boaden (ed.), 2 vols. (London: H. Colburn and R. Bentley, 1831–1832).

Selected Verse of David Garrick, J. D. Hainsworth (ed.) (Armidale, Australia: University of New England, 1981).

Songs, Chorusses, &c. Which Are Introduced in the New Entertainment of the Jubilee. At the Theatre Royal. In Drury-Lane (London: T. Becket and P. A. de Hondt, 1769).

Three Plays by David Garrick, Elizabeth P. Stein (ed.) (New York: William Edwin Rudge, 1926).

Other Alterations and Performance Versions of Shakespeare's Plays

Cibber, Colley, *The Tragical History of King Richard III* (1700), in *Five Restoration Adaptations of Shakespeare*, Christopher Spencer (ed.) (Urbana: University of Illinois Press, 1965), pp. 273–344.

Cibber, Theophilus, *Romeo and Juliet, a Tragedy* (London: C. Corbett and G. Woodfall, 1748), facsimile (London: Cornmarket Press, 1969).

Colman, George, *The History of King Lear. As It Is Performed at the Theatre Royal in Covent Garden* (London: R. Baldwin and T. Becket and Co., 1768), facsimile (London: Cornmarket Press, 1969).

Davenant, William, *Macbeth, a Tragedy* (1674), in Christopher Spencer (ed.), *Five Restoration Adaptations of Shakespeare* (Urbana: University of Illinois Press, 1965), pp. 33–107.

Hamlet, Prince of Denmark: A Tragedy. As It Is Now acted by His Majesty's Servants. Written by William Shakespear (London: J. and P. Knapton, T. Longman, C. Hitch and the Rest of the Proprietors, 1747).

Hamlet, Prince of Denmark: A Tragedy. As It Is Now Acted by His Majesty's Servants. Written by William Shakespear (London: J. and P. Knapton, T. Longman, C. Hitch, and the Rest of the Proprietors, 1751).

Hamlet, Prince of Denmark: A Tragedy. As It Is Now Acted at the Theatres Royal, in Drury-Lane, and Covent-Garden. Written by William Shakespear (London: Hawes and Co., B. Dodd, J. Rivington, S. Crowder, T. Longman, B. Law, T. Caslon, T. Lownds and C. Corbett, 1763).

The Historical Tragedy of Macbeth (Written Originally by Shakespear) Newly Adapted to the Stage, with Alterations [by John Lee], *as Performed at the Theatre in Edinburgh* (Edinburgh: W. Cheyne, 1753).

The Historical Tragedy of Macbeth (Written Originally by Shakespeare) With the Songs, Alterations [by John Lee] *and Additions* (Dublin: W. Whitestone, 1761).

Marsh, Charles, *The Winter's Tale, a Play, Alter'd from Shakespear* (London: Charles Marsh, 1756), facsimile, Valerie Edden intro. (London: Cornmarket Press, 1970).

Otway, Thomas, *The History and Fall of Caius Marius* (1680) [from *Romeo and Juliet*], in J. C. Ghosh (ed.), *The Works of Thomas Otway*, 2 vols. (Oxford: Clarendon Press, 1932), vol. I, pp. 433–519.

The Sheep-shearing, or, Florizel and Perdita. A Pastoral Comedy Taken from Shakespear [altered from *The Winter's Tale* by Macnamara Morgan] (London: J. Truman, 1762).

The Sheep-shearing: or, Florizel and Perdita. A Pastoral Comedy. Taken from Shakespear. As It Is Acted at the Theatre-Royal in Dublin. The Songs Set by Mr. Arne [altered from *The Winter's Tale* by Macnamara Morgan] (Dublin: Peter Wilson, 1767).

Tate, Nahum, *The History of King Lear* (1681), in Christopher Spencer (ed.), *Five Restoration Adaptations of Shakespeare* (Urbana: University of Illinois Press, 1965), pp. 201–274.

The Winter's Tale. A Tragedy [altered by Thomas Hull], in *Shakespeare's Plays. As They Are Now Performed at the Theatres Royal in London; Regulated from the Prompt Books of Each House by Permission*, 9 vols. (London: John Bell and C. Etherington, 1773–1774), vol. V, pp. 149–225.

Other Editions of Shakespeare's Plays and Works Consulted

Antony and Cleopatra. A Tragedy. By Mr. William Shakespear (London: J. Tonson, and the Rest of the Proprietors, 1734).

Bate, Jonathan and Eric Rasmussen (eds.), *The RSC Shakespeare: The Complete Works* (Basingstoke: Macmillan, 2007).

[The 'Bell edition'; notes by Francis Gentleman], *Shakespeare's Plays. As They Are Now Performed at the Theatres Royal in London; Regulated from the Prompt Books of Each House by Permission*, 9 vols. (London: John Bell and C. Etherington, 1773–1774).

Capell, Edward (ed.), *Mr. William Shakespeare, His Comedies, Histories, and Tragedies*, 10 vols. (London: J. and R. Tonson, 1767–1768).

Furness H. H. (ed.), *The Winter's Tale*, 5th edn (Philadelphia: J. B. Lippincott Co., 1898).

Gibbons, Brian (ed.), *Romeo and Juliet* (London: Arden, 1980).

Hanmer, Thomas (ed.), *The Works of Shakespear*, 6 vols. (Oxford: Printed at the Theatre, 1744).

Johnson, Samuel (ed.), *The Plays of William Shakespeare*, 8 vols. (London: Tonson, 1765).

Johnson, Samuel and George Steevens (eds.), *The Plays of William Shakespeare*, 10 vols. (London: C. Bathurst and 32 ors, 1773).

Johnson, Samuel and George Steevens (eds.), *The Plays of William Shakspeare*, 2nd edn, 10 vols. (London: C. Bathurst and 33 ors, 1778).

The Life and Death of King Lear. By Mr. William Shakespear (London: J. Tonson, and the Rest of the Proprietors, 1734).

Malone, Edmond (ed.), *The Plays and Poems of William Shakspeare*, 10 vols. (London: J. Rivington and Sons and 31 ors, 1790).

Pope, Alexander (ed.), *The Works of Mr. William Shakespear*, 6 vols. (London: Tonson, 1725).

Rowe, Nicholas (ed.), *The Works of Mr. William Shakespear* [. . .] *Revis'd and Corrected*, 6 vols. (London: Tonson, 1709).

Steevens, George (ed.), *Twenty of the Plays of Shakespeare, Being the Whole Number Printed in Quarto During His Life-time*, 4 vols. (London: Tonson, 1766).

Theobald, Lewis (ed.), *The Works of Shakespeare*, 7 vols. (London: A. Bettesworth and C. Hitch, J. Tonson and 3 ors, 1733).

Theobald, Lewis (ed.), *The Works of Shakespeare*, 2nd edn, 8 vols. (London: H. Lintott, C. Hitch, J. and R. Tonson and 7 ors, 1740).

Thompson, Ann (ed.), *The Taming of the Shrew* (Cambridge: Cambridge University Press, 2003).

Warburton, William (ed.), *The Works of Shakespear*, 8 vols. (London: J. and P. Knapton, etc., 1747).

Wells, Stanley and Gary Taylor (gen. eds.), *William Shakespeare, the Complete Works* (Oxford: Clarendon Press, 1986).

The Winter's Tale. By Mr. William Shakespeare (London: J. Tonson, and the Rest of the Proprietors, 1735).

Other Works Cited

Anon., *Shakespear's Garland, Being a Collection of New Songs, Ballads, Roundelays, Catches, Glees, Comic Serenatas &c. Performed at the Jubilee at Stratford upon Avon: the Music by Dr. Arne, Mr. Barthelimon, Mr. Allwood, and Mr. Dibdin* (London: T. Becket and P. A. de Hondt, 1769).

Songs, Chorusses, &c. which Are Introduced in the New Entertainment of the Jubilee. At the Theatre Royal. In Drury-Lane. (London: T. Becket and P. A. de Hondt, 1769).

[probably Francis Gentleman], *The Stratford Jubilee, a New Comedy of Two Acts, as It Has Been Lately Exhibited at Stratford upon Avon, with Great Applause, To which Is Prefixed Scrub's Trip to the Jubilee* (London: T. Lowndes and J. Bell, 1769).

Boswell, James, *The Journal of a Tour to the Hebrides with Samuel Johnson, LL.D* (1785) (London: J. M. Dent, 1931).

Boswell's London Journal 1762–1763, Frederick A. Pottle (ed.) (London: Heinemann, 1950).

Boswell in Search of a Wife, 1766–1769, Frank Brady and Frederick A. Pottle (eds.) (London: Heinemann, 1957).

Burney, Frances, *Evelina* (1778), Kristina Straub (ed.) (Boston: Bedford Books, 1997).

Capell, Edward (ed.), *Prolusions, or Select Pieces of Antient Poetry* (London: Tonson, 1760).

Carey, George Saville, *Shakespeare's Jubilee, a Masque* (London: T. Becket and P. A. de Hondt, 1769).

A Catalogue of the Library, Splendid Books of Prints, Poetical and Historical Tracts of David Garrick, Esq. (London: 1823).

Churchill, Charles, *Poetical Works*, Douglas Grant (ed.) (Oxford: Clarendon Press, 1956).

Cibber, Colley, *An Apology for the Life of Colley Cibber, with an Historical View of the Stage During His Own Time, Written by Himself* (1740), B. R. S. Fone (ed. and intro.) (Ann Arbor: University of Michigan Press, 1968).

Colman, George, *Man and Wife, or, The Shakespeare Jubilee, a Comedy, of Three Acts, as It Is Performed at the Theatre Royal in Covent Garden*, 2nd edn (London: T. Becket & Co. and R. Baldwin, 1770).

Dryden, John, *All for Love: Or, The World Well Lost* (1678), Maximillian E. Novak and George R. Guffey (eds.), in *The Works of John Dryden,* vol. 13 (Berkeley and London: University of California Press, 1984), pp. 1–111.

Fielding, Henry, *The History of Tom Jones*, Fredson Bowers (ed.), 2 vols. (Oxford: Clarendon Press, 1974).

Fitzgerald, William Thomas, 'Hint for an inscription to the memory of Johnson and Garrick, who are both buried at the base of Shakespeare's statue, in Westminster-Abbey', *The Bath Chronicle*, 19 April 1792, p. 4.

Miscellaneous Poems (London: Bulmer & Co., 1801).

Goldsmith, Oliver, *Collected Works,* Arthur Friedman (ed.), 5 vols. (Oxford: Clarendon Press, 1966).

Haywood, Eliza, *The Female Spectator*, 4 vols. (London: T. Gardner, 1745), vol. II, p. 8.

Johnson, Samuel, *Poems*, E. L. McAdam, Jr. (ed.) with George Milne (New Haven and London: Yale University Press, 1964).

Miscellaneous Observations on the Tragedy of Macbeth (1745), in Arthur Sherbo (ed.), *Johnson on Shakespeare*, 2 vols. (New Haven and London: Yale University Press, 1968), vol. I, pp. 3–45.

Notes on Shakespeare's Plays, in Arthur Sherbo (ed.), *Johnson on Shakespeare,* 2 vols. (New Haven and London: Yale University Press, 1968), vol. I, pp. 117–524, vol. II, pp. 527–1048.

Preface to Shakespeare (1765), in Arthur Sherbo (ed.), *Johnson on Shakespeare,* 2 vols. (New Haven and London: Yale University Press, 1968), vol. I, pp. 59–113.

Proposals for Printing, by Subscription, the Dramatick Works of William Shakespeare (1756), in Arthur Sherbo (ed.), *Johnson on Shakespeare*, 2 vols. (New Haven and London: Yale University Press, 1968), vol. I, pp. 51–58.

The Rambler, W. J. Bate and A. B. Strauss (eds.), 3 vols. (New Haven and London: Yale University Press, 1969), no. 168 (1751), vol. III, pp. 125–129.

Irene (London: R. Dodsley, 1749), facsimile (Ilkley: The Scolar Press, 1973).

Dictionary of the English Language (1755), 2 vols., facsimile (Harlow: Longman, 1990).

Jonson, Ben, *Works*, C. H. Herford and Percy Simpson (eds.), vol. 3 (Oxford: Clarendon Press, 1927).

Every Man in His Humour: A Parallel-text Edition of the 1601 Quarto and the 1616 Folio, J. W. Lever (ed.) (London: Edward Arnold, 1972).

[Lennox, Charlotte], *Shakespear Illustrated: Or the Novels and Histories, On which the Plays of Shakespear Are Founded, Collected and Translated from the Original Authors. With Critical Remarks*, 3 vols. (London: A. Millar, 1753–1754).

Milton, John, *Poetical Works*, Douglas Bush (ed.) (Oxford: Oxford University Press, 1966).

More, Hannah, *Letters*, R. Brimley Johnson (ed.) (London: John Lane the Bodley Head Ltd., 1925).

Pepys, Samuel, *The Diary of Samuel Pepys*, Robert Latham and William Matthews (eds.), vol. 8 (London: G. Bell and Sons, 1974).

Reynolds, Sir Joshua, *Johnson and Garrick* (London: Printed by Nichols, Son, and Bentley, 1816).

Letters, John Ingamells and John Edgcumbe (eds.) (New Haven, CT: Yale University Press for the Paul Mellon Centre for Studies in British Art, 2000).

Richardson, Samuel, *The History of Sir Charles Grandison* (1753–1754), Jocelyn Harris (ed.), 3 parts (London: Oxford University Press, 1972).

Sheridan, Richard Brinsley, *The Critic*, in Cecil Price (ed.), *Dramatic Works of Richard Brinsley Sheridan*, 2 vols. (Oxford: Clarendon Press, 1973), vol. II, pp. 463–550.

Spencer, Christopher (ed.), *Five Restoration Adaptations of Shakespeare* (Urbana: University of Illinois Press, 1965).

Steele, Richard, *The Conscious Lovers* (1722), Shirley Strum Kenny (ed.) (London: Edward Arnold, 1968).

Thompson, Edward, *Trinculo's Trip to the Jubilee* (London: C. Moran, W. Flexney and R. Riddley, 1769).

Walpole, Horace, *The Castle of Otranto: A Gothic Story*, 2nd edn (London: William Bathoe and Thomas Lownds, 1765).

Correspondence, W. S. Lewis (ed.), vol. 32 (London and New York: Oxford University Press/Yale University Press, 1965).

Whitehead, William, *Poems on Several Occasions* (London: Dodsley, 1754).

Plays and Poems, 3 vols. (London: J. Dodsley, 1774).

[Woodward, Henry], *Songs, Chorusses, &c. As They Are Performed in the New Entertainment of Harlequin's Jubilee, at the Theatre Royal in Covent-Garden* (London: W. Griffin, 1770).

SECONDARY SOURCES

Addison, Joseph, *The Spectator*, Donald F. Bond (ed.), 5 vols. (Oxford: Clarendon Press, 1965), no. 40, 16 April 1711, vol. I, pp. 168–173, no. 45, 21 April 1711, vol. I, pp. 191–195.

Anderson, Dorothy, 'Reflections on librarianship: Observations arising from examination of the Garrick collection of old plays in the British Library', *British Library Journal*, 6 (1980), 1–6.

Annals of the Club, 1764–1914 (London: The Club, 1914).

Anon., *Some Remarks on the Tragedy of Hamlet Prince of Denmark, Written by Mr. William Shakespeare* (London: Wilkins, 1736).

'Remarks on the tragedy of the orphan', *Gentleman's Magazine*, 18 (November 1748), 502–506.

Miscellaneous Observations on the Tragedy of Hamlet, Prince of Denmark (London: W. Clarke, 1752).

The Theatrical Examiner: An Enquiry into the Merits and Demerits of the Present English Performers in General (London: J. Doughty, 1757).

'A teller's account of a crowded house at *Drury Lane* Theatre', in *Theatrical Monitor*, 18 (16 April 1768), 2–6.

'[E]xtract of a letter to a gentleman in London', *The Gentleman's Magazine*, 39 (September 1769), 421–423.

Garrick's Vagary: Or England Run Mad. With Particulars of the Stratford Jubilee (London: Bladon, 1769).

'Monthly catalogue', in 'A society of gentlemen', *The Critical Review: or, Annals of Literature*, vol. 28, (London: A. Hamilton, 1769), pp. 231–237.

Review of Garrick's *Ode upon Dedicating a Building, and Erecting a Statue, to Shakespeare*', *The Gentleman's Magazine*, 39 (September 1769), 447.

Notice of *Hamlet, London Chronicle*, 17–19 December 1772, p. 592.

'The theatre, *Numb.* XVI', *Town and Country Magazine and Universal Repository*, 5 (December 1772), 655–658.

'Theatrical intelligence', *The Morning Chronicle*, 20 September 1779, p. 2.

'A description of the monument erected in Westminster Abbey, to the memory of the celebrated David Garrick', *Universal Magazine*, August 1797, p. 73.

'To David Garrick Esqr. Upon his dedication of a temple to Shakespear', MS poem, ref. Y.d.184 (26), Folger Shakespeare Library.

Avery, Emmett L., 'The Shakespeare Ladies Club', *Shakespeare Quarterly*, 7.2 (Spring 1956), 153–158.

(ed.), *The London Stage Part 2, 1700–1729*, 2 vols. (Carbondale: Southern Illinois University Press, 1960).

Babcock, Robert Witbeck, *The Genesis of Shakespeare Idolatry 1766–1799: A Study in English Criticism of the Late Eighteenth Century* (Chapel Hill: University of North Carolina Press, 1931).

Baker, David Erskine, Isaac Reed (ed.), *Biographia Dramatica or a Companion to the Playhouse*, 2 vols. (London: Rivington, and 7 ors, 1782).

Baretti, Joseph, *Discours sur Shakespeare et sur Monsieur de Voltaire* (London and Paris: J. Nourse, Durand neveu, 1777).

Barker-Benfield, G. J., *The Culture of Sensibility: Sex and Society in Eighteenth-century Britain* (Chicago and London: University of Chicago Press, 1992).

Bartholomeusz, Dennis, *Macbeth and the Players* (Cambridge: Cambridge University Press, 1969).

Bartlett, Ian, 'William Boyce', in *New Grove Dictionary of Music and Musicians*, 2nd edn (London: Macmillan, 2001), vol. IV, pp. 155–162.

Bate, Jonathan, *Shakespearean Constitutions: Politics, Theatre, Criticism 1730–1830* (Oxford: Clarendon Press, 1989).

Shakespeare and the English Romantic Imagination (Oxford: Clarendon Press, 1989).

'The Romantic stage', in Jonathan Bate and Russell Jackson (eds.), *The Oxford Illustrated History of Shakespeare on Stage* (Oxford: Oxford University Press, 2001), pp. 92–111.

Bate, W. Jackson, *Samuel Johnson* (New York and London: Harcourt Brace Jovanovich, 1977).

Benedetti, Jean, *David Garrick and the Birth of Modern Theatre* (London: Methuen, 2001).

Besterman, Theodore, Introduction to *Voltaire on Shakespeare* (1967), in Theodore Besterman (ed.), *Studies on Voltaire and the Eighteenth Century*, 71 vols. (Geneva: Institut et Musée Voltaire, 1955–1973), vol. LIV.

Bindman, David and Malcolm Baker, *Roubiliac and the Eighteenth-century Monument* (New Haven and London: Yale University Press for the Paul Mellon Centre for Studies in British Art, 1995).

Booth, Michael R., Richard Southern, Frederick and Lise-Lone Marker and Robertson Davies, *The Revels History of Drama in English, 1750–1880,* vol. 6 (London: Methuen, 1975).

Boswell, James, *Life of Johnson*, R. W. Chapman (ed.), J. D. Fleeman (corr.) (London, Oxford and New York: Oxford University Press, 1970).

Branam, George C., *Eighteenth-century Adaptations of Shakespearean Tragedy* (Berkeley and Los Angeles: University of California Press, 1956).

'The genesis of David Garrick's *Romeo and Juliet*', *Shakespeare Quarterly*, 35.2 (Summer 1984), 170–179.

Bratton, Jacky, *New Readings in Theatre History* (Cambridge and New York: Cambridge University Press, 2003).

Braybrooke, The Rt. Hon. Lord, 'An evening with Voltaire', *Gentleman's Magazine,* n.s. 34 (November 1850), 571–573.

Brewer, John, *The Pleasures of the Imagination: English Culture in the Eighteenth Century* (London: HarperCollins, 1997).

Bristol, Michael D., *Big-time Shakespeare* (London and New York: Routledge, 1996).

Broadley, Rosie, Colin Harrison, Susan Sloman, Lisa White and Christopher Woodward, Exhibition catalogue *Every Look Speaks: Portraits of David Garrick* (Bath: Holburne Museum of Art, 2003).

Brook, Donald, *The Romance of the English Theatre* (London: Rockliff, 1947).

Brown, John Russell, *Shakespeare: The Tragedies* (Basingstoke: Palgrave, 2001).

Burke, Edmund, *A Philosophical Enquiry into the Origin of Our Ideas of the Sublime and Beautiful,* 2nd edn (London: Dodsley, 1759), facsimile (Menston: Scholar Press, 1970).

Burney, Charles, *A General History of Music*, 4 vols. (London: Burney, 1776–1789).

Burnim, Kalman A., *David Garrick, Director* (Pittsburgh: University of Pittsburgh Press, 1961).

Butler, Martin, 'Jonson's London and its theatres', in Richard Harp and Stanley Stewart (eds.), *The Cambridge Companion to Ben Jonson* (Cambridge: Cambridge University Press, 2000), pp. 15–29.

Carr, Stephen Leo and Peggy A. Knapp, 'Seeing through *Macbeth*', *Publications of the Modern Language Association of America*, 96.5 (October 1981), 837–847.

Cibber, Theophilus, *Dissertations on Theatrical Subjects* (London: Griffiths, 1756).

Cocco, Maria Rosaria, 'Under the mulberry tree: The Garrick/Shakespeare Jubilee of 1769', in Mariacristina Cavecchi and Mariangela Tempera (eds.), *EuroShakespeares: Exploring Cultural Practice in an International Context* (Bologna: University of Bologna, 2002), pp. 7–33.

Conolly L. W., *The Censorship of English Drama 1737–1824* (San Marino: The Huntington Library, 1976).

Copeland, Nancy, 'The source of Garrick's *Romeo and Juliet* text', *English Language Notes*, 24.4 (June 1987), 27–33.

'The sentimentality of Garrick's *Romeo and Juliet*', *Restoration and Eighteenth-century Theatre Research*, 4.2 (Winter 1989), 1–13.

Cumberland, Richard, *Memoirs* (London: Lackington, Allen & Co., 1806).

Dash, Irene G., 'Garrick or Colman?', *Notes and Queries*, 216 (April 1971), 152–155.

'A penchant for Perdita on the eighteenth-century English stage', in *The Woman's Part: Feminist Criticism of Shakespeare*, Carolyn Ruth Swift Lenz, Gayle Greene and Carol Thomas Neely (eds.) (Urbana: University of Illinois Press, 1980).

Dávidházi, Péter, ' "He drew the liturgy, and framed the rites": The changing role of religious disposition in Shakespeare's reception', *Shakespeare Survey*, 54 (2001), 46–56.

Davies, Thomas, *Dramatic Miscellanies*, 2nd edn, 3 vols. (London: Davies, 1784).

Memoirs of the Life of David Garrick, Esq., 2nd edn, 2 vols. (London: Davies, 1780), facsimile (Hildesheim and New York: Georg Olms Verlag, 1972).

Dawson, Anthony B., *Shakespeare in Performance: Hamlet* (Manchester and New York: Manchester University Press, 1995).

Deelman, Christian, *The Great Shakespeare Jubilee* (London and New York: Michael Joseph, Viking, 1964).

Dibdin, James C., *The Annals of the Edinburgh Stage* (Edinburgh: Richard Cameron, 1888).

Dobson, Michael, ' "Remember/first to possess his books": The appropriation of *The Tempest*, 1700–1800', *Shakespeare Survey*, 43 (1990), 99–107.

The Making of the National Poet: Shakespeare, Adaptation and Authorship, 1660–1769 (Oxford: Clarendon Press, 1992).

Dodsley, Robert, *Correspondence 1733–1764*, James E. Tierney (ed.) (Cambridge: Cambridge University Press, 1958).

Donohue, Joseph (ed.), *The Cambridge History of British Theatre, 1660–1895*, vol. 2 (Cambridge: Cambridge University Press, 2004).

'Dramaticus', 'Present state of the stage, with strictures upon the most celebrated performers', *Town and Country Magazine and Universal Repository*, 5 (March 1773), 127–128.

Dutton, Richard, *William Shakespeare: A Literary Life* (Basingstoke: Macmillan, 1989).

Edden, Valerie, intro. to Charles Marsh, *The Winter's Tale, a Play, Alter'd from Shakespear* (London: Charles Marsh, 1756), facsimile (London: Cornmarket Press, 1970).

Fennell, James, Anonymous article in *The Prompter*, 10 (11 November 1789), 58–59.

Fitzgerald, Percy, *The Life of David Garrick from Original Family Papers and Numerous Published and Unpublished Sources*, 2nd edn (London: Simkin, Marshall, Hamilton, Kent & Co., 1899).

Foot, Jesse, *The Life of Arthur Murphy, Esq.* (London: J. Faulder, 1811).

Franklin, Colin, *Shakespeare Domesticated: The Eighteenth-century Editions* (Aldershot: Scolar Press, 1991).

Freeman, Jane, 'Beyond bombast: David Garrick's performances of Benedick and King Lear', *Restoration and Eighteenth-century Theatre Research*, 14.2 (1999), 1–21.

Freeman, Lisa A., *Character's Theater: Genre and Identity on the Eighteenth-century English Stage* (Philadelphia: University of Pennsylvania Press, 2002).

Gentleman, Francis, *The Dramatic Censor; or, Critical Companion*, 2 vols. (London: J. Bell and C. Etherington, 1770).

Shakespeare's Plays. As They Are Now Performed at the Theatres Royal in London; Regulated from the Prompt Books of Each House, by Permission, 9 vols. (London: John Bell and C. Etherington, 1773–1774).

Gray, James, '"Swear by my sword": A note in Johnson's *Shakespeare*', *Shakespeare Quarterly*, 27.2 (Spring 1976), 205–208.

De Grazia, Margreta, *Shakespeare Verbatim: The Reproduction of Authenticity and the 1790 Apparatus* (Oxford: Clarendon Press, 1991).

Green, Susan, 'A cultural reading of Charlotte Lennox's *Shakespear Illustrated*', in J. Douglas Canfield and Deborah C. Payne (eds.), *Cultural Readings of Restoration and Eighteenth-century English Theater* (Athens, GA: University of Georgia Press, 1995), pp. 228–257.

Guthrie, William, *An Essay upon English Tragedy. With Remarks upon Abbé le Blanc's Observations on the English Stage* (London: T. Waller, prob. 1747).

Halio, Jay L., '*Romeo and Juliet* in performance', in Frank Occhiogrosso (ed.), *Shakespeare in Performance: A Collection of Essays* (Newark and London: University of Delaware Press and Associated University Presses, 2003), pp. 58–70.

Harp, Richard and Stanley Stewart (eds.), *The Cambridge Companion to Ben Jonson* (Cambridge: Cambridge University Press, 2000).

Harris, Arthur John, 'Garrick, Colman and *King Lear*: A reconsideration', *Shakespeare Quarterly*, 22.1 (Winter 1971), 57–66.

Haywood, Charles, 'William Boyce's "Solemn Dirge" in Garrick's *Romeo and Juliet* Production of 1750', *Shakespeare Quarterly*, 11.2 (Spring 1960), 173–187.

Hedgcock, Frank A., *A Cosmopolitan Actor: David Garrick and His French Friends* (London: Stanley Paul & Co., 1912).

Highfill, Philip H., Jr., Kalman A. Burnim and Edward A. Langhans, *A Biographical Dictionary of Actors, Actresses, Musicians, Dancers, Managers and Other Stage Personnel in London, 1660–1800*, 16 vols. (Carbondale: Southern Illinois University Press, 1973–1993).

Hogan, Charles Beecher (ed.), *The London Stage Part 5, 1776–1800*, 3 vols. (Carbondale: Southern Illinois University Press, 1968).

Holland, Peter, 'The age of Garrick', in Jonathan Bate and Russell Jackson (eds.), *The Oxford Illustrated History of Shakespeare on Stage* (Oxford: Oxford University Press, 2001), pp. 69–91.

Hume, Robert D., 'Before the Bard: "Shakespeare" in early eighteenth-century London', *ELH*, 64 (1997), 41–75.

Jarvis, Simon, *Scholars and Gentlemen: Shakespearean Textual Criticism and Representations of Scholarly Labour, 1725–1765* (Oxford: Clarendon Press, 1995).

Johnson, Jeffrey Lawson Laurence, 'Sweeping up Shakespeare's "rubbish": Garrick's condensation of Acts IV & V of *Hamlet*', *Eighteenth Century Life*, 8.3 (1983), 14–25.

Kahrl, George M., in collaboration with Dorothy Anderson, *The Garrick Collection of Old English Plays: A Catalogue with an Historical Introduction* (London: The British Library, 1982).

Kastan, David Scott, *Shakespeare and the Book* (Cambridge: Cambridge University Press, 2001).

Kendall, Alan, *David Garrick* (New York: St. Martin's Press, 1985).

Kielmansegge, Count Frederick, *Diary of a Journey to England in the Years 1761–1762*, Countess Kielmansegg (trans.) (London: Longmans, Green & Co., 1902).

Knapp, Mary E., *A Checklist of Verse by David Garrick* (Charlottesville: University of Virginia, 1955; rev. 1974).

Knight, Joseph, *David Garrick* (London: Kegan Paul, Trench, Trübrier & Co., 1894).

Lamb, Charles, *Specimens of English Dramatic Poets Who Lived about the Time of Shakspeare* (London: Longman, Hurst, Reeves and Orme, 1808).

46 contributions to William Hone (ed.), *The Table Book of Daily Recreation and Information* (1827), vol. III of Hone's *Works* (London: William Tagg and Co., 1878).

'On the tragedies of Shakspeare, considered with reference to their fitness for stage representation' (1811), in E. V. Lucas (ed.), *Miscellaneous Prose by Charles and Mary Lamb* (London: Methuen, 1912), pp. 112–130.

Langhans, Edward A., *Eighteenth Century British and Irish Promptbooks: A Descriptive Bibliography* (New York and London: Greenwood Press, 1987).

Lockwood, Tom, 'Edmond Malone and early modern textual culture', *Yale University Library Gazette*, 79 (October 2004), 53–69.

Loehlin, James N. (ed.), *Shakespeare in Production: Romeo and Juliet* (Cambridge: Cambridge University Press, 2002).

Loftis, John, Richard Southern, Marion Jones and A.H. Scouten, *The Revels History of Drama in English*, vol. 5, 1660–1750 (London: Methuen, 1976).

London Stage 1660–1800, The, *A Calendar of Plays, Entertainments & Afterpieces Together with Casts, Box-receipts and Contemporary Comment Compiled from the Playbills, Newspapers and Theatrical Diaries of the Period,* 5 parts, William Van Lennep, Emmett L. Avery, Arthur H. Scouten, George Winchester Stone, Jr., and Charles Beecher Hogan (eds.) (Carbondale: Southern Illinois University Press, 1960–1968).

Lusardi, James P. and June Schlueter, ' "I have done the deed": *Macbeth* 2.2', in Frank Occhiogrosso (ed.), *Shakespeare in Performance* (Newark: University of Delaware Press; London: Associated University Presses, 2003), pp. 71–83.

McDonald, Russ, *Shakespeare and the Arts of Language* (Oxford: Oxford University Press, 2001).

McIntyre, Ian, *Garrick* (London: Allen Lane, The Penguin Press, 1999).

Maclean, Gerald, Donna Landry and Joseph P. Ward (eds.), *The Country and the City Revisited: England and the Politics of Culture, 1550–1850* (Cambridge: Cambridge University Press, 1999).

Madelaine, Richard (ed.), *Shakespeare in Production: Antony and Cleopatra* (Cambridge University Press, 1998).

Maguire, Nancy Klein, 'Nahum Tate's *King Lear*: "The king's blest restoration" ', in Jean I. Marsden (ed.), *The Appropriation of Shakespeare: Post-Renaissance Reconstructions of the Works and the Myth* (Hemel Hempstead: Harvester Wheatsheaf, 1991), pp. 29–42.

Malone, Edmond, 'An historical account of the rise and progress of the English stage', in Edmond Malone (ed.), *The Plays and Poems of William Shakspeare,* 10 vols. (London: J. Rivington and Sons and 31 ors, 1790), vol. I. ii, pp. 1–284.

Marsden, Jean I. (ed.), *The Appropriation of Shakespeare: Post-Renaissance Reconstructions of the Works and the Myth* (Hemel Hempstead: Harvester Wheatsheaf, 1991).

'The individual reader and the canonized text: Shakespeare criticism after Johnson', *Eighteenth Century Life*, 17.1 (1993), 62–80.

The Re-imagined Text: Shakespeare, Adaptation, and Eighteenth-century Literary Theory (Lexington: University Press of Kentucky, 1995).

'Daddy's girls: Shakespearian daughters and eighteenth-century ideology', *Shakespeare Survey*, 51 (1998), 17–26.

'Improving Shakespeare: From the Restoration to Garrick', in Stanley Wells and Sarah Stanton (eds.), *The Cambridge Companion to Shakespeare on Stage* (Cambridge: Cambridge University Press, 2002), pp. 21–36.

Martin, Peter, *Edmond Malone, Shakespearean Scholar: A Literary Biography* (Cambridge: Cambridge University Press, 1995).

Milhous, Judith and Robert D. Hume, 'The Drury Lane Theater Library in 1768', *Yale University Library Gazette*, 68.3–4 (April 1994), 116–134.

[Montagu, Elizabeth], *An Essay on the Writings and Genius of Shakespear, Compared with the Greek and French Dramatic Poets, with Some Remarks upon the Misrepresentations of Mons. de Voltaire* (London: J. Dodsley and 5 ors, 1769).

Morgan, MacNamara, *A Letter to Miss Nossiter Occasioned by Her First Appearance on the Stage: In which Is Contained Remarks Upon Her Manner of Playing the Character of Juliet* (London, 1753).

Murphy, Arthur ('Theatricus'), 'Free remarks on the tragedy of *Romeo and Juliet*', *The Student*, 2 (1750), 58–64.

'On the tragedy of King *Lear*' (12 January 1754), in *The Gray's Inn Journal*, 2 vols. (London: P. Vaillant, 1756), vol. II, pp. 73–80.

Review of *Romeo and Juliet* in 'Postscript. The theatre. no. 10', *The London Chronicle*, 10–12 February 1757, p. 152.

The Life of David Garrick, Esq., 2 vols. (London: J. Wright, 1801).

'Hamlet, with alterations; a tragedy, in three acts', in Jesse Foot, *The Life of Arthur Murphy, Esq.* (London: J. Faulder, 1811), pp. 256–274.

Nichols, John, *Literary Anecdotes of the Eighteenth Century*, Colin Clair (ed.) (Fontwell: Centaur Press, 1967).

Nicoll, Allardyce, *The Garrick Stage: Theatres and Audience in the Eighteenth Century*, Sybil Rosenfeld (ed.) (Manchester: Manchester University Press, 1980).

Noverre, Jean Georges, *Letters on Dancing and Ballets*, Cyril W. Beaumont (trans.) (London: Beaumont, 1930).

Noyes, Robert Gale, *The Thespian Mirror: Shakespeare in the Eighteenth-century Novel* (Providence, RI: Brown University, 1953).

Occhiogrosso, Frank (ed.), *Shakespeare in Performance* (Newark and London: University of Delaware Press and Associated University Presses, 2003).

Odell, George C. D., *Shakespeare from Betterton to Irving*, 2 vols. (London: Constable, 1921).

Oland, William, 'Non-pareil; or, Shakespeare and Garrick', *The Gentleman's Magazine*, 49 (April 1779), 208.

Oman, Carola, *David Garrick* (London: Hodder and Stoughton, 1958).

Orgel, Stephen, 'The authentic Shakespeare', in *The Authentic Shakespeare and Other Problems of the Early Modern Stage* (New York and London: Routledge, 2002), pp. 231–256.

Parsons, Mrs Clement, *Garrick and His Circle* (London: Methuen & Co., 1906).

Pedicord, Harry William, *The Theatrical Public in the Time of Garrick* (Carbondale: Southern Illinois University Press, 1954).

'George Colman's adaptation of Garrick's promptbook for *Florizel and Perdita*', *Theatre Survey*, 22.2 (1981), 185–190.

'*Ragandjaw*: Garrick's Shakespearian parody for a private theatre', *Philological Quarterly*, 60.2 (1981), 197–204.

'Shakespeare, Tate, and Garrick: New light on alterations of *King Lear*', *Theatre Notebook*, 36.1 (1982), 14–21.

Pegge, Samuel, 'Memoirs of Edward Capell, Esq. ', in John Nichols, *Illustrations of the Literary History of the Eighteenth Century*, 8 vols. (London: Nichols, 1817–1858), vol. I, pp. 465–476.

Pope, Alexander, *Literary Criticism of Alexander Pope*, Bertram A. Goldgar (ed.) (Lincoln: University of Nebraska, 1965).

Pope W. J. Macqueen, *Theatre Royal Drury Lane* (London: W. H. Allen, 1945).

Porter, Roy, *Enlightenment: Britain and the Creation of the Modern World* (London: Penguin Books, 2001).

Prescott, Paul, 'Doing all that becomes a man: The reception and afterlife of the Macbeth actor, 1744–1889', *Shakespeare Survey*, 57 (2004), 81–95.

Price, Cecil, *Theatre in the Age of Garrick* (Oxford: Basil Blackwell, 1973).

Rawson, Claude, *Satire and Sentiment 1660–1830* (New Haven, CT: Yale University Press, 2000).

Redgrave, Corin, 'The king and I', *The Guardian*, 17 January 2005, pp. 14–15.

Rintz, Don, 'Garrick's "protective reaction" to a charge of plagiarism', *Restoration and Eighteenth-century Theatre Research*, 14.1 (1975), 31–35.

Rogers, Rebecca, 'How Scottish was "the Scottish play?" *Macbeth*'s national identity in the eighteenth century', in Willy Maley and Andrew Murphy (eds.) *Shakespeare and Scotland* (Manchester: Manchester University Press, 2004), pp. 104–123.

Rosenberg, Marvin, *The Masks of King Lear* (Berkeley, Los Angeles and London: University of California Press, 1972).

'Macbeth and Lady Macbeth in the eighteenth and nineteenth centuries', in John Russell Brown (ed.), *Focus on Macbeth* (London, Boston and Henley: Routledge & Kegan Paul, 1982), pp. 73–86.

Russell, Gillian, 'Theatrical culture', in Thomas Keymer and Jon Mee (eds.), *The Cambridge Companion to English Literature 1740–1830* (Cambridge: Cambridge University Press, 2004), pp. 100–118.

Scheil, Katherine West, *The Taste of the Town: Shakespearean Comedy and the Early Eighteenth-century Theater* (Lewisburg: Bucknell University Press, 2003).

Schoch, Richard W., ' "A supplement to public laws": Arthur Murphy, David Garrick, and Hamlet, with alterations', *Theatre Journal*, 57.1 (March 2005), 21–32.

Scouten, Arthur H., 'Shakespeare's plays in the theatrical repertory when Garrick came to London', *University of Texas Studies in English, 1944* (Austin: University of Texas Press, 1945).

'The increase in popularity of Shakespeare's plays in the eighteenth century: A caveat for interpreters of stage history', *Shakespeare Quarterly*, 7.2 (Spring 1956), 189–202.

(ed.), *The London Stage Part 3, 1729–1747*, 2 vols. (Carbondale: Southern Illinois University Press, 1961).

Shattuck, Charles H., 'Drama as promptbook', in George Winchester Stone, Jr. (ed.), *The Stage and the Page: London's 'Whole show' in the Eighteenth-century Theatre* (Berkeley: University of California Press, 1981), pp. 163–191.

Shaw, Bernard, *Prefaces* (London: Constable, 1934).

Shawe-Taylor, Desmond, ' "The beautiful strokes of a great actor": Garrick and his painters', in Rosie Broadley, Colin Harrison, Susan Sloman, Lisa White and Christopher Woodward, exhibition catalogue *Every Look Speaks: Portraits of David Garrick* (Bath: Holburne Museum of Art, 2003), pp. 11–30.

Shepherd, Simon and Mick Wallis, *Drama/Theatre/Performance* (London and New York: Routledge, 2004).

Sherbo Arthur (ed.), *Johnson on Shakespeare*, 2 vols. (New Haven and London: Yale University Press, 1968).

The Birth of Shakespeare Studies: Commentators from Rowe (1709) to Boswell-Malone (1821) (East Lansing, MI: Colleagues Press, 1986).

The Achievement of George Steevens (New York, Bern, Frankfurt am Main and Paris: Peter Lang, 1990).

'Steevens, George (1736–1800)', in *Oxford Dictionary of National Biography* (Oxford University Press, 2004) online edn, May 2006, http://www.oxforddnb.com/view/article/26355

Spevack, Marvin, *A Complete and Systematic Concordance to the Works of Shakespeare*, 9 vols. (Hildesheim: Georg Olms Verlag, 1968–1980).

Steevens, George, Anonymous 'Letter to Mr. Urban', *The Gentleman's Magazine*, 39 (August 1769), 375.

Writing as 'A man of letters', letter to *The Public Advertiser*, 29 August 1769, p. 2.

Writing as 'Insomnis', letter to *The Public Advertiser*, 15 August 1769, pp. 1–2.

Stern, Tiffany, *Making Shakespeare: From Stage to Page* (London: Routledge, 2004).

Stochholm, Johanne M., *Garrick's Folly: The Shakespeare Jubilee of 1769 at Stratford and Drury Lane* (London: Methuen, 1964).

Stone, George Winchester, Jr., 'Garrick's long lost alteration of *Hamlet*', *Publications of the Modern Language Association of America*, 49 (1934), 890–921.

'Garrick's presentation of *Antony and Cleopatra*', *Review of English Studies*, 13 (January 1937), 20–38.

'*A Midsummer Night's Dream* in the hands of Garrick and Colman', *Publications of the Modern Language Association of America*, 54 (1939), 467–482.

'Garrick's treatment of Shakespeare's plays and his influence upon the changed attitude of Shakespearean criticism during the eighteenth century', Ph.D. Thesis, 2 vols. (Harvard University, 1940).

'Garrick's handling of *Macbeth*', *Studies in Philology*, 38 (1941), 609–628.

'Garrick's production of *King Lear*: A study in the temper of the eighteenth-century mind', *Studies in Philology*, 45 (1948), 89–103.

'David Garrick's significance in the history of Shakespearean criticism: A study of the impact of the actor upon the change of critical focus during the eighteenth century', *Publications of the Modern Language Association of America*, 65.2 (March 1950), 183–197.

'Shakespeare's *Tempest* at Drury Lane during Garrick's management', *Shakespeare Quarterly*, 7.1 (Winter 1956), 1–7.

(ed.), *The London Stage Part 4, 1747–1776*, 3 vols. (Carbondale: Southern Illinois University Press, 1962).

'*Romeo and Juliet*: The source of its modern stage career', *Shakespeare Quarterly*, 15.2 (Spring 1964), 191–206.

'Garrick and *Othello*', *Philological Quarterly*, 45 (1966), 304–320.

'A century of *Cymbeline*; or Garrick's magic touch', *Philological Quarterly*, 54 (1975), 310–322.

(ed.), *The Stage and the Page: London's 'Whole Show' in the Eighteenth-century Theatre* (Berkeley: University of California Press, 1981).

Stone, George Winchester, Jr., and Philip H. Highfield, Jr., *In Search of Restoration and Eighteenth-century Theatrical Biography* (Los Angeles: University of California, William Andrews Clark Memorial Library, 1976).

Stone, George Winchester, Jr., and George M. Kahrl, *David Garrick: A Critical Biography* (Carbondale: Southern Illinois University Press, 1979).

Sutton, R. B., 'Further evidence of David Garrick's portrayal of Hamlet from the diary of Georg Christoph Lichtenberg', *Theatre Notebook*, 50.1 (1996), 8–14.

Taylor, Gary, *Reinventing Shakespeare: A Cultural History from the Restoration to the Present* (London: The Hogarth Press, 1990).

'Afterword: The incredible shrinking Bard', in *Shakespeare and Appropriation*, Robert Sawyer and Cristy Desmet (eds.) (London: Routledge, 1999), pp. 197–205.

Todd, Janet, *Sensibility: An Introduction* (London: Methuen, 1986).

Tomarken, Edward, *Samuel Johnson on Shakespeare: The Discipline of Criticism* (Athens, Georgia: The University of Georgia Press, 1991).

Van Lennep, William (ed.), *The London Stage Part 1, 1660–1700* (Carbondale: Southern Illinois University Press, 1965).

Vickers, Brian (ed.), *Shakespeare: The Critical Heritage*, 6 vols. (London and Boston: Routledge & Kegan Paul, 1974–1981).

'The emergence of character criticism, 1774–1800', *Shakespeare Survey*, 34 (1981), 11–21.

'Shakespearian adaptations: The tyranny of the audience', in *Returning to Shakespeare* (London and New York: Routledge, 1989), pp. 212–233.

Victor, Benjamin, *The History of the Theatres of London and Dublin from the Year 1730 to the Present Time*, 3 vols. (London: T. Davies, 1761; T. Becket, 1771).

Walsh, Marcus, *Shakespeare, Milton, and Eighteenth-century Literary Editing: The Beginnings of Interpretative Scholarship* (Cambridge: Cambridge University Press, 1997).

Warner, Richard, *A Letter to David Garrick, Esq., Concerning a Glossary to the Plays of Shakespeare, On a More Extensive Plan than Has Hitherto appeared. To which Is Annexed, a Specimen* (London: Printed for the author, 1768).

Warton, Joseph, article on *King Lear*, *The Adventurer*, 113 (4 December 1753), 253–258.

Wells, Stanley, *Shakespeare for All Time* (London: Macmillan, 2002).

Williams, Simon, 'Taking Macbeth out of himself: Davenant, Garrick, Schiller and Verdi', *Shakespeare Survey*, 57 (2004), 54–68.

Woodfield, Ian, *Opera and Drama in Eighteenth-century London: The King's Theatre, Garrick and the Business of Performance* (Cambridge: Cambridge University Press, 2001).

Woods, Leigh, 'Crowns of straw on little men: Garrick's new heroes', *Shakespeare Quarterly*, 32.1 (Spring 1981), 69–79.

Garrick Claims the Stage: Acting as Social Emblem in Eighteenth-century England (Westport, CT, and London: Greenwood Press, 1984).

'Garrick's King Lear and the English malady', *Theatre Survey*, 27.1–2 (1986), 17–35.

Young R. V., 'Ben Jonson and learning', in Richard Harp and Stanley Stewart (eds.), *The Cambridge Companion to Ben Jonson* (Cambridge: Cambridge University Press, 2000), pp. 43–57.

Index

Act to Restrain Abuses of Players 31
Adam, Robert 5
Addison, Joseph 50, 89, 122
Alchemist, The (Garrick's alteration) 29, 89
Allen, Ralph 48
All for Love 101
All's Well That Ends Well 116
Anatomist, The 21
Anderson, Dorothy 168
Anti-Midas, a Jubilee Preservative 196n.21
Antony and Cleopatra (Garrick and Capell's alteration) 4, 13, 48, 77, 100–3, 105, 163
  cuts 100–1
  failure of 101–2
Apotheosis of Garrick, The 93
Appel à toutes les nations de l'Europe 154
Arne, Thomas 72, 88, 107
As You Like It 87, 89
audiences
  misbehaviour and riots in 23–4, 28
  patriotism of 23–5, 77, 103, 110
  preferences of 20–2, 28, 39, 77, 80, 97, 105
  seating arrangements for 22, 25, 26

Babcock, Robert Witbeck 167
Bandello, Matteo 73
bardolatry 5, 11, 43, 107, 169
Baretti, Guiseppe 73
Barry, Ann 62
Barry, Spranger 66, 69, 75, 88, 123, 130
Bate, Jonathan 62, 107, 169
Bate, W. Jackson 44
Bath Chronicle, The 62, 165
Bath Theatre Royal *see under* Theatre Royal, Bath
Batoni, Pompeo 167
Beauclerk, Topham 16
Beaumont, Francis 18
Beaux' Stratagem, The 89
Bell, John, *see under Shakespeare's Plays as they are now performed*
Bellamy, George Anne 68
Bergmann, Fredrick Louis *see under* Pedicord, Harry William
Berry, Edward 153
Besterman, Theodore 154
Betterton, Thomas 140
Bibliography of the English Printed Drama to the Restoration 168
Bickerstaffe, Isaac 22
Biographia Dramatica 161, 201n.58
Blakes, Charles 153
Boaden, James 8, 47, 150, 160
Boaistuau, Pierre 73
Booth, Michael 20
Boscawen, Frances 168
Boston Public Library 114
Boswell, James 6, 16, 27, 28, 89, 168
Boswell, James, the younger 168
Boyce, William 72, 87
Branam, George C. 71, 79
Bratton, Jacky 163
Brewer, John 16
British Library 168, 169
British Museum 61, 168
Brooke, Arthur 73
Brown, John Russell 133
Buckingham, George Villiers 89
Burke, Edmund 16, 134
Burlington, Dorothy, Countess of 69
Burney, Charles 168
Burney, Frances 27
Burnim, Kalman A. 57, 123, 129, 148, 150
Butler, Martin 32

Caius Marius, The History and Fall of 12, 63–4, 66, 70, 74–5
Canongate Playhouse, Edinburgh 61
Capell, Edward 5, 13, 47, 48, 77, 96–7, 98, 99–100, 100–3, 136, 137, 138, 152, 163, 168
  typographical marks, Capell's system of 102–3
Cardenio 13

Carey, George Saville 112
Carter, Elizabeth 168
Carter, George 93
Catharine and Petruchio 78, 81, 116
Cato 17
censorship 28, 39, 96–7, 114
Centlivre, Suzanna 21
Chamier, Anthony 16
Charlotte, Queen 111
Chetwood, William 13
Chetwynd, Edward 96–7
Chinese Festival, The 24, 58
Cibber, Colley 24, 59, 138, 166
Cibber, Susanna 68, 69, 75, 89, 189n.30
Cibber, Theophilus 63–4, 79
Clandestine Marriage, The 17, 21
Clive, Catherine (Kitty) 38, 69, 189n.30
Club, The 14, 15, 16–19, 135, 139
Cocco, Maria 107
Coffey, Charles 21
Coleridge, Samuel Taylor 167
Colman, George, the elder 17, 77–8, 93, 96, 113–14, 121–3, 128, 196n.20
Comedy of Errors, The 116, 164
Congreve, William 27
Conolly, L. W. 96–7
Conscious Lovers, The 167
Copeland, Nancy 64, 68, 74
Coriolanus 116
Country Girl, The 27
Country Wife, The 27
Courtyard Theatre, Stratford-upon-Avon 170
Covent Garden *see under* Theatre Royal, Covent Garden
Critic, The 158–9
Critical Review, The 112
Cross, Richard 95, 102, 120
Cymberline 4
  Garrick's alteration 7, 35, 75, 77, 103, 105
  Marsh's alteration 91

Dash, Irene 86
Davenant, William 29, 44, 46, 48–51, 55, 60, 61
Dávidházi, Péter 107
Davies, Susanna 38
Davies, Thomas 8, 14–15, 21, 26, 28, 36, 41, 52, 55, 59, 80, 89, 106, 121, 128, 136, 143, 149, 151, 153, 158
Devil to Pay, The 21
Dibdin, Charles 117
Dictionary of the English Language 5, 7
Dobson, Michael 10, 158
Doctor Faustus 60
Dodsley, Robert 97
Double Falsehood 13
Dramatic Miscellanies 143
dramatic theory 80, 140, 152–3, 158
Drummer, The 89
Drury Lane, *see under* Theatre Royal, Drury Lane
Dryden, John 29, 101, 109

Eastward Ho! 41
Edden, Valerie 91
editing of Shakespeare, in eighteenth century 6–7, 11, 13, 14
Essay on Acting, An 53–4, 55
Essay on the Writings and Genius of Shakespeare 19, 156
Evelina 27
Every Man in His Humour 29–31, 41
  Garrick's alteration 14, 31–42, 52, 89

Fairies, The see under A Midsummer Night's Dream
Fair Quaker of Deal, The 89
Fairy Tale, A 78, 94
Falstaff 110–11, 117, 167
Farquhar, George 89
Fennell, James 71
Ferney 154, 155
Fielding, Henry 4
Fitzgerald, Percy 8
Fitzgerald, William Thomas 165–6
Fleetwood, Charles 44
Florizel and Perdita 5, 90
  see also The Winter's Tale (Garrick's alteration)
Folger Shakespeare Library 100, 141
Foote, Samuel 97, 167, 196n.20
French, James Murphy 24
Furness, Horace Howard 79
Fuseli, Henry 55

Gainsborough, Thomas 48, 88, 168
Garrick, David 3–5, 16–19, 130, 157
  alteration, principles of 14, 19, 29, 31, 64, 72
  collection of old English plays 5, 31, 47, 60, 76, 97–8, 99, 136, 137, 138, 168–9
  monument and tomb in Westminster Abbey 8, 165
  paintings of 37, 48, 55, 59, 167–8
  roles:
    Abel Drugger 29
    Antony 4, 101
    Benedick 4, 116, 117
    Don Felix 21
    Hamlet 4, 44, 119, 148, 157, 158
    King Lear 4, 27, 44, 119, 120, 125–7, 133–4
    Kitely 14, 35–7, 41, 42

Garrick, David (cont.)
Leontes 4, 81–2, 86, 94
Macbeth 4, 52, 53, 57–9, 62, 157
Othello 4, 35
Posthumus 4, 35, 103
Richard the Third 4, 19, 44, 59
Romeo 4, 66–8, 75
Shakespeare, idolisation of 4–5, 6, 75, 77, 107, 119, 128, 155, 166, 169
Garrick, Eva Maria 4, 47, 77, 168
Garrick, George 3, 176n.42
Garrick's Folly 107
Garrick's Vagary 112
Genesis of Shakespeare Idolatry 1766–1799, The 1176
Gentleman, Francis 57, 59, 80–1, 93, 112, 125, 128, 153, 162
Gentleman's Magazine, The 3, 57, 112
Gentle Shepherd, The 87
George III, King 111
Gibbon, Edward 16
Goldsmith, Oliver 16, 17–18, 21, 76
Goodman's Fields Theatre 19, 62
Good Natur'd Man, The 17
Green, Susan 107
Greg, W. W. 168

Halio, Jay L. 68
Hamlet 4, 75, 101, 102, 111, 140, 152, 159, 169
Garrick's alteration 6, 105, 139–53, 160–1, 164
critical reactions to 8, 9, 158
French influence on 140, 153, 155, 157
grave-diggers, Osric and fencing match, omission of 139, 147, 153, 157, 158
preparation copy for 140–5, 145–7, 151, 160
restorations in 145–7, 149, 157, 160, 204n.107
Hawes text 140, 143, 145, 149, 151
Hughes-Wilks text 140, 145
Hampton 5, 115, 168
Handel, George Frideric 87
Hanmer, Thomas 45, 61
Harris, Arthur John 123, 128
Harlequin's Invasion 25
Harlequin's Jubilee 118
Harvard Theatre Collection 129–30
Havard, William 153
Hawkins, Sir John 16, 76
Hawkins, Thomas 98
Hayman, Francis 119
Haymarket Theatre 19, 94, 112
Haywood, Eliza 12
Hazlitt, William 167
Hedgcock, Frank 9
Henderson, John 6, 130
History of English Poetry 98
History of the Theatres of London and Dublin, The 194n.3
Hoadly, John 158
Hogan, Charles Beecher 123
Hogarth, William 59, 167
Holland, Peter 11, 57, 107, 150, 158, 169
Hopkins, William 78, 113, 115–16, 129, 130
Hull, Thomas 91–3, 94, 164
Hume, Robert D. 10, 12, 43–4
Hunt, William 113
Huntington Library 95, 96, 97, 114

Irene 21, 153
Isle of Dogs, The 41
Ivy Lane Club, The 15

Jarvis, Simon 5
Johnson, Jeffrey 144
Johnson, Samuel 5, 6, 7, 13, 15, 21, 23, 44, 47, 64–5, 70, 73, 76, 80, 81, 99, 110, 122, 135, 143, 152, 153, 162, 163, 165, 166–7, 168
and *Macbeth* 44–6, 46–7, 57, 61
Garrick, relationship with 3, 16–17, 18, 90, 98–9, 104, 163
The Club, membership of 15, 16, 135
Jonson, Ben 14, 18, 29–31, 41, 88, 89, 98, 109, 155
Jubilee at Stratford-upon-Avon, the 5, 54, 103, 106–7, 111, 112, 135–6, 167
Jubilee, The 21, 25, 106, 113–18

Kahrl, George M. 97, 155
Kastan, David Scott 104
Kean, Edmund 62
Kelly, Hugh 18, 23
Kemble-Devonshire Collection 114
Kemble, John Philip 6, 62
King Henry the Fourth 110, 111
King Henry the Fifth 7, 116, 169
King Henry the Sixth 116
King John 116
King Lear 4, 111, 119, 169
Bathurst text, the 120, 124, 129, 130–3
Colman's alteration 121–3, 125, 128, 134
Garrick's alteration 120, 121–30, 128–9, 135
Fool, omission of the 119, 128, 135
happy ending 9, 119, 128, 134
restorations in 120, 121, 123, 125, 127–8, 129, 133
sensibility in 127, 134–5
Tate's alteration 13, 42, 119, 120–1, 121–2, 123–4, 128, 135
King Richard the Second 13, 116, 138
King Richard the Third (Cibber's alteration) 4, 59, 138, 150

King's Theatre 77
Knight, Joseph 8–9, 79

Lacy, James 25, 70
Lamb, Charles 166, 167, 168
Langhans, Edward A. 114, 123, 129
Langton, Bennet 16
Laplace, Pierre-Antoine, de 155, 158
Larpent Collection, *see under* Huntington Library
Lee, John 61–2, 64
Lennox, Charlotte 73–4
Lethe 21
Letter to David Garrick, Esq., A 6
Letter to Miss Nossiter, A 72, 74–5
Lever, J. W. 35
Lichtenberg, Georg Christoph 157
Lincoln's Inn Fields Theatre 29, 50
Literary Club, The, *see under* The Club
Lives of the Poets 15
Lockwood, Tom 168
Loehlin, James N. 66, 72
London Chronicle, The 158
London Stage, The 9, 29, 75, 87, 102, 173n.27
Lord Chamberlain's Office 28, 31, 39, 95, 96
Loutherbourg, Philippe Jacques de 21
Love for Love 27
Love's Labours Lost 116

McDonald, Russ 60
McIntyre, Ian 39, 54, 57, 107
Macbeth 4, 117, 164
  Davenant's alteration 44, 46, 48–51, 55, 60, 61
  Garrick's alteration 29, 33, 43, 44–7, 51–60, 62, 63, 75, 101, 139
    cuts in 54–7
    Macbeth, death scene for 53, 57–9, 60, 61, 62, 68
    Lady Macbeth, treatment of 55–7
    Porter, omission of 52
    witches, handling of 51–2, 55
  Lee's alteration 60–2
Macklin, Charles 60, 62, 111–12
Madelaine, Richard 102
Making Shakespeare: from Stage to Page 116
Malone, Edmond 14, 18, 99, 164–5, 168
Man and Wife, or, The Shakespeare Jubilee 113–14, 115, 116–17
Marlowe, Christopher 60
Marmontel, Jean François 155
Marsden, Jean I 10, 75, 84, 104, 134, 159, 166–7
Marsh, Charles 64, 90–1, 93, 94, 95
Masks of King Lear, The 133
Measure For Measure 116
Memoirs of the Life of David Garrick, Esq. 15, 21
Mendez, Moses 87
Merchant of Venice, The 24
Merry Wives of Windsor, The 117
Midsummer Night's Dream, A 117
  Garrick and Colman's alteration 77–8
  opera, *The Fairies* 24, 77
Milton, John 109
Miscellaneous Observations on Macbeth 44–6
Montagu, Elizabeth 19, 156
More, Hannah 135, 142, 151, 168
Morellet, Abbé André 155
Morgan, Macnamara 68, 72, 74, 86, 87, 88, 90, 93, 94, 95
Morning Chronicle, The 158
Much Ado about Nothing 4, 89, 116
Murphy, Arthur 8, 14, 48, 53, 71, 74, 159–60

Necker, Suzanne 156
Neville, Richard 156
Nossiter, Isabella 72, 74–5, 87
Noverre, Jean Georges 24, 58–9
Nugent, Dr Christopher 16

Ode upon dedicating a building, and erecting a statue, to Shakespeare, An 5, 54, 60, 106, 107–12, 113, 116, 167
Odell, George 9, 123
Oland, William 3
Oman, Carola 9
Orgel, Stephen 11, 53
Origin of the English Drama, The 98
Othello 4, 35, 138
Otway, Thomas 12, 63, 74–5
Oxford Shakespeare, The 2, 121

Padlock, The 21
Paris 153, 154, 155
Parsons, Mrs Clement 9
Pastor Fido, Il 87
Pedicord, Harry William 20, 25, 123, 128
  and Bergmann, Fredrick Louis 1, 2, 54, 62, 65, 68, 81, 100, 129, 143–4, 145, 148
Pepys, Samuel 50
Percy, Thomas 98
Piozzi, Hester (*see under* Thrale, Hester)
Polly Honeycomb 28, 96
Pope, Alexander 7, 14, 45, 109, 165
Pope, W. J. Macqueen 9
Powell, William 90
Prescott, Paul 52
Prior Park 48
Pritchard, Hannah 38, 55, 62, 87, 94, 189n.30
Prolusions 102

Prompter, The 64
Provok'd Wife, The 89
Public Advertiser, The 25, 28, 135–6
'P.W.' 6

Quin, James 4, 44, 48, 50, 51, 60, 110, 167

Ragandjaw 181n.38
Rambler, The 46
Ramsay, Allan 87
Ramus, Nicholas 130
Ravenscroft, Edward 21
Recruiting Officer, The 89
Redgrave, Corin 134
Rehearsal, The 89
Reliques of Ancient English Poetry 98
'Retaliation' 17–18
Reynolds, Sir Joshua 16, 17, 20, 37, 76, 104, 168
Rich, John 71
Richardson, Samuel 83, 189n.27
Romeo and Juliet 4, 111
  Theophilus Cibber's alteration 63–4, 66, 70
  Garrick's alteration 7, 21, 29, 33, 43, 63–75
    cuts in 65, 70–1
    Juliet, funeral procession for 71–2
    Rosaline, handling of Romeo's love for 66, 70–1, 73
    tomb scene 66–9, 73, 74–5
  Marsh's alteration 64, 91
  Otway's alteration, *see under Caius Marius*
Romeos, battle of the 21, 69
Rosenberg, Marvin 55, 133–4
Roubiliac, Louis-François 168
Rowe, Nicholas 14, 163
Royal Shakespeare Company 169
  RSC Complete Works, The 169, 170
Russell, Gillian 107

Salmon, Edward 182n.64
Scope, Revd Dr 46
Scouten, Arthur 10
'Scrub's Trip to the Jubilee' 112
Seven Years War 23, 25, 153
Shadwell, Charles 89
Shakespeare Club, The 15
Shakespear Illustrated 73
Shakespeare, William 4
  see also under titles of individual plays
Shakespeare's Garland 112, 115
Shakespeare's Jubilee, a Masque 112
Shakespeare's Plays as they are now performed at the Theatres Royal in London (the Bell edition) 13, 63, 80, 93, 120, 127, 162–3
Shakespeare's plays, eighteenth-century editions of
  Capell, 1767–1768, 76, 99, 103
  Hanmer, 1744, 64, 76, 80, 91
  Johnson, 1765, 45, 76, 110, 122, 133, 138, 145, 160, 162
    Preface 98
  Johnson and Steevens, 1773, 1778, 104, 133, 136, 137, 138, 147, 162, 163–4
  Malone, 1790, 14, 164–5
  Pope, 1725, 14, 64, 76
  Rowe, 1709, 14, 76, 180n.24
  Steevens, 1766, 98, 136
  Theobald, 1733, 1740, 45–6, 52, 61, 73, 76, 80, 81
  Warburton, 1747, 46, 47, 73, 76, 81, 162
Shattuck, Charles H. 123
Shaw, Bernard, *see under* 'bardolatry'
Shawe-Taylor, Desmond 59
Sheep-Shearing, The 87–8, 90, 93, 94, 95
Shepherd, Simon 167
Shepherds' Lottery, The 87
Sheridan, Richard Brinsley 21, 90, 158
Sheridan, Thomas 62, 64, 196n.21
She Stoops to Conquer 17
Smith, William 157
Smock Alley Theatre, Dublin 62
Spectator, The 50
Stage Licensing Act 19, 95–6
Steele, Richard 167
Steevens, George 5, 16, 98, 102, 104, 106, 135–9, 160–1, 162, 163, 168
  influence on Garrick's alteration of *Hamlet* 13, 138–9, 147–8
Stern, Tiffany 116
Stochholm Johanne M. 107
Stone, George Winchester 9, 10, 45, 46, 51, 58, 66, 71, 79, 95, 100, 101, 123, 127, 129, 140, 145–7, 148, 155, 167
Stratford-upon-Avon, *see also* under Jubilee 48, 104, 111, 170
Stratford Jubilee, The 112
Suard, Jean Baptiste Antoine 111

Taming of the Shrew, The 116
  Garrick's alteration, *see under Catharine and Petruchio*
Taswell, James 153
Tate, Nahum 13, 42, 119, 120–1, 121–2, 123–4, 128, 135, 166
Taylor, Gary 79
Tempest, The 117
  Garrick's alteration 77, 105
  opera 24, 77

Theatre Royal, Bath 62
Theatre Royal, Covent Garden 17, 26, 42, 60, 61, 69, 87, 91, 94, 95
  competition with Drury Lane, *see under* Theatre Royal, Drury Lane
Theatre Royal, Drury Lane 4, 19, 26, 34, 45, 53, 60, 89, 95, 97, 168
  capacity 25
  competition with Covent Garden 19–20, 21, 69, 70, 71, 75, 90, 94, 100, 106, 113–18
  lighting 26–7
    see also under 'audience'
Theatrical Fund 130
Theobald, Lewis 13, 45, 80, 98, 109, 163
Thompson, Ann 78
Thompson, Edward 194n.3
Thrale, Hester 16, 89–90
Timon of Athens 116
'Tis Well it's no Worse 22
Titus Andronicus 116
Tomarken, Edward 139
Tom Jones 4
Tonson, Jacob 13, 81, 95, 100, 104
Town and Country Magazine, The 157, 158
Trinculo's trip to the Jubilee 194n.3
Trinity College, Cambridge 99
Troilus and Cressida 116
Two Gentlemen of Verona, The 116

unities, classical, *see under* dramatic theory

Vanbrugh, Sir John 89
Veigel, Eva Maria *see under* Garrick, Eva Maria
Vickers, Brian 10, 54, 64, 79, 167
Victor, Benjamin 194n.3
Volpone 40
Voltaire, François-Marie (Arouet) 109, 111, 154–7
  Shakespeare, views on 137, 154, 155–6

Walker, John 95
Walker, Robert 13
Wallis, Mick 167
Walpole, Horace 17, 104, 109, 203n.93
Walsh, Marcus 5–6
Warburton, William 13, 31, 46–8, 61, 64, 80, 102, 152, 162, 163
Ward, Sarah 38
Warner, Richard 6, 104
Warton, Thomas 98
Wells, Stanley 12, 57, 60, 169
Westminster Abbey 8, 18, 165
Westminster Magazine, The 158
Weston, Thomas 112
Whalley, Peter 98
Whitehead, William 28, 39
Wilks, Robert 140
  see also under Hamlet, Hughes-Wilks text
Winter's Tale, The 4, 116
  (*see also Florizel and Perdita, The Sheep-Shearing*)
  Colman's revision of Garrick's alteration 93–4
  Garrick's alteration 13, 78–90, 94, 95, 105, 163
    cuts 81
    pastoralism of 86, 87–8
    prologue to 78–80
    sentimentality in 82–3, 84–5
    song for Perdita 89–90, 135
  Hull's alteration 80, 91–3, 94
  Marsh's alteration 90–1, 93, 94, 95
Woffington, Peg 26
Wolfit, Donald 169
Wonder, The 21
Woodward, Henry 21, 42, 94, 118, 153
Word to the Wise, A 23
Wren, Sir Christopher 25
Wycherley, William 27

Yates, Mary Ann 102

Zoffany, Johan Joseph 55